Technology Education in New Zealand

This book aims to develop understanding of technology education in New Zealand. It is New Zealand's story of technology education in the 21st century and will assist teachers and teacher educators in developing technology education programmes. It explores the philosophy of and rationale for technology education and the relevant theory underpinning technology education. The background to recent changes to the technology curriculum are outlined and aspects of *Technology in The New Zealand Curriculum* are explored, including sections on the technological areas, strands and components of technology. The process of planning a unit of work is explained thoroughly and modelled to assist teachers who are new to teaching technology in New Zealand. The authors take a unique, dual narrative approach to explore two students' journeys through their technology education. This is complemented by teachers' commentary, making explicit links to teacher thinking and theory, and explaining planned student practice. Wholly dedicated to the New Zealand context, this is essential reading for preservice and qualified teachers alike.

Wendy Fox-Turnbull is an associate professor at the University of Waikato and Deputy Head of School for Te Kura Toi Tangata – School of Education. Wendy was chair of the Technology Education New Zealand (TENZ) Council from 2006 to 2018 and has convened two TENZ conferences (TENZ 2005 and TENZ/ICTE 2017) and one international technology research conference (PATT 2013) in Christchurch. She previously taught at the University of Canterbury's College of Education, in Technology Education, primary and secondary, Professional Inquiry Studies and Inquiry Learning, from 1997 to 2017. In 2015 Wendy was awarded the TENZ Outstanding Contribution to Technology Education Award and is one of six living recipients. Research special interests include authentic learning in technology education, the place of women in technology-related careers, the role and nature of effective conversations in learning and teaching, and learning approaches for the 21st century. Wendy has presented regularly at PATT and other international conferences and has published in a range of journals and books in the field of technology education. Wendy is a registered and certified primary teacher.

Elizabeth Reinsfield is a senior lecturer at the University of Waikato. Dr Reinsfield's research interests include cross-generational perceptions of innovation, and teachers' engagement with and enactment of curriculum. In 2019, Liz led the Mātanga project – a national professional learning programme (PLP) for Early Childhood, Primary and Secondary technology teachers in New Zealand to engage with, make meaning of, and enact the curriculum. This was particularly pertinent because of the recent curriculum revision, and consequent emphasis on digital technology. As a result of this work, she was given the Technology Education New Zealand (TENZ) Award: Outstanding Teacher Educator in Technology. In 2020 she was also awarded the Teacher Education Forum of Aotearoa New Zealand (TEFANZ) Emerging Teacher Educator Award.

Alistair Michael Forret has been involved in Technology Education in New Zealand (TENZ) since its beginning in 1992. He was involved in writing the early versions of the Technology Curriculum and was one of the teacher educators at the University of Waikato who prepared the initial "wave" of facilitators to introduce the 1995 Technology Curriculum. Mike has worked in initial teacher education for over 20 years, initially at Hamilton Teachers' College and then at the University of Waikato where he taught preservice teacher education courses and supervised postgraduate research in technology and science education. Mike retired from the university in 2016 and is a director of a web services and development company.

Technology Education in New Zealand
A Guide for Teachers

Wendy Fox-Turnbull,
Elizabeth Reinsfield and
Alistair Michael Forret

LONDON AND NEW YORK

First published 2021
by Routledge
2 Park Square, Milton Park, Abingdon, Oxon OX14 4RN

and by Routledge
605 Third Avenue, New York, NY 10158

Routledge is an imprint of the Taylor & Francis Group, an informa business

© 2021 selection and editorial matter, Wendy Fox-Turnbull, Elizabeth Reinsfield, Alistair Michael Forret

The right of Wendy Fox-Turnbull, Elizabeth Reinsfield, Alistair Michael Forret to be identified as the authors of the editorial material, and of the authors for their individual chapters, has been asserted in accordance with sections 77 and 78 of the Copyright, Designs and Patents Act 1988.

All rights reserved. No part of this book may be reprinted or reproduced or utilised in any form or by any electronic, mechanical, or other means, now known or hereafter invented, including photocopying and recording, or in any information storage or retrieval system, without permission in writing from the publishers.

Trademark notice: Product or corporate names may be trademarks or registered trademarks, and are used only for identification and explanation without intent to infringe.

British Library Cataloguing-in-Publication Data
A catalogue record for this book is available from the British Library

Library of Congress Cataloging-in-Publication Data
Names: Fox-Turnbull, Wendy Helen, author. |
Reinsfield, Elizabeth, author. | Forret, Alistair Michael, author.
Title: Technology education in New Zealand : a guide for teachers /
Wendy Helen Fox-Turnbull, Elizabeth Reinsfield, Alistair Michael Forret.
Description: Abingdon, Oxoin ; New York, NY : Routledge, 2021. |
Includes bibliographical references and index.
Identifiers: LCCN 2020041378 (print) | LCCN 2020041379
(ebook) | ISBN 9780367473334 (hardcover) | ISBN
9780367418977 (paperback) | ISBN 9781003034933 (ebook)
Subjects: LCSH: Technology—Study and teaching—New Zealand. |
Curriculum planning—New Zealand.
Classification: LCC T168.5 .F68 2021 (print) | LCC T168.5 (ebook) |
DDC 607.1/093—dc23
LC record available at https://lccn.loc.gov/2020041378
LC ebook record available at https://lccn.loc.gov/2020041379

ISBN: 978-0-367-41895-3 (hbk)
ISBN: 978-0-367-41897-7 (pbk)
ISBN: 978-0-367-81680-3 (ebk)

Typeset in Galliard
by KnowledgeWorks Global Ltd.

Contents

List of figures and tables	vii

1 Introduction   1

Rationale and aim 3
Structure of the book 5
Outline of chapters 5

2 Underpinning philosophy and perspectives of technology in New Zealand   9

Technology and humans 9
Summary 22

3 Rationale for and nature of technology education in New Zealand   24

Introduction 24
Rationale for teaching technology 24
Technology as an academic subject 29
The evolution of technology education 31
Technological literacy – technacy in New Zealand 34
Ways of thinking and knowledge for technology practice 38
Teaching approaches 59
Social interaction and talk in technology 74
Sources of funds of knowledge (FOK) 86
Summary 90

4 Implementing the technology curriculum in New Zealand   96

Introduction 96
Technology in the New Zealand curriculum 96
Hangarau 97

vi *Contents*

Te whariki 98
Technology as a learning area in The New Zealand
  Curriculum 99
Technological areas 101
Transformations 116
Immediate contexts for learning 117
Strands and components 119
Flow charting 132
Planning units of work in technology 140
Technology education in early childhood 169
Summary 170

5 Classroom narrative   173

Early years (4 years old) 173
Years 1–3 (5–7 years old) 175
Years 4–6 (8–10) 181
Years 7 and 8 190
Years 9 and 10 197
Year 11: design and visual communication 205
Year 13: designing and developing material outcomes 206
Summary 208

6 Epilogue   209

Index   214

Figures and tables

Figures

2.1	S.S. Dunedin in port	11
2.2	The GTS cycle	17
3.1	Perspectives of technological determinism	36
3.2	Wider contexts for learning technology	38
3.3	Pacey's model of technological practice	49
3.4	Gawith's model of technology practice	50
3.5	Kimbell's reflective activity capability model of technological practice	51
3.6	An example of a linear design process	51
3.7	An example of a cyclic design process	52
3.8	An example of a messy or complex design process	53
3.9	Examples of the students' "Immigrant biscuit" portfolios and outcomes	70
4.1	The organising structure of technology in the NZC	100
4.2	Ministry of Education's first draft proposed models for technology education and Hangarau Matihiko published 2017	108
4.3	Ministry of Education's released draft technology education and Hangarau Matihiko published later in 2017	109
4.4	The relationship between the technological areas and the domain-specific specialist areas in senior secondary	115
4.5	The brief development process	124
4.6	An example of a key task list	127
4.7	A simple task list for junior students	128
4.8	Savoury Yoghurt Herringbone example	132
4.9	"High vis for dogs" an example of a simple flow chart	133
4.10	An example Scratch-like code computer programme	135
4.11	Fox-Turnbull model of student TP	137
4.12	Characteristics of technology	139
4.13	Flugs for Cuddles at School brainstorm	146
4.14	Website for Hobbit Harriers brainstorm	147
4.15	Flugs for Cuddles at School scoping	148

viii   *Figures and tables*

4.16 Website for Hobbit Harriers scoping	149
4.17 Flugs for Cuddles at School pathway	150
4.18 Website for Hobbit Harriers pathway	151
4.19 Technology unit planner template	152
4.20 Technology unit planner template guidelines	154
4.21 Level 1 Flugs for Cuddles technology unit plan	156
4.22 Level 6 website for Hobbit Harriers technology unit plan	158
5.1 Examples of pull-along toys	174
5.2 Bee-Bots on the farm	179
5.3 Savoury yoghurt given brief	182
5.4 Questionnaire taken home	183
5.5 Taste test form used by the students	184
5.6 A range of props shown to the students	187
5.7 One child's sketch of a microphone	188
5.8 Biscuit colour chart	191
5.9 A base recipe that might be used in this unit	193
5.10 Nutritional panel for base biscuit recipe	194
5.11 Example of te reo readers	198
5.12 Sensory evaluation diagram	204

Tables

1.1 Differentiating technology education and educational technology	2
3.1 Information search process model	66
3.2 Authentic activities and pedagogy within the immigrant biscuit context	72
3.3 Sophistication and flexibility of thinking across two achievement objectives	81
3.4 Potential behaviours underpinning success in technology	82
3.5 TOCF nature of technology level 4 NZC	83
4.1 Technology components and levels adapted from NZC	97
4.2 Links between the 1995, 2007 and 2017 technological areas	102
4.3 Immediate contexts of learning for technological areas at each NCZ level	118
4.4 Potential attributes and related specifications	125
4.5 Critical path example for making a developing a new muffin type showing optimal and alternative time interval allocations	130
4.6 The lesson slice	162
4.7 Learning intentions with context separated	164
4.8 Muddled and contest-free learning intentions	164
5.1 An example of a CCP pathway: fast foods	202

1 Introduction

Technology is all around us. It is an integrated part of what it is to be human. In fact, technology separates us from other living species. Building, manipulating and modifying our environment to meet specific needs is an innate human behaviour. You only need to observe a group of very young children in a sandpit or playing with blocks to see that we build and "intervene" in our world as soon as we are physically able. It therefore makes sense that in school we should learn about technology. Technology education in this book refers to the learning area of the curriculum that helps children understand the influences of technology on their past, present and future world as well as developing the capability to skilfully and ethically design, develop and evaluate technologies within authentic contexts.

Technology education is a learning area that deals with the ways people develop their technological environment to enhance their experiences of, and in, the world. The world today is technological; people engage with and use technology from the minute they are born, some even before. It therefore makes sense that students are educated about technology, learn how it is developed, how it influences and impacts on their lives and how to develop it ethically and sustainably. For students to be happy and to flourish in a technological world, it is important that they become technological literate.

The term technological literacy, sometimes known as technacy, is defined in a number of different ways, but essentially means to acquire a level of literacy that is needed to understand and operate within today's technological world. Not only do people need to read and write (language literacy), engage with and use numbers (numeracy or number literacy), they also need to be able to engage with, critique and develop technology (technological literacy/technacy). Knowledge in technology is often difficult to define, but includes not only "knowing that" but also "knowing how." Early philosophers of technology often identified knowledge deployed in the development of artefacts as being borrowed from science, but we now know that technology is a body of knowledge in its own right and that people who use technology have knowledge and understanding that differs from that of technology developers. These knowledge categories are particularly relevant to technological knowledge; "those who do" and "those who use" technology.

2 Introduction

Table 1.1 Differentiating technology education and educational technology

Technology education Students learn ...	Educational technology Teachers and students learn ...
the impacts of technology on their and others' lives and the environment	educational technologies are tools to facilitate learning
the influences of technology on humans and the environment	that different pedagogical approaches can be deployed
to critique existing technology to inform future practice	to use technology to enhance teaching and learning
to plan and undertake technological practice	that educational technologies facilitate different ways of doing and thinking
to design ethical and authentic technological outcomes	that educational technology does not include designing and developing these tools only using them for learning
to develop the above outcomes	technologies influence ways of learning
to evaluate designed outcomes using stakeholder feedback and developed attributes and specifications	to evaluate technologies used to enhance teaching and learning
to develop technological literacy	that educational technologies include distance learning as well as enhanced face-to-face learning

Technology education is not to be confused with educational technology, which involves children using technology as a learning tool. Table 1.1 summarises the key ideas differentiating technology education and educational technology. It is important to understand these before we begin to think about teaching technology.

Technology education explicitly deals with the technological processes of investigating, designing, making and appraising technological solutions for identified problems or recognised opportunities within any given social and cultural context. Programmes of learning in technology use authentic learning contexts and models for inquiry-based learning, facilitating the integration of numerous curriculum areas. Technology is interdisciplinary and requires student technologists to work in an integrated manner. This symbiotic relationship with a number of other curriculum areas means that through technological practice, students will deploy knowledge from a range of other disciplines in meaningful contexts thus enhancing understanding of technology and other curriculum areas. Technology education has been a part of the New Zealand curriculum (NZC) since the publication of New Zealand Ministry of Education's (MoE) *The New Zealand Curriculum Framework* published in 1993. Technology was included for the first time in this publication as one of the then eight curriculum areas. A draft technology curriculum followed in 1995 with *Technology in the New Zealand Curriculum* published in 1997. This was the first time technology in any form was a part of the primary (Years 1–6) curriculum in New Zealand, although compulsory implementation was delayed due to industrial action by

Introduction 3

the Post Primary Teachers' Association (PPTA) with formal gazetting of the curriculum occurring in 1999.

At the time of implementation, the MoE offered a number of professional learning and development (PLD) contracts to assist teacher professional development. This occurred at a time when other curriculum areas were also undergoing changes and the programmes offered were "opt" in programmes so not all teachers received professional development in technology. In primary schools, technology was a completely new subject; however, in intermediate schools the specialist "manual" (woodwork, metalwork, food and textiles teachers) became "technology" teachers overnight with little or no training or no concept of technology. Many did not understand the philosophical understandings of technology and how it differed from previous technical skill-based programmes. The issue of a lack of understanding of technology in primary and intermediate schools continues today for many teachers of technology and gives rise to the need for this book.

To exacerbate this issue, since its introduction the technology curriculum has undergone two other significant changes, the first following the Ministry of Education Curriculum Stocktake resulting in the publication of *The New Zealand Curriculum* in 2007. The second occurring in 2017 giving digital technologies a stronger presence within the technology curriculum. The book explores these changes and curriculum development in later chapters. A special feature of the book is the culminating section presented as a narrative. A narrative approach explores technology through the eyes of two students, one male and one female as they journey through their technology education schooling. Written in the first person it gives the students' perspective on their learning experiences and assessment of technology education. Running parallel to this narrative is a narrative of the various technology teachers the students encounter during their schooling. It makes explicit links to teacher thinking, curriculum, research theory, and explains what their students are required to do and why? Planning, implementation, evaluation and assessment of technology education learning are included in the teachers' narratives. The aim of the narrative is to develop an engaging text for student teachers and practicing teachers alike.

Rationale and aim

Teacher knowledge in technology has two distinct categories: technological content knowledge (TCK) and pedagogical content knowledge (PCK). Both categories play an important role in teachers' ability to teach technology effectively and students' attitudes and achievement in technology. We are concerned that student teachers of technology and teachers new to New Zealand often have limited or narrow understanding of technology that influences their ability and confidence to teach technology.

This book aims to develop understanding of technology education in New Zealand. It is New Zealand's story of technology education from the late 20th century

4   *Introduction*

into the 21st century. It informs primary and secondary student teachers, teachers, school and technology education programmes and senior management teams, and is informed by and organised through the Pre-service Technology Teacher Education Resource (PTTER) framework, developed by initial teacher education (ITE) educators from the six universities in New Zealand that have ITE programmes and subsequently published in the *International Journal of Technology and Design Education* (Forret et al., 2011).

The PTTER framework consists of four cornerstones recommended for framing technology teacher education programmes. These include sections of the philosophy of technology, a rationale for its inclusion in the curriculum, the nature of the technology curriculum in New Zealand and guidelines for its implementation in both primary and secondary classrooms. The aims and principles of *The New Zealand Curriculum* published by the New Zealand MoE in 2007 and the updated *Technology in the New Zealand Curriculum* statement published in 2017 also by the MoE underpin this book (MoE, 2017b).

During the last 12 years, technology in the NZC has undergone two significant changes. Additional changes to senior secondary assessment have added complexity. The 2007 iteration added two new strands for learning (Technological Knowledge and the Nature of Technology) and saw the introduction of new achievement objectives for all strands. After the implementation of the 2007 NZC, there was a significant review of the New Zealand Qualifications Authority (NZQA) framework, to align senior secondary school assessment with the newly introduced achievement objectives. Because of the review of unit and achievement standards, there was a considerable change in practice in assessment for teachers of secondary school technology from 2011 to 2013.

As alluded to above, the NZC has very recently undergone other significant changes, including a rewritten curriculum statement, the addition of the two new technological areas – computational thinking and designing and developing digital outcomes – and a reformation of the previous technological areas. The purpose of this 2017 change is to strengthen the place of digital technologies in the curriculum.

At the beginning of 2019, national standards were removed from primary schools. This too affects technology as it provides opportunity for primary teachers to lessen their focus on achievement in reading, writing and mathematics, to focus on teaching a broad and balanced curriculum of all eight learning areas, including technology education and other subjects such as science, health and social studies. New Zealand has had national standards for nine years. Many existing teachers have not taught technology or have forgotten how to plan and implement quality learning to address this area of the curriculum.

Future changes are also predicted, with a further review underway to align senior secondary school practices with contemporary and innovative approaches to learning and still further revision of the senior secondary achievement standards. The above MoE actions and policy changes have also impacted teacher education. As student teachers come to grips with new ideas about technology, they find that the curriculum requirements are very different to their precious ideas and experiences. During professional experiences in schools, student teachers should be given the opportunity to observe and implement quality practice. Student teachers need to understand technology and how to implement it successfully. Current teachers need to become familiar with recent modifications to the technology curriculum, including implementation of digital technologies. Given that schools' engagement with the recent changes is variable, the latter cannot be assured. This book therefore supports student teachers and teachers to connect recent relevant theory with practice. The last textbook published for technology teacher education in the New Zealand context was edited by Janet Burns in 1997. Technology in the NZC has several unique features compared to other countries. This book covers a number of these unique features that are not necessarily covered in more generic books related to technology education. Pre-service student teachers: Early Childhood, Primary and Secondary sectors, teachers in New Zealand new to teaching technology, foreign teachers of technology employed to teach technology in New Zealand, international and national researchers of technology education will find this book of value.

Structure of the book

This book has four further sections based on the four cornerstones of the PTTER framework (Forret et al., 2011).These cornerstones are deemed necessary for successful teaching of technology in New Zealand. To be successful, teachers of technology must understand the underpinning philosophy of technology, have a strong rationale for teaching technology, know and understand technology content including deep and meaningful connections within it and finally how it is best implemented in the classroom.

Outline of chapters

Chapter 1: Introduction

This chapter gives a brief overview of what can be found in the book. To establish a clear understanding of technology education it initially defines technology and differentiates between technology education and education technology. It gives a brief overview of the pathway to the current curriculum documents relevant to technology education before stating the rationale and aims of the book. Because technology has roots in a wide variety of camps such as technical education, computer science and home economics it is critical that this chapter outlines the perspectives taken in subsequent chapters. It also outlines how the book is organised and its link to the PTTER framework. This framework uses four cornerstones to framing technology teacher education programmes. They are philosophy of technology, a rationale for its inclusion in the curriculum,

6 *Introduction*

the nature of the technology curriculum in New Zealand and guidelines for its implementation in both primary and secondary classrooms.

Chapter 2: Underpinning philosophy and perspectives of technology in New Zealand

The relationship between people and technology underpins this chapter. Before technology can be taught with clarity and depth teachers must have a clear understanding of technology and the relationship it has to people, society and culture. So much of today's technology is developed to make money or seize power. It is easy to forget that technology is ultimately about people. Culture and customs influence technologies people engage in. Technology impacts human lives significantly. This chapter is a timely reminder of this. The second half of the chapter touches on the process people use to generate technological outcomes. These ideas are explored further in subsequent chapters. The chapter concludes with a discussion about fundamental differences between science and technology. Science and technology are closely related and inform each other however it is important to recognise that they have different practices, knowledge and skill bases. Technology intervenes in the world. Science explores and aims to understand the world.

Chapter 3: Rationale for and nature of technology education in New Zealand

This chapter begins by exploring and critiquing the original six key rationale given for implementing technology into the New Zealand context, finding them as relevant today as they were when they were first identified. These rationale allude to a number of pedagogical approaches and key learning ideas with implications and applications for technology. These too are discussed in this chapter. Technology is an academic subject in the New Zealand curriculum however it is often mistaken as a subject for those who are struggling academically. Understanding the academic content technology means understanding relevant theoretical and knowledge bases. Technology is about identifying and solving technological issues with an academic and practical duality. This chapter explains and discusses technological literacy and practice introducing a number of models of technology practice. Current problem-based student-centered pedagogies are of particular interest and relevance to technology. This chapter concludes with description of a number of key teaching approaches some of which are illustrated.

Chapter 4: Implementing the technology curriculum in New Zealand

Chapter 4 is dedicated to explaining and illustrating all aspects unique to Technology in the New Zealand curriculum including Te Whāriki, our early childhood curriculum (ECE) and Marautanga o Aotearoa our Māori medium curriculum. It does not explicitly include how *The New Zealand Curriculum* (NZC) 'front end' such as principles, values and key competencies are present and or taught through. When using this chapter student teachers, teachers and teacher educators should do so through the framework of this front end. Technology should offer students multiple opportunities to engage with and learn through the NZC principles, values and key competencies. With this in mind Chapter Four outlines the framework and all components of technology education in New Zealand with the intent to assist those new to teaching technology to understand its structure and implementation of the curriculum. A unit planning process including steps for preplanning and a unit template are also offered in this chapter. Each recommended step in the unit planning process is modelled at levels 1 and 6 of NZC. These represent learning from the beginning and end of the compulsory sector. The immediate context for the L1 unit is 'Flugs for Cuddles' and at L6 Website for Hobbit Harriers. The chapter concludes with a brief explanation of technology in the ECE sector.

Chapter 5: Classroom narrative

Technological practice is a means to realise students' thinking and design ideas in order to solve technological problems. This chapter is organized as a narrative in which two fictitious children work their way through early childhood education, primary and secondary schools. Some of the units are loosely based on actual experiences of the authors. The childrens' experiences and activities in technology education are described. In parallel to this runs teacher commentary about the planning and thinking that has gone into the technology learning undertaken by the students. Our narrative begins when our two imaginary children who are in their last year in early childhood education (Early Years). It then tracks them through their technology learning in Years 1-3 (Junior Primary School), Years 4-6 (Middle Primary School), Year 7-8 (Intermediate School); Year 9-10 (Lower Secondary School) and Year 11-13 (Senior Secondary School). Our children, Cooper and Aria are four years old when our narrative begins. Cooper is a European male and Aria a Māori female.

Chapter 6: Epilogue

This chapter is an epilogue rather than a conclusion. It reiterates our purpose for the book and explains technology's checkered journey in New Zealand. It also recaps the fundamental shifts in thinking to move from teaching and learning programmes that are based on skill development to programmes that are problem-based. It proceeds by giving a quick summary of the key ideas presented in each chapter. The chapter concludes with a reminder that the book is a means to support technology teachers at various stages of their professional journey. It recommends that Chapter 5 is used in conjunction with the New Zealand

8 *Introduction*

curriculum (NZC) achievement objectives and their Indicators of Progression found in Technology Online.

Bibliography

Burns, J. (Ed.). (1997). *Technology in the New Zealand curriculum – perspectives on practice*. Auckland: The Dunmore Press Ltd.

Forret, M., Fox-Turnbull, W., Granshaw, B., Harwood, C., Miller, A., O'Sullivan, G., & Patterson, M. (2011). Towards a pre-service technology teacher education resource for New Zealand. *International Journal of Technology and Design Education*, early access online (December). http://link.springer.com/article/10.1007/s10798-011-9199-8#page-1.

Ministry of Education (MoE). (1993). *The New Zealand curriculum framework*. Learning Media.

Ministry of Education (MoE). (1995). *Technology in the New Zealand curriculum*. Learning Media.

Ministry of Education (MoE). (2007). *The New Zealand curriculum*. Learning Media.

Ministry of Education (MoE). (2017a). *Te whāriki a te kōhanga reo*. Ministry of Education.

Ministry of Education (MoE). (2017b). *Technology in the New Zealand curriculum*. Ministry of Education. Retrieved 20 February from http://nzcurriculum.tki.org.nz/The-New-Zealand-Curriculum/Technology.

2 Underpinning philosophy and perspectives of technology in New Zealand

Technology and humans

Wherever you happen to be while reading this, take a moment to look around and consider how many things around you are human-made. Assuming you are inside as you read this, there are likely to be tables, chairs, sofas, light fittings, books, pens, cell phones, computers, the various items of clothing you are wearing, carpet, curtains, the actual building you are in and so on. It doesn't take long to realise that virtually everything around you, or on you, is the result of human ingenuity and endeavour. If you happen to be outside while reading this, the list is likely to be just as long. When you start to look more closely and think more deeply about the 'made' world in which we live, and usually take for granted, you soon find yourself asking questions like, "Why are things the way they are? Where did they come from? Who decided they should be the way they are? How and why were they made, and by whom?" To understand the nature of technology, that is, to understand what technology is as a human endeavour, and how it is practised, we need to ask and answer these sorts of questions, to consider the world in which you live and challenge what you take for granted. Developing your own self-awareness helps you better understand both technology and technology education.

The nature and perspectives of technology

A good place to start in our quest to understand the nature of technology is for you to think about your view of technology and see how this compares with others' views. It is likely that, unless you have been intimately involved in technological practice, your view of technology has, like much of society, been influenced by how technology is described in the media and marketing or you may have undertaken technology at school and made "stuff," sometimes pretty much the same as everyone else in the class because you were told by your teacher what to make and sometimes you might have even been told why you were making it.

While there is variation in the perceptions of technology, common views of technology tend to include three main features. First, technology is commonly

10 *Philosophy and perspectives of technology*

considered to be associated with electronics and computing. When a teacher is asked what subject they teach and they reply *technology*, the inquirer will usually assume that they teach their students about computers and information and communication technology and, while this may be the case, it often is not. It is perhaps inevitable that when many people think of technology, they make associations with high-tech electronic devices such as computers, cell phones and televisions.

A second common view, associated with the first, is that technology refers to things or artefacts. In addition to electronic devices, many people also recognise other human-made things as technology – such as cars, buildings, bridges and other physical constructions. While many technological outcomes are indeed physical things, technology is not simply a collective synonym for these items.

A third common view is that technology is a modern development that has a relatively short history. Such assumptions relate to a high-tech, electronic view of technology or to technological outcomes that have only been developed within the last century or so.

While the above views are partially accurate, they represent a narrow view of technology. One of our main aims in this book is to help you develop a deeper, broader and more comprehensive understanding of technology and technology education.

Technology and human development

When reflecting upon the human-made things around you, it is also worth considering the ways in which your life would be different had these technological outcomes not been developed. We are so used to having technological artefacts and systems around us that we seldom stop to consider the real impact they have on our everyday life. As an example, let's look at refrigeration. Up to 54% of New Zealand houses have had their own, or access to a shared, refrigerator, since the 1950s (Department of Statistics, 1956). Now, virtually every contemporary New Zealand household has at least one refrigerator and probably a freezer as well. We simply expect to be able to keep food and drink fresh for long periods of time and think nothing of being able to do this. The freezer allows us to keep meat, dairy products and numerous other foodstuffs fresh and ready for our use for a long period of time. Think for a moment how your life would change if refrigeration was not available.

Doing this takes you back to what life was like in the time of your great grandparents. Milk had to be bought daily. Special treats, like ice cream, had to be bought just before the meal in which it was to be consumed. Meat, fish, fruit and various other foods had to be bought more regularly because they could not be kept for long periods of time without them deteriorating in quality. This meant that the number and types of available foods, shopping patterns, the type and location of shops, and the sorts of meals that were prepared, were quite different from today. The very existence of the ubiquitous modern supermarket depends on refrigeration.

Philosophy and perspectives of technology 11

Figure 2.1 S.S. Dunedin in port (Wikimedia Commons, the free media repository)

Think of all the things you keep in the fridge – milk, cheese, butter and/or margarine, meat, fish, fruit, drinks, eggs, leftovers and much more – and how having a fridge shapes the way you live. What would you do if you didn't have a fridge? While refrigeration has clearly changed the way we eat, shop and much else in our daily lives, it has also been responsible for much of New Zealand's economic prosperity.

In 1882, the sailing ship S.S. Dunedin (Figure 2.1) delivered the first cargo of frozen meat from New Zealand to Britain. This voyage, from Port Chalmers to London, took three months during which the cargo was kept frozen by a Bell-Coleman refrigeration system driven by a steam engine that used three tons of coal a day. The successful delivery of the S.S. Dunedin's cargo paved the way for the trade in frozen meat and dairy products that became the cornerstone of New Zealand's economy.

Refrigeration is important not just for exporting frozen meat, dairy and numerous other products such as fish, fruit and flowers, it is also a necessity for the farms that produce these products. New Zealand dairy farming depends on refrigeration. Without it, there would be no practical way to safely store or transport large quantities of milk. One of the reasons New Zealand has such a well-established road network is that milk tankers can access farms to collect milk. Similarly, other industries like brewing and wine making also depend on refrigeration and it would not take much thought to list many other ways in which refrigeration is important in our contemporary lives.

Thus, the advent of refrigeration has changed our way and quality of life, changed the layout of our towns and cities, and underpins much of New Zealand's economic success. The reason refrigeration has had such an impact is that it has successfully helped to solve a problem that humans have grappled

12 *Philosophy and perspectives of technology*

with for millennia, the problem of food preservation. When humans developed farming and agriculture, we were able to produce a surplus of food, but, as food production is cyclic and linked to the seasons, it became necessary to develop ways to store/preserve food during times of plenty so that it was available during times of shortage, particularly in winter. Techniques for preserving food such as drying, salting, pickling and the making of preserves (jams) have been practised for thousands of years and are increasingly a skill left to gourmets or those with a passion for cooking. The relatively recent development of refrigeration allows us to fairly effortlessly preserve and store food. The above example of refrigeration, and we could have chosen any one of numerous other technological developments, serves to illustrate some important points about the nature of technology, each of which we will discuss further:

1 Technological developments draw on existing knowledge and skills and evolve over historical time.
2 There is a strong and mutually forming relationship between technology and society.
3 Technology is value-laden and values driven.

Technological development

A brief look at any contemporary technology shows that new developments are built on existing knowledge and capabilities. While the S.S. Dunedin's 1882 voyage was a first in transporting frozen meat to Britain, the ability to do this required a number of already available technological capabilities. Some of the most obvious are that it was necessary to be able to build a ship capable of carrying the cargo and be able to navigate it safely from New Zealand to Britain. Knowing how to build a Bell-Coleman compression refrigeration system was also needed along with the capability to build and operate a steam engine. Refrigeration on its own would be of little use without the other technological developments that made the voyage possible.

While, in 1882, the S.S. Dunedin and the technology employed in her historic voyage were very *modern* for the time, each of the necessary components listed above have a long history of development. Shipbuilding has been practised for thousands of years. Although, in 1882, the Dunedin was a modern ship, the knowledge and skills employed in her design and construction have been developed over a very long time. Similarly, although the first commercial steam engine was developed in 1712 by Thomas Newcomen, there is evidence that ideas for a rudimentary steam engine had been developed by Hero of Alexandria as far back as the 1st century AD. In 1882, refrigeration was a relatively new development, with the first closed vapour-compression refrigeration system being described in 1805 and the first working system being built by Jacob Perkins in 1834. Māori had their own means of preservation, where food was stored in *whata*, which were elevated platforms with thatched tops to protect the food from vermin and extreme weather.

Philosophy and perspectives of technology 13

We could consider the technological knowledge and capability needed to build a ship, steam engine and refrigerator, and how each of these developments is the culmination of numerous other developments. Refrigerators are not driven by steam engines. For refrigeration to become available as a household appliance, several other developments needed to occur with the most obvious being electricity generation – the electric motor that drives the pump in the fridge and the electrical grid that delivers electrical energy to all corners of the country. As we think about technological developments, we soon begin to realise how interconnected and interdependent they are. New developments and solutions soon lead to further developments and solutions, each building on what has already been achieved.

Technology and society

The above example of refrigeration illustrates the close relationship between technological development and our style and quality of life. Even within the few generations in which refrigeration has been developed and become an integral part of our lives, we can see the changes that have occurred. Changes in technology are driven by our needs and wants and changes in society are caused by our adoption of new technological developments. This notion is called technological determinism.

If we look way back into the history of human development, we can see how intimately connected are our technological capability and our survival and development as a species. What has given humans our survival edge and allowed us to become such a successful species is our ability to make tools and change and shape our environment to meet our needs and wants. This ability is what sets us apart from other species. It is not that other species do not use tools or change and shape their environment but no other species does this to the extent, or with the complexity, that humans do. Jacob Bronowski (2011) began his account of the evolution of human civilisation with the statement that:

> Man is a singular creature. He has a set of gifts which make him unique among the animals: so that, unlike them he is not a figure in the landscape – he is a shaper of the landscape. In body and in mind he is the explorer of nature, the ubiquitous animal, who did not find, but made his home in every continent (p. 19).

Our ability to live in virtually every environment on the planet from the frozen arctic to arid deserts, rain forests, temperate grasslands and high altitude mountains is due to our ingenuity in using the resources available to construct solutions to meet our needs. Mark Cosgrove (1989) defined human technology as "the way humans use intellectual capabilities and physical resources to solve problems of survival, well-being and quality of life" (p. 3).

Technological capability set humans on a different evolutionary path from other animals. It provided us with a distinct survival advantage that has, to some

14 *Philosophy and perspectives of technology*

extent, overridden our natural biological evolution. It changed our primordial ancestors to such an extent that John Dakers (2006) commented that "the trajectory of our evolution, physically, intellectually, and culturally, is a direct result of tool use and technological development" (p. 146).

A good indication of the close relationship between human and technological development is the way in which human history is often described in a series of Ages, starting with the Stone Age, Bronze Age, Iron Age and more recently the Industrial Age and Information Age (also known as the Computer Age or Digital Age). All of these historical periods align with particular types of tools, technological capabilities and outcomes that characterise that period of our history. The way we live and the quality of our lives is directly connected to the tools we make and the technological capability they afford us to, as Cosgrove put it, solve problems of survival, well-being and quality of life.

While the technologies we develop to meet our needs and wants, change and shape our lives, it is also the case that our needs and wants determine the technologies that we develop. Our need/want to preserve and store food has led us to develop various food preservation techniques, including refrigeration. Our need/want for transport has led to the development of the wide variety of modes of transport we see today. Our health needs/wants have led to the array of medicines and techniques now available, and so on.

Technology and values

An important point here is that, because technology is driven by our needs/wants/desires, technology is essentially driven by our values, and technological outcomes are heavily value-laden. We use the word *values* here in its broadest sense, meaning the range of principles, beliefs and preferences, that determine what we value. We are not referring simply to monetary value, although making money is clearly a part of the human spectrum of wants and desires.

Solving problems of survival, well-being and quality of life is a values-infused endeavour. When we use words like well-being and quality of life, not everyone will have the same perspective on their meaning. An individual, or group, perspective on this is determined by their values, what one person considers an improvement in their quality of life may be perceived by someone else as a reduction in their quality of life. This means that there is diversity in the technological outcomes that people develop, correlating with a variation in wants and desires.

Diversity is part of what makes our "made" world so interesting and also means that there are many ways to approach technological development. We can respond to technological challenges in a variety of effective and successful ways – there is always more than one way to achieve a technological goal.

From an educational perspective, this is particularly pertinent because it means that, in technology, there is not one right answer to solving a technological problem. For many students this may be contrary to a lot of what they have experienced at school where much of their time is spent trying to come up with

Philosophy and perspectives of technology   15

the *right* answer. In technology, there is always more than one way to achieve the goal and several of these may be excellent, but different, solutions.

Imagine for a moment that you are faced with the challenge of producing safe, reliable, economical, eco-friendly, comfortable and affordable transport, and presumably this is the actual goal of a number of technologists. We can see that different groups of technologists would produce different responses (solutions) to this challenge. We could evaluate these solutions to identify their relative strengths and weaknesses and decide which solution we feel best meets the established goals. The process of designing and building a vehicle, as well as evaluating it, is inevitably one of competing goals, or values. One solution may be very eco-friendly, but expensive to buy, while another might be very affordable but doesn't meet the highest safety standards. We can imagine lots of possible variations based on the response of different teams engaging in the challenge. Even if several vehicles rated the same in all identified criteria, which is unlikely, there would still be preference differences according to the individual's emotional response to the overall design, colour and aesthetic appeal of the vehicle.

Thus, we can see that technological development is driven by our values. The technological outcomes that are retained by society and become part and parcel of our everyday lives are those that best meet our needs and resonate with our values. Similarly, we can see how technological outcomes represent the decisions their designers and builders have made, and that these are a reflection of the values that guided those decisions.

Let us now return to the three common views of technology discussed earlier and see what we make of them in light of what we have said about technology so far. It is understandable that many people might have a here-and-now, high-tech view of technology that focuses on the latest, exciting technological outcomes. After all, these are the products and systems that we see around us, and the ones that are most prominently advertised and discussed in the media. However, technological outcomes encompass much more than just high-tech digital electronics and our view of technology needs to recognise this.

For similar reasons, it is understandable that many people might think of technology as a general name for all the human-made things that surround them but you can see from the above definition of technology that technology refers to the whole process by which we solve problems of survival, well-being and quality of life and not just the outcomes of this process. This is why, as you might have noticed, we refer to human-made artefacts and systems as technological outcomes. To us, it is misleading to refer to a computer, bicycle, or clothes peg, as technology. These are technological outcomes, the result of a process of evolving technological development.

Humans have always engaged in technology. At any point in history we could call the current technological developments *modern* (just as, in 1882 the S.S. Dunedin was a modern ship), but, as we have seen, a broader perspective shows us that technology as a human enterprise has always been a part of human development and, in that sense, is in fact, an ancient endeavour.

16   *Philosophy and perspectives of technology*

The scientific name given to our species is *homo sapiens*, which is Latin for wise person or man the knower. In light of the close developmental relationship we have with our technological capability it has been suggested that a better name for our species would be *homo faber* – man the maker.

Technological practice

How do we go about the process of creating technological products and systems that meet our needs and wants? Earlier, we looked briefly at a challenge of producing safe, reliable, economical, eco-friendly, comfortable and affordable transport. This sort of description of the task in hand is called a *Design Brief*. Within the design brief, a technologist aims to describe clearly what we are trying to do by identifying the goals for the project. In our current brief we have identified safety, reliability, economy, environmentally friendly, comfort and affordability as characteristics of a successful outcome; these are the characteristics we value in the vehicle we are trying to develop.

Although this list of criteria may seem clear, the brief is still generic and missing some very important information. For example, for whom is the vehicle being designed, for what will it be mainly used and in what type of environment will it be used? Knowing who the client, or end user is, and the purpose and context for which the product is intended is crucial information to developing a successful outcome.

Also, when we say we want a vehicle that is economical to run, what exactly do we mean? What level of economy are we looking for? In order to achieve this goal, we will need to specify this precisely – for example, we could identify kilometres per litre for a petrol/diesel vehicle, kilometres per battery charge for an electric vehicle. This identifies the specifications to aim for. Some design criteria, like fuel economy, can be specified quantitatively and objectively. Comfort is much more qualitative and subjective and requires developers to be in touch with what the end user wants and needs – their values.

As we discussed earlier, technological development evolves by building on, and extending, existing knowledge and capability. In developing our design brief and its associated specifications, we will need to investigate whether there are any existing products, techniques or knowledge that can be researched and inform our ideas. Finding out all we can about previous (if any) or associated approaches to our problem is always a good starting point.

At the beginning, our brief will contain initial specifications for our vehicle but, as we work through the design and development process, it is likely that we will modify these and maybe add new specifications. Throughout the process of developing our solution, we will likely be involved in research (including market research), planning, project management, designing, modelling, making and evaluating. Each of these activities involves bringing a range of knowledge and skills to the task of developing our outcome and, at some point, after much developmental work, we will have final specifications from which our product or system can be constructed.

Philosophy and perspectives of technology 17

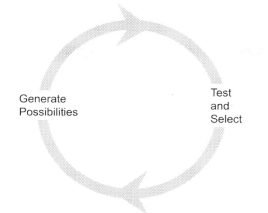

Figure 2.2 The GTS cycle

The development process

The process we use to go from our initial design brief and specifications to a final outcome can follow a cyclic or iterative process. We might identify a possible solution, try it out, see if it works and meets the intended goals. If it does, great, it's done. If not, using what is learned from this experience can be used to come up with a new possible solution. Try that out and see if it works and meets the intended goals. If it does, great, we're done. If not, using what is learned from this experience can be used to come up with a new possible solution … and so on until you are satisfied with your solution. This process can be described as a developmental cycle of generating-testing-and-selecting (GTS cycle), as shown in Figure 2.2.

A more detailed description of the process might include some, or all, activities like research (including market research), planning, project management, designing, modelling, making and evaluating, but, at its core, this is a process of generating possible solutions, testing them, selecting what works and generating new possibilities based on what you have learned. It seems very simple, and it is, but it is also extremely effective and we will look at each part in more detail.

Generation of ideas

When faced with a problem you do not already know how to solve, the only way forward is to try something new, and this requires you to generate some possible solutions that can then be considered against the original brief. The more ideas you can come up with the better. If you only have one idea, the chances of it being the ultimate solution are small, but out of many ideas may come one exceptional solution – each idea will likely contribute something important to the overall development of the final outcome.

18 *Philosophy and perspectives of technology*

As mentioned earlier, a good starting point is to find out all we can about existing (if any) approaches to our problem, or to similar problems. This type of research helps to focus our attention on design details and to see possible improvements. Working in a team is helpful in generating ideas. Each member of a design team will see things differently and have different ideas, adding to the pool of possibilities. Brainstorming and discussion are good for ideas generation and development. Listening to others' ideas is a good way to stimulate your thinking and spark new ideas.

Testing-and-selecting

Testing-and-selecting lies at the heart of technological development and is something we all do all the time, often unconsciously, as we make decisions and solve problems. Testing-and-selecting can happen quickly and informally as we encounter something new and consider what we think of it. In a brainstorming session with other members of a design team, you may test-and-select many ideas. Testing-and-selecting in this case means assessing your initial response to an idea or design. You may like a particular idea/design; think it has value, while disliking and rejecting another idea. As discussion goes on and some ideas begin to be more favoured, testing becomes more rigorous in relation to the particular pros and cons of a design, in relation to the design brief.

Beyond the testing-and-selecting of a brainstorming session, ideas that have been selected for further development can be tested in a variety of ways, including two-dimensional and three-dimensional drawings, computer, or physical modelling. Drawings are a great way to share and test ideas. Drawings make it easier to see how design ideas will look and work (form and function) and to try out variations of a design in terms of shape, size, colour or material – without the cost of actually constructing it. Further testing of form, function and feel may require the construction of physical models. For products with which people will physically interact (touch, manipulate, handle, read, operate), physical models are essential for testing their functionality, look, feel and user friendliness.

The ultimate modelling test is to build a *prototype*. Unlike other physical models, which are often not complete working models having been built to test characteristics such as dimensions, look, feel and aesthetics, a prototype is built to look and operate exactly as the proposed final outcome and provides the ultimate test of all the ideas and work that has gone into the design and construction of the outcome. Of course, what you learn from building a prototype may mean that the development process is not over and that further changes to the design are required.

As with the generation of ideas, testing-and-selecting is also more effectively done in teams. Just as members of a team have different perspectives, experiences and knowledge that support the generation of more, and more varied, ideas so a team enhances testing-and-selecting by providing different ways of looking at (evaluating) ideas. The more thoroughly an idea is tested the better the outcome will be.

Philosophy and perspectives of technology   19

Any test or selection requires that there be something to test for; some criteria by which to select and, as we already know, technology is driven by values. As a design team goes through the GTS process, getting closer and closer to a successful outcome, they are guided by their values.

The values guiding the GTS cycle; the values that possible solutions are being tested for and selected on, are explicitly stated in the design brief and specifications that define the desired outcome. These values reflect the values of those involved in the development process, their principles, beliefs and preferences, including ethical, moral, cultural, economic, political and other values. When, as is usually the case, technological outcomes are aimed at the needs and wants of a client or potential customers, the values of the end user are a key component of the development process. Designers need to understand the needs and wants of their customers and respond to these in the outcomes they develop. The GTS process is therefore driven and directed by a combination of values that are ultimately embedded in the resulting solution.

The cutting room floor

Along with the common views of technology discussed earlier, many people think that the main part of developing innovative technological solutions is to come up with a bright idea and the rest will somehow follow automatically. We enjoy the heroic stories of how innovators and inventors came up with the ideas that underpin new technological developments and it is enticing to think that we can sit around dreaming up new ideas and that this will create great new products and make us rich. However, what we seldom see, or think about, is what is sometimes referred to as the *cutting room floor.*

Moving pictures (movies) can be made by taking many photographs of a scene one after the other very quickly (24 or more photos per second). To view the movie, the images are viewed one after the other at the same rate. Although we are viewing individual images, each image is only seen for a short time and our persistence of vision gives us the impression of smooth motion.

Today, movie making and editing is done digitally on computers but in the early 20th century the captured streams of images were formed into long reels of celluloid film. Because a movie is shot in scenes (parts), the final film had to be put together by physically cutting and pasting lengths of film in the right order to create the proper sequence of the movie. The room in which this editing was done was called the cutting room and the term "cutting room floor" has become synonymous with the footage not included in the finished film. Movie scenes often have to be redone because some aspect of the acting, sound, lighting, set or costume, is not quite right – or the director thinks of a better way to shoot the scene. As new scenes are shot, the film goes back to the cutting room and a new version of the movie emerges. When we eventually see the movie in a cinema, we see the end result of all this work, not the re-shot scenes, editing, and film that is left on the cutting room floor.

20 *Philosophy and perspectives of technology*

Having a good idea is just the start of what can often be a long and difficult journey. This technological journey can also be illustrated by vacuum cleaners. The currently available models in appliance stores are based on the cyclonic filtration system, first introduced by James Dyson in his Dyson brand of cleaners, who got the idea for his new vacuum cleaner by observing cyclonic industrial filtration and extraction systems used in spray-painting facilities, and then adapting this idea to a system that worked effectively in a domestic vacuum cleaner – this did not happen quickly. Over a two-year period, Dyson made over 2000 models in brass and aluminium before he succeeded in making an efficient cyclone vacuum system.

Every technological development has its own version of a cutting room floor. While having great ideas is a key part of technological development, without which we could not move forward, the journey from initial idea to a successfully realised outcome can involve a great deal of hard work and many iterations. This is summed up effectively by Thomas Edison who is famously reported to have commented that "Genius is one percent inspiration and ninety-nine percent perspiration." When asked about all the tests and trials he had to do to come up with something that worked, he said, "I have not failed. I've just found 10,000 ways that won't work."

The GTS process is developmental in nature. With each revolution of the cycle, something new is learned, new possibilities are generated and the way forward becomes clearer. Even when the initial design brief is very clear and detailed, it is common for the end result to vary significantly from that initial brief. We don't know what we don't know – it is not until we embark on the developmental process that we begin to learn how to improve our initial designs. As we learn more about how to do what we are trying to achieve, not only does the way forward become clearer but the goal itself can also change as we see the task from a perspective of greater knowledge and understanding.

Technology and science

Today, it is commonplace to see science and technology appear in the same sentence or statement. New technological developments and innovations are often connected to scientific research and development. Because of this close connection, people are sometimes unclear about the differences between technology and science, thinking that they are perhaps the same or misunderstanding their differences. While technology and science today often work together as we try to solve problems to better understand the world around us, at times, the distinction between the two enterprises is somewhat blurred. It is important, therefore, to consider the nature of science and its relationship with technology.

Along with our ability to create tools to shape and change the environment to meet our needs and wants, another key characteristic of humans is our curiosity; our urge to understand and explain the world around us, and this is what drives science. While technology might be represented to be the pursuit of practical solutions for survival, well-being and quality of life, science is our endeavour to

Philosophy and perspectives of technology 21

understand and explain the world (and universe) around us – a means to explain why things are the way they are and why things happen as they do. Humans are innately curious and continuously seeking answers that help us to understand the world around us.

When faced with things we don't understand and cannot immediately explain, we commonly respond by making up stories that make sense of what we see or experience. This characteristic is seen throughout human history in the myths, legends and religious accounts that have been handed down through the ages across cultures. Ancient philosophers (e.g. Greek and Roman, more than two thousand years ago) spent a lot of time thinking and writing about the world around them and putting forward possible explanations for what they saw and thought about how "things" worked. Their approach was to put forward logical and rational explanations, which would then be debated among those interested in the idea. Some views would gain support within the community and be perpetuated, while others would be abandoned. Generally, what was missing from this approach, however, was support from evidence. It was not until the 16th century with the work of Galileo and Newton that an evidence-based approach to developing scientific explanations began to take over.

Modern science also retains the discussion and debate characteristics of the ancient philosophers, but there is also an expectation that there is the collection of valid and reliable evidence to support those ideas and explanations. Whenever we consider the endeavour of science we bump into the notion of *theory*, which can be represented as *making up stories to explain things*. A theory therefore is a possible explanation and, as we have seen, people have been doing this in one form or another for thousands of years. Theory can often be misunderstood within society however – and taken as some sort of guess, as the opposite of a fact, because "it's just a theory." On the contrary, the reason that a theory becomes accepted within the scientific community is that it is supported by a valid explanation that is consistent with the available evidence. The reason your cell phone works is because our scientific understanding of electromagnetic waves is reliably accurate. Of course, there are other aspects of the world and universe about which we are not so sure. While the general public like to know whether something is right or wrong, or true or false, scientists realise that even when they are highly confident in the veracity of their theory, there is still much to learn. No explanation is perfect and scientists understand that however good their current theory might be, it will certainly be improved in the future.

As with technology, the process by which science develops its explanations is through a process of GTS. In the case of science, the generative part refers to generating possible explanations. Testing-and-selecting applies to scientific investigation to gather valid and reliable evidence that supports or refutes the theory being tested. A particular difference between technology and science is the value-laden and context-dependent nature of technological outcomes. We saw earlier that because technological outcomes are a response to societal needs and wants, these outcomes can vary widely from one country and

22   *Philosophy and perspectives of technology*

culture to another, not just because of different values – although this is a very significant factor – but also because of the available physical and human resources and geographical, economic, political, conditions. In contrast, scientific outcomes – understanding and explanation – are not value and context specific. In other words, and as an example, the scientific understanding of electromagnetic waves that underpins the operation of a cell phone is the same anywhere in the world. Science-based knowledge in this circumstance can be viewed as being universal.

So, technology and science are different, they are aimed at different outcomes and their outcomes are important in their own right. However, it is not difficult to see how the outcomes of each can enhance the other. Understanding the cause of a disease helps us develop new drugs and methods of treatment, understanding the atomic and molecular structure of matter helps us develop new materials with which to design and build, and so on. On the other hand, the development of high-speed computers allows large amounts of research data to be processed and analysed in ways never before possible, advances in glass and optics technology afford the building of ever more capable telescopes, new sensors and instrumentation make it possible to detect and measure physical quantities with greater accuracy and reliability than ever before. Together, technology and science can be more effective to address societal problems. Their relationship is one of mutual support and synergy.

Summary

While technology is often viewed through the lens of the modern, high-tech examples we see around us, in this chapter, we have seen that technology has been around for a very long time and has always been an integral part of human survival and development. Rather than simply a description of artefacts, technology describes an innate human activity through which we solve problems of survival, well-being and quality of life.

Technological practice draws on existing knowledge and skills while, through this practice, new knowledge and skills are generated. Over time, our technologies evolve and improve through a strong and mutually forming relationship between technology and society in which we develop the technologies that meet our meds and wants, and the technologies we develop reflect our values. It is important to recognise the value-laden and values-driven nature of technology.

The chapter concluded with a discussion about fundamental differences between science and technology. While today, science and technology are closely related and inform each other, it is important to recognise that they have different practices and unique knowledge and skill bases. Technology's unique knowledge, skills, history and philosophy indicate the importance of technology as an academic subject in its own right. The following chapter describes the rationale of technology education in schools including theoretical content knowledge that informs technology and pedagogical content knowledge for its successful implementation in the classroom.

Bibliography

Bronowski, J. (2011). *The ascent of man*. The Random House Group.

Cosgrove, M. (1989). *Learning science from technology*. University of Waikato, Hamilton, New Zealand.

Dakers, J. (Ed.). (2006). *Defining technological literacy: Towards an epistemological framework*. Palgrave Macmillan.

Department of Statistics. (1956). *The New Zealand official year-book 1956*. Statistics New Zealand. https://www3.stats.govt.nz/New_Zealand_Official_Yearbooks/1956/NZOYB_1956.html.

3 Rationale for and nature of technology education in New Zealand

Introduction

Government policy and Ministry of Education (MoE) encourages teachers in New Zealand to be legitimate curriculum decision makers. There are tensions that exist between the teaching of the technology curriculum, which is socially organised and affected by teachers' perceptions of the subject. An official curriculum outlines practices that carry specific meanings and importance within a society, and it reflects a country's social, cultural, political and economic discourse to determine what is considered to be official and legitimate knowledge.

This chapter looks at technology in the New Zealand curriculum (NZC). It begins by looking at why we should teach technology and why it is a relatively recent addition to the learning areas. Six key rationales for implementing technology identified as arguments for the initial implementation of technology education are as equally, if not more, relevant today than they were in the early 1990s when first added to the curriculum. These rationales allude to a number of pedagogical approaches and key learning ideas with implications and applications for technology. These too are discussed in this chapter.

Although a relatively recent addition to the curriculum, in its current form, technology education in New Zealand grew out of technical education. The history of the curriculum, including its technical beginnings, is discussed in the chapter. Understanding its beginnings will assist teachers and student teachers to understand the number of challenges for the implementation of the technology curriculum. The chapter concludes with a description and exploration of a range of pedagogical ideas to assist in the successful implementation of technology, based on the philosophical assumption that technology is constructed within sociocultural and historical contexts, by using inquiry-based and constructivist approaches to learning.

Rationale for teaching technology

In 1993, Alister Jones and Malcolm Carr developed a rationale for technology education. They state that technology is a major influence in the lives of all people and communities. Technology ranges from the very simple to the very complex and that, in today's world, it is increasingly important that people are aware of the impact technology has on their lives. Understanding the nature of technology has implications for teachers and learners alike, particularly as an individual's perception of technology is heavily influenced by their lived experiences and engagement with technology.

In New Zealand, there is an aging demographic of teachers, who might be more likely to associate the subject with its technical beginnings and adopt a traditional approach to its enactment (Counts., 2017). According to Reinsfield and Williams (2017), technology education is heavily influenced by political agenda and the perception that its role is to develop students who can contribute to the national workforce, particularly in the trades. Such a driver is disparate to the aims of the NZC, which states that the intent of technology education is to "develop a broad technological literacy that will equip [students] to participate in society as informed citizens and give them access to technology related careers" (MoE, 2007, p. 32).

Understandings of the subject can be interpreted as the result of professional, parental or students' cultural capital (Sullivan, 2001). According to Bourdieu (1986), cultural capital can be represented in three forms – through the dispositions of mind and body, through cultural goods in an objectified state (such as teacher-generated resources) and through institutional discourse. For example, school-aged students may expect learning in technology to involve only practical work because this is what their parents described the subject to be. The tension with this thinking is that it is not reflective of the nature of the subject, as it is conceptualised within the current NZC.

Compared to most other learning areas, technology is a relatively recent addition to the NZC. The nation underwent major curriculum reforms in the early 1990s that saw the establishment of the NZC framework. This framework provided overarching guidance for the development of curricula in New Zealand. It contained seven essential learning areas and for the first time included technology for all students from Years 1 to 10. At this time, six rationales for developing technology education included economic, pedagogic, motivational, cultural, environmental and personal. These provided a strong argument for the inclusion of technology in compulsory education.

Rationale 1: Economy

Economic justification for the place of technology in the curriculum emerged from the understanding that the country could no longer continue to be the "garden for England." Before its entry into the European Economic Unit, Great Britain was a major importer of New Zealand produce and our major source of income. In the 1990s, the New Zealand government realised there was a need for diversification within the economy. To do this New Zealanders needed to become innovative developers of goods and services that did not necessarily rely on our primary industries. It was envisaged that the introduction of technology education could assist in developing innovative, creative thinkers. Technology

26 Rationale for and nature of technology education

education in secondary schools can provide pathways to accommodate a range of workforce needs. At times this creates a professional tension for some teachers. For example, teachers who come from a trade background might value quality outcomes and skill development over process and technological thinking which can lead to a philosophical conflict between the academic and practical enactment of the technology curriculum. Shortages in disciplines such as information and communication technology, science, technology, engineering, and mathematics, have been aligned with an unprecedented and immediate societal need to overcome skills shortages in the trades. These wider pressures can affect secondary teachers, who are sometimes required to make a decision about whether they prepare students for technology-related careers, or alternatively, focus on their enactment of the curriculum.

The tension between vocational (trades) and general education in secondary schools suggests a duality between the two philosophical approaches, which are often taught in the same environment, by the same teachers and to the same students; however, the pragmatics of the subject's implementation can mean that to separate teaching into different concepts or pathways is not always straightforward. Technology education and vocational education have differing purposes and contrasting pedagogical approaches, which have not yet been fully acknowledged in some school contexts.

Economic justification for the implementation of technology in the curriculum is more pertinent today than it was at the time of the subject's introduction. In 2017, digital technologies were given greater prominence in the curriculum. Expertise and skills in the designing and developing of digital technologies, to support learners to become digitally fluent, and creators of digital outcomes, is promoted as a means to assist New Zealand in becoming an increasingly economically prosperous nation.

Rationale 2: Pedagogy

The pedagogical rationale for implementation grew from the recognition that intelligence is not only academic in nature. Technology education, as opposed to its predecessor technical education, introduced the notion of multiple intelligences. To be successful in technology education, students need to understand and facilitate a dynamic relationship between academic, practical intelligence, and skill. Pedagogically, technology enables students to be engaged in real-life problem solving to develop technological outcomes (products and systems) that impact and influence people, communities and environments within their lives. The notion of authentic learning, explored later in this book, is motivational and engaging for students when solving authentic problems. Developing quality technological items to solve technological problems gives rise to many genuine reasons for being engaged in curriculum areas other than technology. What better reason to learn to measure if a student is designing and developing a pattern for a new school uniform or developing a landscape design for a part of their school or local park. What better reasons for learning to write letters and emails if students need to contact experts in the field to assist with technology projects they are working on. Other frequently utilised skills and knowledge in science, social science, health and oral language assist students' motivation for learning as they see real-world reasons for their engagement.

Rationale 3: Motivation

Closely related to the pedagogical rationale, the motivational rationale for implementing technology is very powerful. The authors of this book have experienced first-hand how motivational for students it is to undertake authentic technological practice and engage in helping others. In one technology study, Wendy asked her students to design and develop an aid to assist a one-handed person peel potatoes. As a part of the learning focus, Wendy interviewed a member of her running club who had lost an arm in a shark attack while diving in the Chatham Islands some years earlier. In the interview, recorded and later shown to the students as part of the research project, the amputee, Dougal (not his real name) expressed his dismay at not being able to undertake simple tasks for himself, such as buttering his toast. He cried as he told her that he was now not even able to change his baby's nappies. The resulting video, shown to the Year 4 students before they undertook their design task, had a huge impact; motivation and enthusiasm for the task and concern for Dougal were evident throughout the unit.

Rationale 4: Culture

The cultural rationale for the implementation of technology is possibly more relevant today than in the early 1990s. New Zealand is one of the most culturally diverse countries in the world. In education, we focus on meeting the individual learning needs of all students, guided by the principles of equality and inclusion and Te Tiriti o Waitangi (the Treaty of Waitangi) – ensuring the specific rights of Māori. We are therefore both a bicultural and multicultural nation. Two versions of the curriculum were developed (*The New Zealand Curriculum* and Te Marautanga o Aotearoa) with a view to acknowledge both the Māori and Pakeha world views. Such curriculum development is in keeping with the spirit and intent of the Treaty of Waitangi and New Zealand's bicultural heritage. As stated earlier technology is more than "high tech" products, we commonly associate with it. All technological products and systems are designed and developed *by* people, *in* a particular context; this therefore includes technologies of indigenous peoples from all around the world.

Such diversity requires schools and teachers to be culturally responsive – to recognise and value students' interests and circumstances. Culturally responsive pedagogy is a means to establish effective relationships between teachers and students. For some teachers, however, the development of positive relationships might not be something they highly value, particularly if they are already experiencing professional difficulty, when engaging with the curriculum. In New

28 *Rationale for and nature of technology education*

Zealand, acknowledging *cultural locatedness* is an important way for teachers to support the notion of Tangata Whenuatanga – to recognise the bicultural nature of our country and the unique and valued knowledge that each student brings with them to the classroom. For example, teachers in New Zealand are required to provide contexts for learning, where the identity, language and culture of Māori learners are affirmed – educators need to be responsive to students' interests and circumstances. Such contexts can use peoples' knowledge of the local context, tikanga (traditions) and language and provide opportunities to enact both a local and living curriculum, where students are positioned to drive their own learning.

Technology offers opportunities for students from diverse cultures and backgrounds to draw on their "Funds of Knowledge" (FOK) to contribute to their technological practice. The theory of FOK takes the view that learning does not just happen but is a social process bound within a wider social context. People have wide knowledge, developed through their life experiences. The knowledge that students come to school with can enhance their learning and facilitate useful interactions between knowledge found inside and outside the classroom. The more teachers know about the home and cultural activities and experiences of their students, the better informed they will be, and the better able to maximise learning opportunities and to make the most of knowledge and skills already accessible to some students. Teachers can make more of the learning in their classrooms if they understand that students bring with them knowledge from their families, culture and background. This is particularly valuable when students are working collaboratively with others, and it provides opportunities to value and use knowledge and skills often marginalised by society.

Rationale 5: Environmental

The environmental rationale for implementing technology is becoming increasingly more relevant by the day. Technology education does not only focus on the designing and development of technologies, it also includes understanding the ethical and environmental implications, impacts and influences of technologies. In other words, it encourages students and technologists to contemplate whether they *should* design and develop particular technologies – despite being able to. Many of the world's environmental disasters are technological in nature. The following examples provoke thought around what should/could have been done differently to avoid these problems:

- Agent Orange https://www.history.com/topics/vietnam-war/agent-orange-1
- Pacific Garbage Patch https://www.nationalgeographic.org/encyclopedia/great-pacific-garbage-patch/
- Exxon Valdez https://www.history.com/topics/1980s/exxon-valdez-oil-spill
- Bhopal Gas https://www.britannica.com/event/Bhopal-disaster
- Chernobly Power Plant Explosion https://www.nationalgeographic.com/culture/topics/reference/chernobyl-disaster/

Rationale 6: Personal

The final but by no means the least important rationale for implementing technology into the curriculum is the personal justification. We all live in a technological world. Chapter 2 mentions the ubiquitous nature of technology, it is everywhere and many of us would not be alive today without it. Trying to imagine ourselves in a world without any technology, somewhat embarrassingly, leaves us with no clothes, footwear, processed foods, medications and bedding, just to name a few. One of the main aims of technology education is to enable us to flourish in our technological world. Technology education empowers us to make decisions about how we engage with and consume technologies as well as design and develop it. We want technology to empower us not to capture or constrain us. Technology education assists this.

Technology as an academic subject

While technology has a sound theoretical and knowledge base, it also enjoys a duality with practice. Theories of technology and technological practice that we have discussed earlier in this chapter indicate a language and knowledge base specific to technology education and therefore an academic subject taught in its own right.

Technology has regularly changed as a curriculum area but must be conceived as distinct from, and more inclusive than, traditional technical subjects. It claims intellectually demanding content, fosters fundamentally important cognitive processes, is modern in reflecting advanced industrial practice and the inclusion of a wide range of disciplines and modes of study, including cultural and economic. The inclusion of technology is seen as a key to economic development in countries looking for economic growth.

Contemporary pedagogy in technology

Despite the long-time emphasis on knowledge recall and test performances as a measure of success in schools, more recently there has been a focus on how to prepare students for their future lives within a technological world. In 2007, Guy Claxton suggested that effective 21st-century learners need to be capable of being:

- curious and questioning;
- resilient and focused;
- open-minded and flexible;
- imaginative and creative;
- critical, sceptical and analytical;
- methodical and opportunistic;
- reflective and self-evaluative;
- keen to improve their products and performances;
- collaborative but independent.

30 *Rationale for and nature of technology education*

There are a number of attitudes, skills and dispositions vital for success in today's technological world. These include critical thinking, problem solving, adaptability, initiative, entrepreneurialism, effective communication, analysing information, openness, flexibility of thinking, curiosity, imagination, confidence and self-belief. Learning and progress can be measured through three dimensions: robustness, breadth and richness. Building learning power within children occurs through the development of these attitudes, skills and dispositions within four domains: resilience, resourcefulness, reflectiveness and reciprocity. Within these dimensions sit a number of capabilities particularly relevant to technology education. These include: noticing, perseverance, managing distractions and absorption in the resilience domain; making links, questioning and imaging in resourcefulness; planning and distilling in reflectiveness and collaboration, empathy, and interdependence in reciprocity. Increasing children's curiosity, sense of adventure, perseverance and independence along with teaching children how to be better learners also increases their capabilities for learning.

Technology education offers a range of rich and culturally bound contexts for learning. It engages students in the social construction of outcomes. It facilitates the making of connections, working cooperatively and collaboratively with peers and relevant others. It involves practical engagement in worthwhile and real-world projects. Technology projects are frequently collaborative, requiring cooperative work and shared processes and therefore require more varied approaches to learning than the traditional approaches often used in primary and secondary classrooms. The skills required to work in cooperatively and collaboratively link strongly to attitudes and dispositions mentioned above and *The New Zealand Curriculum* values, principles and key competencies. Capable and effective learners should be able to demonstrate a range of attitudes and dispositions. These link closely to what happens in quality technology education. Varied teaching approaches in technology, deploying the above dispositions and capabilities will engage and motivate students to develop new knowledge and skills much of which can be transferred to a range of other learning situations.

Within real-world contexts, as students determine technological needs and opportunities, design and develop technological outcomes in consultation with key and minor stakeholders they work in authentic practices. Authentic technology practice is real to the students, their lives, and to situations they may encounter in the future workplace. For example, a context in New Zealand in which students design and develop a range of flavoured cottage cheeses, is something that students could relate to as dairy products are a significant part of New Zealand culture and economy. In other words, it is an authentic context because students could imagine they, or someone they know, may, or could, do this professionally. The same study might not be as relevant in Asian or Pacific communities where cheese is not a common aspect of culture.

As technology projects are undertaken, students gain an appreciation of the bigger picture of their current and future worlds, use principles, values and key competencies while they create and innovate, and possibly work with various

Rationale for and nature of technology education 31

digital technologies. The socially embedded nature of technology integrates a variety of skills, ethics and cross-cultural themes, offering opportunities for students to participate in and understand many local, national or global community issues. This involvement integrates a much wider range of authentic learning experiences than is traditionally offered in primary and secondary schooling. Supportive and professionally aware technology teachers guide and facilitate a much wider range of skills and process learning than most classroom teachers. As such their teaching can extend deeply into the realm of lifelong learning for successful living in the 21st century.

The first iteration of the technology curriculum *Technology in the New Zealand Curriculum*, published by the MOE in 1995 gave us a useful list of characteristics of learning in technology. They indicate clear connections to Claxton's 21st-century learning key ideas. The characteristics of learning include:

- Technology builds on students' existing knowledge and skills, values, interests and aspirations.
- Technology develops real, identified needs or problems, and with multiple solutions. There is no single "right answer."
- Lateral thinking and willingness to test divergent options are encouraged.
- Students should experience the satisfaction of developing a range of outcomes.
- Developments are advanced by sharing ideas, presenting concepts and evaluating possible solutions.
- Teacher's knowledge, experience and skills provide input to assist in refining ideas, selecting resources and achieving quality in products, as well as guiding students towards viable solutions.
- Teachers support, guide, challenge and learn with the students, interacting with their thinking and helping to clarify ideas.
- Learning in technology encourages risk taking. Students' ideas should be accepted and valued, and students challenged to realise their aspirations.
- Technology provides opportunities for students to show initiative, make choices and take more responsibility for their own work.
- Technology requires students to work cooperatively and collaboratively with each other, their teachers and other adults.
- The teacher's role is to motivate, encourage, support and provide feedback to students.
- Technology offers opportunities for a wide range of people in the community to provide specialist input.

The evolution of technology education

Knowledge of the history of the development of the *Technology in the New Zealand Curriculum* is essential in order to gain a full understanding of the debate and theoretical underpinnings that went into its development. Its development came after a long path of discussion, research, debate and implementation

32   *Rationale for and nature of technology education*

programmes. Technology's inclusion has brought with it many challenges and changes for teachers, schools and the MoE.

Technology education does not have a long tradition in comparison to some other areas of the curriculum. To represent the subject's nature in New Zealand, it is important to consider how it has evolved since its inception, as well as to review some of the influences that impact its interpretation in a school setting. Technology education provides unique opportunities to engage students in their learning through conceptual *and* practical means. The role and status of technology education has evolved, but its cross-disciplinary nature means that there is no single theoretical perspective that can define it. Regardless of how it is defined, technology education can expose students to knowledge that is developed as a result of working with materials, through the development of a concept or outcome, and in response to an identified problem, need or opportunity. The way that this learning occurs should be considerate of students' interests, alongside the official curriculum, and not determined solely by the teacher, community perceptions or political agenda.

The subject's formative years in New Zealand

New Zealand's schooling system has been heavily influenced by colonisation and a British philosophy. British public school structures were often adopted with many secondary schools reflecting elitist perspectives and endorsing the view that the working classes were predisposed to more menial tasks. In 1905, the first New Zealand-based technical school was opened. This school offered practical subjects for those students who were deemed unsuitable for the academic nature of secondary schooling and directed these individuals towards the trades. Such an attitude reflected the philosophy of England and Wales where technical education was historically aligned to economic and political agenda as well as to employment. This attitude continues to be pervasive in New Zealand and technology education is regularly positioned as a subject that can cater solely to the needs of lower ability students rather than to accommodate a diversity of academic and social learning approaches.

During the 1980s, the government endeavoured to decentralise governance and resources in education. This political move was presented as an opportunity for educational professionals to become more empowered and to improve both social and academic outcomes for students. The supporting Picot and Tomorrow's Schools reports reflected, instead, an increasing influence of the Treasury on educational policy. This translated to a context where, "recent official policy discourses on student achievement have stressed the importance of teachers and the impact that effective teaching can have on student life chances and on national economic performance" (p. 107). The challenge for teachers in such a climate was how to manage any disparity that may be caused as a result of political drivers. In technology education, there was the risk that teachers will retain existing thinking or default to past practices that perpetuate stereotypical and traditional perceptions of the nature and position of the subject.

Rationale for and nature of technology education   33

Technology in the New Zealand Curriculum became mandatory in January 1999. Technology is now compulsory for all students until the end of their tenth year at school. In the late 1970s and early 1980s there were several early international conversations about the need for technology in the curriculum. In New Zealand in 1990 when the National Party (New Zealand conservative political party) launched education as a major policy in its manifesto. At this stage it was not clear whether technology would be a separate subject or combined with science. In 1991, Don Ferguson from the MoE undertook extensive research culminating in a series of discussion papers for circulation within the Ministry and beyond. These literature review based discussion papers investigated definitions of technology education and the international growth of technology as a subject, its purpose and content. Also in 1991, Dr. Lockwood Smith, the then Minister of Education, announced that technology should be a separate curriculum area rather than an extension of science. In August the Ministry invited and received over 150 submissions about technology. Response to technology inclusion in the draft National Curriculum Framework was mostly positive.

In 1992, Terry Guy, an education consultant, investigated international developments and the current New Zealand situation in technology education and subsequently developed a framework for the curriculum. Possibilities for implementation and organisation of technology education in schools were discussed. The Centre for Science & Mathematics Education Research (CSMER) at the University of Waikato tendered for, and won, a contract to develop policy papers. Alister Jones was responsible for this work, working closely with Ferguson during the development of these papers.

The New Zealand Curriculum Framework published in April 1992 confirmed technology as one of the seven essential learning areas. In July the Centre for Science, Mathematics and Technology Education Research (CSMTER) was awarded the contract for the development of the draft curriculum. Over 200 teachers were involved in the development process which was managed by Jones and Eleanor Hawe from Auckland College of Education, in close liaison with Steve Benson from the MoE. Eleven writing groups with 85 writers in consultation with reference people, including teachers, technologists, engineers, university lecturers and other community groups, wrote the draft curriculum trialled by Jones in 1994.

In 1995, the NZC aimed to establish technology education as a core subject rather than a means of occupational training. Don Ferguson stated that, "from the outset, technology was seen as something distinct from technical education, [e.g. workshop, craft and home economics]" (p. 6). This curriculum reduced the emphasis on the acquisition of technical skills and focused on developing students' understanding of factors that influenced the process of manufacturing. This iteration of the curriculum centred on the notions of technological knowledge, problem solving and citizenship. The attempts to counter a traditional view of technology education, raise its academic profile and generate new understandings of its purpose appeared limited in their

34 *Rationale for and nature of technology education*

effect. The subject remained technicist in nature and traditional pedagogical approaches persisted.

Technology in the New Zealand Curriculum was published in October 1995, having undergone a number of significant changes. The number of strands was reduced from six to three. Contexts of study were added and learning experience examples were reduced to those successfully trialled. Design and graphics became a component in the remaining seven technological areas rather than one of its own. It was planned to gazette the curriculum statement in December 1996 with full implementation from 1997; however, the new Minister of Education, Hon Wyatt Creech, announced, in May 1996, an easing of curriculum timelines in response to concerns over teacher workloads. This included further transition years for technology in 1997 and 1998. In July 1997 Creech announced that the newly proposed date for gazetting the technology curriculum was to be at the end of 1998 for full implementation in 1999. In fact, Technology in the NZC was finally gazetted in January 1999.

Any change in curriculum requires teachers to reflect on the currency of their practice and can lead to resistance to, or acceptance of, the change. Despite community recognition that some teachers had found the change in curriculum difficult to navigate, the new technology curriculum then consolidated the epistemological shift which had begun in 1995. Conceptually, technology education became a subject that recognised the theoretical and conceptual dimensions connecting the different specialist areas that had both technical and vocational beginnings.

Technology education in New Zealand is distinct from other countries because curriculum development has historically focused on the nature of its content rather than the means it is communicated to practitioners for implementation in their classroom. This curriculum more explicitly acknowledged the relationship between technological development and society, either historically, in the present day, or in the future. The focus on the nature of technology provides an opportunity for teachers to consider how learning contexts might enable students' creative, innovative and future-oriented thinking.

Technological literacy – technacy in New Zealand

In their review of technology education in New Zealand, Alister Jones and Vicki Compton indicated that international research trends and policy thinking, rather than teachers' existing or consolidated understandings and practices, influenced curriculum change. Technological literacy is a concept that underpins international and the current NZC. Technology Online defines technologically literate young people as having a broad understanding of how and why things work; understanding how technological products and systems are developed; critically evaluating technological developments and trends; designing and evaluating their own solutions in response to needs and opportunities. Technological literacy or Technacy can also be viewed as a means to support students to function in a technological and future-focused society. Such a focus

Rationale for and nature of technology education 35

provides opportunities for a reciprocal relationship between technology and society because it:

- considers technology from a historical perspective or as socially constructed in nature;
- can be used to provide learning, which focuses on the development of technologies and techniques that apply in our constructed world, to encompass the processes, ways of thinking, and organisation of socio-technological contexts;
- provides a generic context for specialist areas (like textiles) within technology, which have alternative connotations associated with the learning;
- accommodates dynamic learning to enable students' participation in a developing global and digital community.

It can logically be anticipated that teaching in the future should look very different, with virtual and "on demand" teaching approaches becoming commonplace. This was never more clearly illustrated than during the COVID-19 lockdown when all educational institutions closed, and learning moved online where possible. To become technologically literate, students need to understand the relationship between technology and society because the world is changing at an alarming and ever increasing rate. If people are left behind they run the risk of becoming alienated. We need to develop technological literacy, to understand our technology infused new world, and live a meaningful existence within it.

The evolution of technology is inevitably shaped by societal need or demand. Arnold Pacey suggested there was also a political dimension, consisting of "hardware, practical skills, technical knowledge … organisational … and cultural aspects connecting values and beliefs" (p. 7).

Technological determinism can be used to reflect the differing trends in socio-technological evolution and *ways of thinking* about technology. Figure 3.1 identifies a range of engaging and future-focused ways to explore alternative and innovative learning opportunities to develop students' technological literacy.

Artefactual determinism is a view that artefacts shape societal relationships with technology. For example, there is mystery, and many hypotheses have developed over time, about the Egyptian pyramids. The tools developed to enable their construction would have been designed to address a particular need.

Technical determinism refers to discourse in a social setting that influences societal engagement with technology. The social and economic discourse influences what is considered to be legitimate knowledge in a country. For example, Genetically Modified crops and foods are believed to offer a range of benefits, including:

- lower pesticide costs;
- less environmental pollution from pesticides and herbicides;
- higher productivity and new crop varieties to alleviate hunger in developing countries).

36 Rationale for and nature of technology education

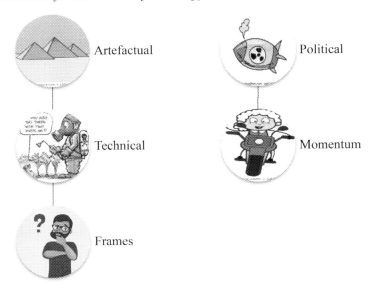

Figure 3.1 Perspectives of technological determinism

However, much opposition has arisen from the general public concerning both the potential for environmental risk, as well as food safety. This technological development has not been trusted as legitimate by many, because of the liability of its newness.

Technological determinism can reflect particular political intentions. The atom bomb is an inherently political artefact that, by its very existence, demands a high level of control to ensure that it doesn't negatively affect the world. The atom bomb was developed to ensure that those in power, with self-perceived qualities of good judgement, could "win a race" and end World War II. In such circumstances, innovation can gain momentum.

Technological momentum is a concept used to present the view that as technological systems become more established, people are less likely to critique its place in society. The bicycle is an example. Originally, it was perceived by some as immoral because of the tendency for women to show their ankles when using it. Bicycles are now an accepted artefact in most communities, reflecting the notion of technological frames. *Technological frames* include the nature, role and application of the technological artefact or system, within a particular context.

Bronwen Cowie and Rachel McNae state that exposing students to a range of differing perspectives about technology is likely to require a change in teaching and learning for some teachers, to accommodate the:

> … rapid pace of technological advancement and global connectivity [which] has prompted further calls mandating the revision of current education practices to meet and shift futurist predictions and ideals about how young people prepare for and engage with their futures (p. ix).

Fostering innovation

Technological innovation is a quality at the heart of New Zealand's national sense of self. The thinking process that results in innovation is messy and iterative, and often mediated through physical action. The way that we support technological thinking in the younger generation represents a tension between our historical sense of self and an evolving identity as future-focused innovators. New Zealand highly values innovation, particularly when this process of generating, developing and realising new ideas is aligned with economic advantage – such as during the America's Cup. There is an established connection between technological thinking and the ability to innovate through critical and creative problem solving that could be re-directed towards the country's social advantage – such as through the development of solutions which limit the effects of poor living conditions.

In some New Zealand schools, students experience a linear process of technological thinking and development. For example, they are encouraged to use food or wood as a material to replicate products in a pre-defined way, with little expectation that they think critically or creatively. Conversely, internationally, there is a current preference for high-tech solutions to problems, suggesting a local need to develop this kind of critical thinking.

Recent government investment in the digital aspect of technology education implies a national priority for school age students to become creators of digital solutions. There is a risk that by adopting a singular focus on high-tech solutions, other forms of thinking will become marginalised, as might the role of traditional indigenous knowledge in technological innovation. In order to create solutions appropriate to their context, we need to be able to think and do in a range of different ways that enable technological innovation.

The transformative nature of technology assists us to anticipate and define future-focused learning to which students should be exposed in a classroom. Some teachers revert to trusted content because they are confident that, by doing so, they are more likely to address the curriculum requirements. Instead, teachers could be focusing explicitly on the concepts and principles that pertain to technology and its ever-evolving place in society. Technology education can be taught within a range of authentic large contexts, as identified in Figure 3.2.

Concepts within these types of large contexts can include technical performance and processes, disciplinary knowledge, conceptual approaches to problem solving, real-world contexts and responsive pedagogies that are personalised, learner-centred and determined by students' interests. In New Zealand, teachers also identify in their planning, how students' learning addresses the curriculum's key competencies.

Key competencies

The addition of "key competencies" to the national curriculum resulted from the Organisation for Economic Co-operation and Development's (OECD) Definition and Selection of Competencies (DeSeCo) project. The DeSeCo

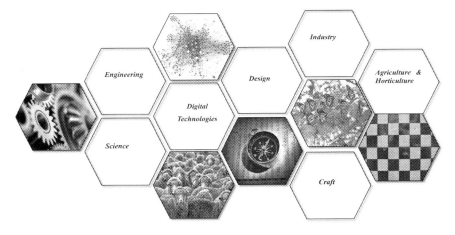

Figure 3.2 Wider contexts for learning technology

report emphasised the need for students to have an active role in their education and proposed that by embedding future-focused competencies into their learning, students would be more likely to use them in order to shape society. The key competencies identified in the New Zealand 2007 curriculum are: thinking; using language, symbols and text; managing self; relating to others; and participating and contributing. There are two obvious key competencies that align with this future-focused context although all are relevant to a holistic approach to technology education. The first key competency of pertinence is "thinking," described as "using creative, critical and metacognitive processes to make sense of information, experiences and ideas." The second is the "participating and contributing" competency that encourages attention to "the roles, and responsibilities … contributing to the quality and sustainability of social, cultural, physical, and economic environments." Both provide a context for teachers to focus students' learning on the relationship between technology and society.

Technology education has the potential to engage students in authentic learning, which can make a difference to their school and local community, and can foster understanding about the way that technology interacts with the wider society to generate understanding of future-focused issues. However, there are enduring and outdated perceptions of the purpose of technology education in New Zealand, and these alternate views influence teachers' existing practices and pedagogical choices.

Ways of thinking and knowledge for technology practice

Teachers' ways of thinking are likely to connect to their lived experiences and mediated by their sociocultural context. The way teachers receive and understand, or experience, particular phenomena might lead to the promotion of

Rationale for and nature of technology education   39

dominant views making understanding considered contestable. Such a perspective is of interest because the "core concepts" presented within the technology curriculum should be the underpinning theory driving students' learning in the subject. The curriculum provides a means for teachers to plan and structure students' evolving understanding in the subject. To make meaning of and then enact these concepts, teachers will inevitably draw upon existing knowledge or seek to establish new understandings. To do so, they are likely to engage with ritual, inert, conceptually difficult, or alien knowledge.

Ritual knowledge is described as being routine and systematic in nature. Within technology education, this might be represented by a teacher who views the subject as being technical in nature and expects students to reproduce existing products, by focusing on a manufacturing process and the development of quality outcomes. Inert knowledge can include information that can be retrieved as required but not used actively. For example, experienced teachers are likely to use established and specialised content knowledge, which may be associated with the function or properties of materials. This knowledge is only activated as and when it is needed.

The pertinence of some knowledge may become troublesome, if teachers have difficulty making connections with the technological concepts as they are presented in the curriculum. This could be because practitioners find some information conceptually difficult, thus causing a retreat to ritual knowledge, with a rationale that it addresses their students' learning needs. For some teachers, the knowledge being presented in the curriculum is alien to them, or they might not even recognise that the concepts presented are contrary to the way that they perceive the subject. This may be because the knowledge conflicts with their beliefs, or because of its perceived conceptual focus, which they do not value. The ways that teachers value knowledge in technology education, as represented through their engagement with the curriculum or emerging practice, can be associated with their self-concept and/or professional identities.

Self-concept and professional identity

Self-concept is a notion that considers an individual's belief or conviction, especially when they are provided with a choice. It is multi-faceted and hierarchical and investigated by studying perceived self-esteem or the dynamics of a teacher's relationships with others. A teacher's self-concept and the way they describe their practice can be explored through their ability to function effectively in uncertain situations. Self-concept is pertinent here because teachers' understanding of the nature of technology education is perceived to have a direct correlation to their emerging professional practice. A teacher's self-concept evolves as the result of the school context within which they teach and their sense of professional belonging and as a result of their values, abilities, aspirations, interests, needs and history.

It might be assumed that the curriculum would define the nature of technology education in New Zealand. There appears, however, to be a disparity in the

40 *Rationale for and nature of technology education*

way that technology teachers view their subject, which is at times contrary to the curriculum and aligns more with their own professional experiences or previous iterations of curriculum policy.

A hidden curriculum

Michael Apple suggests the unintended but emerging consequences of a political text can lead to a hidden curriculum in a school. A hidden curriculum is curriculum learned but not explicitly taught. The hidden curriculum can influence the ways that knowledge is socially constructed, and, in turn, the practices in a school context; it can manifest as "norms and values that are implicitly, but effectively, taught in schools and that are not usually talked about in teachers' statements of end" (p. 78). In the case of technology education, there is the risk that despite suggestions otherwise, teachers might be promoting solely practical and skill-based activities instead of the notions advocated for in the current curriculum.

The purpose of the NZC was to establish the direction for student learning in schools, to provide guidance, and allow schools to shape pedagogy in their context. The drivers for change were to develop an education system to reduce underachievement in education by equipping New Zealanders with 21st-century skills. The NZC stock-take of 2007 indicated education in New Zealand should refocus on developing human capability, with a view to supporting the structure of a prosperous and inclusive society. The report also recommended curriculum be reviewed in light of teachers' workload issues, and that there should be explicit connections made between learning, pedagogy and assessment. Teachers in New Zealand were positioned as empowered professionals and legitimate decision makers who were able to design appropriate learning for their students within their school contexts.

There were several new directions within the NZC but pertinent here, is the emphasis on *learner-centred pedagogies*. Learner-centred pedagogies enable the nature of education to be responsive to the school's students and community. From a learner-centred perspective schools should be democratic environments where learners are enabled to work together to solve real-life or authentic issues, with a view to become contributing members of society. The notion of authentic practice is defined here by Wendy Turnbull as being authentic to the children's cultural world, both current and possible in the future, and authentic to the practice of technologists as closely as possible, given the maturity level and physical skills of the students being taught.

For students to gain the most from their learning in technology education, outcomes should be negotiated *with* or determined *by* them. The challenge however is that to effectively manage the learning in an authentic context, teachers need to be able to respond to the direction that students choose to follow in their learning. Just-in-time teaching (JiTT) is a means to manage such a process.

JiTT is a pedagogical strategy that is usually associated with e-learning platforms to enable teachers' understanding of their students' learning needs

Rationale for and nature of technology education 41

to improve academic outcomes and increase engagement. Whilst this notion is often represented as being a means to foster students' learning outside of the classroom, prior to formal lessons, JiTT is also an enabling concept for technology teachers to support the fostering of an active learning environment. This pedagogical approach is also significant because teachers are positioned to support students' learning, *rather than direct it*. For example, rather than the teacher deciding what skills and knowledge learners should be exposed to in Year 9 then teaching them out of context, the students could instead:

- Explore their own learning context from a problem-based perspective, and to address a need or opportunity.
- Identify what they need to know and develop understanding at a time that makes sense to the learner.
- Construct knowledge collaboratively or individually to facilitate a successful concept or outcome.

For some technology teachers, however, this may present some challenges because it is likely to present an approach that is contrary to their perceptions of the purpose of the subject. In a context where there are teachers working collaboratively to support students' learning, this approach is likely to be easier to realise.

Regardless, a students' engagement with technological concepts (from the curriculum) should drive the knowledge and skills that are acquired to empower their learning in a personally meaningful way. In this context, it is primarily the teacher's responsibility to provide guidance, have understanding of the curriculum concepts, and determine how this translates to the specialist content knowledge (in their area of technology). The ways that teachers navigate this process, however, will determine whether they react to, anticipate, or respond with the support or skills that students need to know as the learning occurs.

Authenticity and technology

Early in the discussions in technology education considered the necessity for authenticity in technology and defined this at two levels. The first level of authenticity considered the objects and the data, a factual level of authenticity. These may have been simplified, compared to the real thing, but were true to life. This means that students would be involved in the use of authentic tools and information but practice would occur within the bounds of the classroom. The second level of authenticity involved the degree to which the tasks performed by the students were authentic. Tacit knowledge (knowing how) is fundamental to technologists and their practice and gained from experience rather than academically. Activity is said to be authentic if it is (i) coherent and personally meaningful and (ii) purposeful within a social framework and

42   *Rationale for and nature of technology education*

thus mirroring the practice of technologists. These two levels differ to those above. The first as "real" to the students may be: real to their own lives or real to situations that they may encounter in the future workplace. The second "real" to technology practice. The latter two ideas of authenticity underpin *Technology in New Zealand Curriculum* and inform technology in the NZC today. A range of learning theories support and inform notions of authenticity. These are explored below before we look more closely at the types of authentic learning necessary for technology.

Authentic practice and culture: related theories

Vygotsky's constructivist theory considers the construction of knowledge within a cultural framework. A number of other theories advocate the placement of learning in authentic practice and underpin thinking in technology education. These include the theories of Enculturation, Expert Knowledge including procedural and conceptual knowledge, situated cognition, apprenticeship and cognitive apprenticeship. Vygotsky's Anchored Instruction also advocates the use of experts or experienced practitioners as a key component of learning. Finally, Karen Zuga suggests that Feminist theory acknowledges that women have a more holistic method of knowing and doing which, in turn, lends itself to learning within authentic contexts.

Constructivism

An individual's ability to make representations within their framework of knowledge occurs within their cultural framework which is tested and altered as new knowledge comes to light. Solving authentic problems enhances learning as the relevance of, and the need for, students' work is explicit. Problem solving is an essential part of this process. Schemata, knowledge structures in memory, are altered through experience and instruction. Constructivist theorists have long perceived that the construction of knowledge occurs through interaction with the environment; therefore merely presenting students with new information and experiences in the classroom is insufficient to promote learning.

There is a clear difference between technology education and its predecessor technical studies or "manual training." Technology education is orientated towards the social constructivist philosophy that technical processes or skills should be taught only as the need to know them arises, in order to solve a social problem. "Manual training" programmes were skill-based where students learned and practised skills in isolation. In technology, students collaboratively participate in problem-solving processes to meet identified needs. For example, when students are solving problems using practices that are authentic to a specific culture of technological practice their knowledge frameworks are more likely to be stronger as they are able to make connections to real practice and need.

Enculturation

Learning must involve activity, concept and culture as they are all interdependent. Traditionally, students were asked to use tools in isolation, having little idea of the culture of the practice for that tool. The culture of a practice determines the way a practitioner does it. To learn to use a tool as practitioners do, students must enter the culture of the community of practice, like an apprentice. Successful learning becomes a process of enculturation. Much school activity is very different from the activity of practitioners. It should not be. Learning should be a process of enculturation but, frequently, when authentic activities are transferred to the classroom, their context is inevitably lost and they become classroom tasks and part of the school culture, quite contrary to the aim of education today which should prepare students for their future world.

Expert knowledge: procedural and conceptual

The development of expert knowledge comes with persistent solving of problems in relevant areas. Technology education is concerned with complex and interrelated problems involving multiple variables that are technical, procedural, conceptual and social, with the potential to enable students to solve problems in authentic situations, thus participating in active and reflective activities. Two main types of knowledge: conceptual knowledge – knowledge of concepts, and procedural knowledge – knowledge about processes, and sometimes skills are relevant to the notion of authenticity in technology. Procedural knowledge includes knowledge of design processes, problem solving, strategic thinking and the knowledge and use of technological principles within context. It is a major component in successful learning in technology. Conceptual knowledge includes knowledge of concepts and facts but not in isolation. Learning and understanding both types of knowledge in parallel must be a part of the enculturation process.

Situated cognition

The theories situated cognition and cognitive apprenticeship also strengthen the argument for technology programmes to reflect authentic technological practice. These theories highlight the issue of the disjunction between traditional classroom learning and cognition in practice. It is important to understand the acquisition of knowledge and investigate the difference between the knowledge of novices and experts. Understanding the difference between classroom learning and cognitive practice is critical as learning is most successful when embedded in authentic meaningful activity making use of physical and social contexts. Situated cognition encompasses thinking as activity carried out within a community of practitioners. Creative thinking by teachers is required to model and guide the students in this manner. There is an advantage of situated cognition for technology education as it is a useful

44 *Rationale for and nature of technology education*

model for integration of the curriculum. Technology education programmes using authentic learning are excellent vehicles for integrating other curriculum areas (explored in more depth later in this chapter). Students given authentic opportunities to measure, speak, write reports, discuss and consider social and health issues during the process of studying technology find learning in other areas more accessible. Authentic practice is very different to the traditional classroom practice. There are several reasons for this. In schooling individual knowledge and achievement is the norm with emphasis placed on individual achievement, even within group work. Incentives outside school lead to learning that is self-motivated or commercially driven. Intellectual and emotional factors are separated in formal learning but fused in a more informal setting as, outside a school setting, problems are multi-faceted and solutions need to be defined before they can be investigated. At school, however, problems are usually pre-formulated and given with appropriate data. Also, at school, external tools are sometimes purposefully excluded but in the real world the success of a problem-solving exercise may well depend on the external tools available.

Apprenticeship models of learning: traditional and cognitive

Invention, discovery and refinement of problems are the hallmarks of the most successful instructional programmes. The notion of learning through participation and collaborative thinking processes is the root of the apprenticeship model of learning, which involves the successful modelling of expert practice. The idea of apprenticeship is that the learner is initially positioned to undertake extensive observation of an expert. Over time the learner does more and more while the support of the expert is slowly withdrawn. This approach aims to give the learner control over her/his own learning, engaging in critical analysis. The expert begins by modelling effective strategies or making explicit their tacit knowledge. Vygotsky referred to this help as "scaffolding." It enables the learner to engage in the activity with increased confidence and competence. Critical to the process is the provision of authentic dilemmas which may be real or imaginary. The same applies to the teaching of technology, which must reflect the real world of technological activity and must be informed by actually practised technology processes. Problems should be ones students want to solve, are real and relevant to them, engage their interest, and for which they can take responsibility. Problem solving becomes the resolution of meaningful problems and dilemmas in the context of guidance and negotiation with teachers.

Cognitive apprenticeship learning theory aims to enculturate students into authentic practices through activity and social interaction. Using scaffolding the teacher gradually withdraws support, as the learner becomes more proficient at the task. This gradual withdrawal of help as the learner's abilities and confidence increases is called "fading." Cognitive apprenticeship programmes develop students through situated learning, enabling students to observe, engage and invent or discover strategies in context.

We can compare cognitive apprenticeship with traditional apprenticeship as it uses many instructional strategies of traditional apprenticeship with emphasis on cognitive skills rather than physical skills. The primary components of a traditional apprenticeship model, coaching and fading remain in cognitive apprenticeship. The strength of apprenticeship is the importance of real activities, performed by the expert and copied by the learner. Cognitive apprenticeship uses these same strategies but during the coaching stage the expert shows the students how to complete the tasks or solve the problem while verbalising the activity within a real context. Students learn the complexity of the expert's thinking, that they make many mistakes and take many changes of direction in their thinking during the problem-solving process. Articulation of expert thinking is critical, and later in this chapter we further explore the role conversation plays in learning. In addition to the phases mentioned, lessons should increase in complexity and diversity, providing an environment to promote intrinsic motivation, cooperation and competition.

Anchored instruction

Another theory that strengthens the argument for technology programmes to involve students in authentic technological practice situated within a specific technological culture is the theory of anchored instruction. The theory suggests that students have a body of knowledge that they don't use unless reminded. The term for this untapped knowledge is "inert knowledge." Imagine a situation where students were given 10 minutes to read an article and learn from it as much as possible. All begin reading from the beginning until the time is up. Later they acknowledged that they knew about the strategies of skim reading and consultation of headings but did not use these skills spontaneously. A major goal of anchored instruction is to overcome the problem of inert knowledge. Sound thinking and problem solving depend on more expertise than general knowledge so it is important that general and specialist knowledge function in close partnership. Authentic activities are defined as "ordinary practices of culture" and anchored instruction tasks are described as projects that simulate apprenticeships, comprising authentic tasks as is essential in technology education. Anchored instruction can translate to JiTT approaches to learning to foster understanding of a new concept, in a differentiated manner, and acknowledge students' previous experiences and interests in technology.

Feminist theory

It is not difficult to believe Karen Zuga's claim that most of the authentic learning occurs in a male dominated field using a male understanding of learning and knowing. However, girls do better when the education system is seen serving girls. The designing and making of technological outcomes is directly related to the profession of engineering. It is perceived as desirable that engineers have a variety of characteristics including those that are typically associated with being

46 *Rationale for and nature of technology education*

"female" such as considering social and moral issues, and empathy. However, in the Western world female numbers are very low in engineering careers. Girls need to be encouraged into engineering careers especially those fields traditionally dominated by males such as civil, mechanical and software engineering. If women are to be attracted to a study of technology both the value and purpose of technology and the way in which it is taught must change. We suggest a change in the structure and practice of real-world technology is needed. Thinking to include feminist ways of knowing and doing is not new but it recognises that subject matter is continually changing and that human behaviour evolves to meet these changing needs. Aspects of the understanding of societal change need to be incorporated into ideas and attitudes within the classroom. Authentic technological practice at both personal and cultural levels within the classroom allows students to integrate knowledge, skills and culture into design processes. We therefore strongly advocate technology as a problem-centred, culturally situated learning. In order to do this thoughtful, critique of existing practices must be carefully undertaken. In many cases technological developments thought to advantage women have, in fact, disadvantaged them. Those involved in technological practice and development must be aware of the full implications of technology for women. In the NZC, the technology strand "Nature of Technology" is critical here. Technological activity in our schools must involve developing students' understanding of the impacts technology has on people and the environment and how society and culture impact technological development. In the previous sections we have looked at the authenticity of technological practice and culture, now let us turn our attention to authentic teachers and pedagogy.

Authenticity in technology

An important message about the nature of activities that students undertake is that authentic learning engages children and encourages learning. Technology, as a learning area that enjoys an academic and practical duality, also enhances learning in other learning areas by acting as a vehicle for authentic use. What better reason for learning to write a structured report if your proposed design needs to be communicated to a local council or school's Board of Trustees. Technology has a unique knowledge base and contributes to students' awareness of innovation and creativity, and technology's role and impacts on the economy, society and the environment.

We know technology education for students needs to be "authentic"; however, the exact meaning of "authentic" in *Technology in the New Zealand Curriculum* and NZC is not clearly defined and has caused much confusion for teachers over the years. The next sections investigate three aspects to authenticity:

1 authentic to technological practice – the practice of technologists;
2 authentic to the cultural, social and historical world of the students;
3 authentic teachers and pedagogy.

Authentic technological practice

In authentic technology activity, students need to be involved in practices which reflect understanding of the culture of real technological practice. These skills and this knowledge are far less relevant and meaningful if taught in isolation. Students must (and have a right to) understand the relevance and place of their learning. In technology, this means to develop understanding, knowledge and skills of authentic technological practice, therefore teachers of technology should model the practice of technologists, immersing themselves in design processes similar to that used in industry and business to solve issues and develop technological outcomes, solving unfamiliar technological problems for the students. Teachers must not be afraid to make errors or have difficulties finding solutions. By serving as a role model, technology teachers can show students how to collect and use information to solve technological problems and help them realise that not all problems have straightforward and simple solutions. The nature of technology practice can be theorised through the study and understanding of models of technological practice, a number of which are discussed in the following sections.

Models of technological practice

Given the importance of understanding technological practice to design and deliver authentic programmes of work, teachers of technology must have a good theoretical and practical understanding of technological practice. The technology curriculum defines technology as "intervention by design: the use of practical and intellectual resources to develop products and systems (technological outcomes) that expand human possibilities by addressing needs and realising opportunities" (Ministry of Education, 2007, p. 32). There are four models of technological practice, from two differing perspectives, which we believe are useful to understanding the practice of technologists, and assist understanding of how technology should be taught. These perspectives are the *macro* and *micro* views of technological practice.

THE MACRO VIEW

Technological practice can be represented through a macro or holistic approach. Gawith's (2000) and Pacey's (1983) models offer a view of technological practice that encompasses the social and cultural backgrounds, and circumstances of the technologist, the client and other stakeholders. Fox-Turnbull (Chapter 4) also offers a macro view of technology practice in the classroom encompassing the role of a teacher. She considers how the school environment might constrain students' technological practice.

Culture and society, while often overlooked, are vital components of technology. The following story illustrates the integral relationship between culture and technology. Washing dishes, a simple task undertaken on a daily basis, is

48   *Rationale for and nature of technology education*

culturally situated and influences the technological products and systems bought and used in its undertaking. The following story illustrates the impact of culture on the technologies engaged with.

One day after a food activity with a group of secondary ITE students, Wendy (one of the authors) reminded them to do the dishes. One student, from India, said to her:

> "Here, you do the dishes in a funny way!"
> "What do you mean?" she replied.
> "Well you fill a sink with hot water and dishwashing liquid and put all the dirty dishes in that water to wash them. When washed you dry them with a tea towel."
> "Isn't that how everyone does the dishes?" Wendy asked.
> "Oh no!" The student said, "In India where I am from we rinse all the plates under warm running water from a tap, put a little soap on each dish and wash them again under the warm running water. No tea towels, the dishes are then left on the bench to dry." Wendy pondered this response and then said,
> "If I did that here I would use all the hot water and have to have a cold shower at night." The student smiled and replied
> "Oh yes! Where I come from in India it is so hot that when I run the tap the water is always warm."

At that moment, Wendy understood for the first time that the way she did the dishes was a part of her culture. It therefore influenced the technologies she used for the task. She has told this story to many of her students and has since heard of other culturally situated stories about doing dishes. In England for example dishes are often washed in a plastic basin in the kitchen sink, in others countries dishes are washed once a day when water is delivered to the house.

The two models of technological practice presented here included cultural activity and practice as a vital component. Pacey's model of technology practice (Figure 3.3) was used in the mid-1990s, when technology education was first being introduced in New Zealand. It has stood the test of time and still offers an excellent holistic view of technological practice as well as identifying a typical, more restricted view of technology.

Pacey's model suggests that when technologists are engaged in developing technological outcomes they are taking into consideration three factors: cultural, organisational and technical.

When undertaking technological development from a cultural perspective, technologists need to consider the stakeholders' cultural influences and impacts. A stakeholder is a term used in the technology curriculum to describe a person or group of people who have a vested interest in a technological outcome or its development. In order for technological development to be successful and useful, the outcome needs to be embedded within the acceptable values, ethical codes and beliefs of that group and align with the values and beliefs of the technologist.

Pacey's Model of Technological Practice

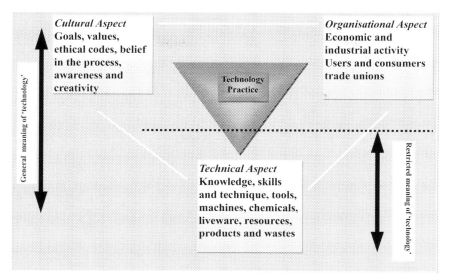

Figure 3.3 Pacey's model of technological practice

For example, when engineers in America were designing electricity systems for New Zealand, they needed to avoid nuclear options. When a company is developing items for sale in a tourist shop in New Zealand, they need to consider associated Māori protocols and customs, to be respectful of ti kanaga Māori.

Technologists must also reflect upon their own ethical beliefs and values when designing and developing technological outcomes. Personal beliefs and values may lead a technologist to select organically grown food in a new food product or ethically produced cotton before selecting it as a material in the construction of a garment. This does not, however, necessarily align with the requirements of the brief. Within organisational aspects, technologists must also consider issues such as the legal constraints or industrial guidelines. For example, workers must be treated fairly; work limited hours and be paid at least a minimum wage. Technologists also need to coordinate with others for a range of reasons. Materials need to be supplied on time, people with specificialist skills and knowledge have to be communicated with and organised. The third aspect, the technical aspect, is associated with a traditional view of technology as making "stuff." In this aspect, technologists deploy a range of knowledge, skills, resources and tools to design and develop their outcomes.

Gawith identified seven elements describing students' technology practice as seen in Figure 3.4. The first three elements, society, work and environment, involve the context within which the technologists (students) were working. Purposeful action described the methodology. The remaining four elements, organisation, information, resources and techniques, involved the skills, knowledge and actions

50 *Rationale for and nature of technology education*

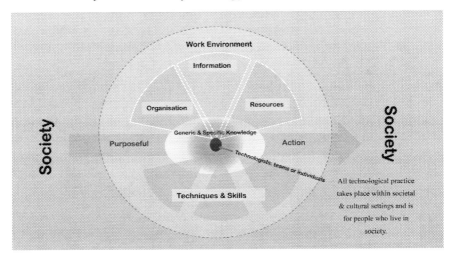

Figure 3.4 Gawith's model of technology practice

of the individual technologist or technology team. Gawith's research identified that technologists structured their knowledge into a framework that reflected a range of subsystems used to break down complex problems and develop technological solutions.

THE MICRO VIEW

The micro view of technology practice focuses on the physical act of developing technological outcomes. Technological practice through a micro approach looks at how technologists actually work through the process of developing solutions to meet identified needs or opportunities. The micro approach considers what the technological process is actually doing – such as the design process for a specific project or series of projects. Kimbell's Reflective Active Capability model, as shown in Figure 3.5, is one model that represents this practice and suggests that as technologists work through a specific project they oscillate between reflective thinking, problem solving in their head, to actively manipulating information, materials and energy to develop desired outcomes. Kimbell places the scenario at the centre of the technologist's practice rather like Gawith's Purposeful action. Kimbell suggests a series of development phases from the first initial discussions and issue identification to the realised final product.

In technology education in the classroom we need students to be technologists but obviously they cannot work at the same level of expertise as the professionals. There are a number of constraints and factors that alter students' technology practice. The nature of students' technological practice is explored in Chapter 4.

Also indicating a micro view are the design models we mentioned in Chapter 2. There is no one single design process as the practice of every technologist differs

Rationale for and nature of technology education 51

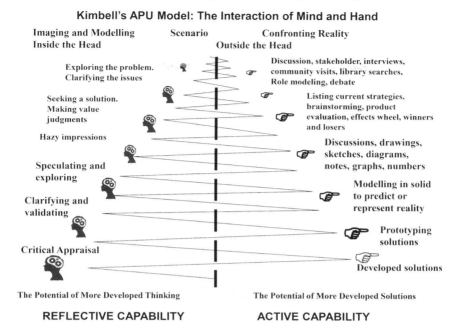

Figure 3.5 Kimbell's reflective activity capability model of technological practice

from that of others. There are, however, a number of useful diagrams which represent generic design processes. There are three main types: linear, circular, and messy or complex. One of each of these is presented below.

A linear design process

As its name suggests, this model (Figure 3.6) represents the design process as a straight line. This model is useful for beginners who are working through design processes for the first time. It gives a clear indication of the stages undertaken during design. One disadvantage of this model is that it does not accurately

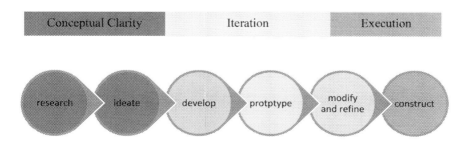

Figure 3.6 An example of a linear design process

52   Rationale for and nature of technology education

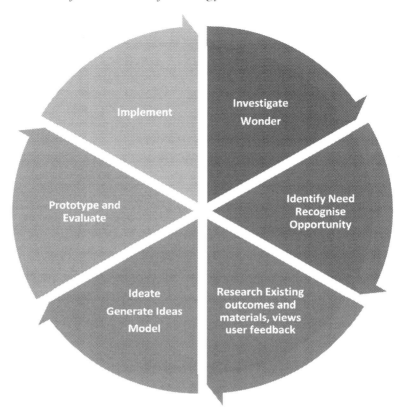

Figure 3.7 An example of a cyclic design process

represent the way many ideas are visited and revisited a number of times during a real design process.

Cyclic design process

The cyclic design model (Figure 3.7) conceptualises design as a continuation, revisitation of design and design ideas. It infers that the design process never ends, as continual improvements or modifications are made to design to meet emerging needs. Unlike the linear model, it allows for the revisiting of designs and ideas but it does not allow for the real messiness that is integral to iterative design processes.

Messy or complex design process

Closest to the reality of actual design processes, Figure 3.8 indicates the unpredictable nature of design and developing technological outcomes. When technologists are working through a design, they frequently do not know where

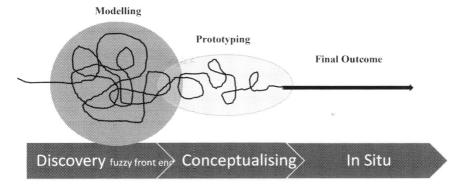

Figure 3.8 An example of a messy or complex design process

they will end up nor how they will get there. They go back and forth; take unexpected twists and turns, which sometimes culminates in fully developed ideas that are then taken into prototype development. At this stage, the process begins again but on a higher and less flexible level as prototypes are fully functional, one-off technological models that can be used for testing and refining technological outcomes.

All models of technology practice and design process models mentioned above are a means to situate the nature of technological practice and to inform teachers' decision-making when professionally engaging with the curriculum.

Authentic technology practice as outlined above will be different from traditional classroom practices. There are several reasons for this:

- In-school emphasis is placed on individual achievement, even within group work. Individuals are therefore not really encouraged to work socially.
- Incentives outside school lead to learning that is self-motivated or commercially driven. Problems encountered are authentic and relevant rather than artificially constructed.
- Intellectual and emotional factors are separated in formal learning but fused in a more informal setting.
- Outside the classroom problems are multi-faceted. Solutions are defined before investigation.
- In-school external tools are frequently excluded (due to age of students, skill development safety and costs) but the success of a problem solving may depend on the external tools available.

Our challenge therefore is to make sure that technology is holistic rather than fragmented. We need students' technological practice to be as close as possible to that of technologists in the field. This means that students should understand the place of a specific task in relation to the whole design process, rather than a fragmented view of each part in the process. To develop this understanding

54 *Rationale for and nature of technology education*

students need to be aware of the whole process and how the components are linked together. This is best done in situations authentic to practice and culturally situated within students' current or possible future worlds.

Culturally authentic activity

Another aspect of authenticity is related to the current and possible future world of each student. Meeting authentic needs of students is vital and achieved if students are undertaking technological development that they can see as relevant to and useful for their current or "possible future" lives. In other words, the contexts within which the students are undertaking technology practice need to be connected to the students' social and cultural worlds. For example, students in New Zealand asked to design nuclear powered vehicles or igloos could hardly be seen as authentic given our stance on nuclear power and our geographical location, but students designing solar powered vehicles and low cost, quality houses for Auckland or Christchurch could be considered authentic.

The "motivational" rationale for the implementation of technology is particularly relevant to this notion of authenticity and an early indication as to its intended meaning. Learning situated in authentic technology practice motivates students to achieve. In later decades of the 20th century, the importance of developing an inclusive curriculum was highlighted. Undertaking technology practice linking to cultural worlds of the students gave opportunity to learn about and value the cultures of all students.

Girls are interested in human aspects of technology and also think more holistically than boys. A starting point for a technological activity can then be through the identification of needs and opportunities related to human needs and social issues within their local communities. This, however, does not mean that technology needs to be about the students themselves, nor that they also design and make technologies they need or want as is often the case. It is easy to see why teachers may think that all technological activity needs to relate directly to the students themselves but culturally authentic does not necessarily mean about the students themselves but should look further into the wider community or to possible future worlds of the students, while still remaining culturally authentic. For example, many people with disabilities depend on technology. Students understand that they, their peers or people they know now or in the future may have to learn to live with disabilities. They may have particular interest in designing products and systems to allow access to learning and to services in the community. Students with disabilities often have greater experience of technology which gives them the opportunity to demonstrate leadership in the classroom, with their experiences a starting point for technological activities. This means that students with disabilities can lead peers in technology education to produce appropriate outcomes. Technological activity should not restrict students but rather allow them to tackle meaningful technological problems thus emphasising the potential for the curriculum to be inclusive of minority groups and authentic to them.

Rationale for and nature of technology education 55

Authentic teachers and pedagogy

Authentic pedagogy is grounded in authentic experience and facilitates socially created knowledge. This includes the development of complex and rich tasks, interaction with technological communities of practice, using cognitive and metacognitive instruction and thinking, the affective and emotional aspects of learning, active and collaborative participation, and dealing with meaningful problems and issues. Learning needs to be significant, meaningful and seen to involve the interests of students. We need to avoid situations where students are not using their minds well and doing work that has no intrinsic meaning or value to them beyond achieving success in school. Learners function best in environments that are intriguing, multi-sensory and dynamic. There are five standards of authentic instruction to appropriately engage students in their learning:

1 higher-order thinking – students manipulating information;
2 depth of knowledge, working with significant and meaningful concepts, developing arguments, solving problems and working with complex understandings;
3 connectedness to the world – the larger social context of the students' lives and facilitate use of personal experience contexts or real-world public problems;
4 substantive conversation-discussion and debate on topics, sharing of ideas and dialogue builds on participants' contributions;
5 social support involving high expectations, respect and inclusion for all students in the learning process, encouraging risk taking and resilience to master higher learning.

In order to do this, teachers must undertake careful planning for the construction of knowledge. They need to enable students to organise, synthesise, interpret, explain or evaluate complex information in addressing a concept, problem or issue. Students need to be encouraged to consider alternative solutions, strategies, perspectives or points-of-view. Teachers need to have strong disciplinary content knowledge and model understanding ideas, theories and perspectives considered central to the discipline. Methods of inquiry, research, or communication characteristic of the discipline should be scaffolded and used, students also need to be able to elaborate on their understanding, explanations or conclusions. Finally, students must be able to see the value of their learning beyond school. To assist this, students should address problems or issues similar to ones that they have encountered or are likely to encounter in life beyond the classroom. To conclude, students need to communicate their knowledge, present products or performances, or take some action for an audience beyond the school setting.

Interactivity between students and the wider community is fundamental in shifting the focus of learning away from the teacher. Everyday situations provide students with opportunities to make decisions about the nature, content and pace of their learning. Learning must occur in an atmosphere of mutual trust,

56 *Rationale for and nature of technology education*

where the teachers become learners along with their students, interact with them in authentic ways and believe in their students.

Some cautions arise in connection with "real-world" contexts for learning as many do actually guarantee truly authentic teaching and learning. Many "real-world" situations can seem phony, second-hand and inauthentic to students. This is extremely important for teachers to consider when giving students opportunities for first-hand experiences with attention given to what "ought to be" happening in a particular scenario. Teachers and their students must adhere to what most people would consider as appropriate and genuine. The "world beyond the classroom" may not be always considered authentic.

What are some of the key ideas to define "real-world" or "real-life" problems? They provoke emotional commitment through a strong personal frame of reference to ensure students are motivated. Endearment and empathy generated by the situation will invariably lead to strong engagement. Issues are open-ended with multiple pathways, strategies and solutions possible (Renzulli et al., 2004). The final recommended solutions should lead to change in actions, attitudes or beliefs, which target a real audience. Authentic pedagogy makes use of disciplined inquiry exemplified by successful practitioners. Students will use their skills to examine, test, deliberate over and really think hard about the information and activity they observe. "Real-world" problems and scenarios require the prolonged higher-order and inquiry thinking necessary to engage students. It is not what *is* in the world beyond the classroom that is important but what *ought to be*, and as such, authenticity will become a value judgement. Learners need to consider connections between their own views, experiences and understandings, to those of accepted experts in the field. As a result, greater credence is given to the knowledge they construct motivated by the level of engagement that is genuine and legitimate. It is the value of these experiences and the level of the engagement and inquiry that connect with and so effectively fulfil the intentions of the NZC.

Authentic pedagogy must have student ownership of learning at its heart. Student interest and ideas should drive the content of authentic study if it is to be of real value and integrity. A classroom with many groups and communities can provide the "authenticity-making" roles. Teachers should plan for group tasks as well as individual learning. Teaching cooperative and collaborative skills must be included as part of the teaching and learning process. Successful teachers will need to develop the required skills and abilities to engage, guide, encourage and support children's learning. In 2004 Slavkin detailed six suggestions for authentic pedagogy. These are:

1 teachers ability to help students accurately review experiences;
2 application of skills on new settings;
3 authentic pedagogy with complex tasks;
4 shared responsibility for learning between teacher and student;
5 understanding there are multiple ways to look at material;
6 teacher and student involvement to ensure learning occurs with information applied practically.

Rationale for and nature of technology education   57

Authentic teachers need to keep up to date and aware of curriculum and education developments and the variety of possible opportunities that exist for students' involvement and engagement. The NZC presents a wide scope for teacher effectiveness. It offers multi-faceted and wider-ranging content. Teachers can no longer remain ensconced in their discipline and adopt a content-driven industrial model delivery. They must integrate key competencies and values into their learning areas and consider how they will teach using the outlined effective pedagogies to meet the individual needs of their students involving them in authentic teaching practices as outlined above. As professionals, teachers must ensure that their teaching pays particular attention to what is best for the students and their understanding, to help them make better sense of the world in which they live. We have modified and embellished Slavkin's original list of ten suggestions for creating a motivational classroom that we believe might be useful, particularly for student teachers of technology. These include:

1 an openness to perceiving new information about students and looking at them as individuals in unique ways;
2 the provision of multi-dimensional classroom, open spaces and break-out spaces give students a choice of learning environment, in technology including access to multi-material facilities;
3 evaluation of students privately using critical reviews, avoiding cultural and personal bias;
4 the effective evaluation of individual learners using authentic practice based assessment practices;
5 the asking of open-ended questions about students' abilities, FOK and experiences from the beginning of the unit;
6 listen attentively to students, using prompting and probing questions for greater depths of understanding;
7 assisting students to identify their own abilities, strengths and potentials;
8 assisting students to feel competent and confident in multiple areas;
9 provision of new challenges and comments about have has been achieved and what the next learning steps are;
10 the teaching of strategies and skill to accomplish technology practice and related tasks, not just for factual knowledge or skill acquisition.

Authenticity is a moral ideal. Authentic teachers care about teaching, want to work well with students, believe in the value of what they do and have a professional respect for students. They must engage with the larger questions of the purpose and role of education and convey how their subject matter matters in the real world. They will connect learners in substantive authentic conversations or dialogue around significant issues and are guided more by caring for the education of students than by their own self-interest. Teachers need to become conversant with formative assessment practices and the principles of active and inquiry-based learning and integration. Students need to take a considerable role in their own learning. Authentic teachers facilitate this through the use of

58 *Rationale for and nature of technology education*

learning intentions or objectives, questioning, construction of success criteria, self and peer assessment practices and the use of ongoing formative assessment. Student involvement increases as they become aware of the purpose, intent and scope of their learning. The use of explicit learning intentions tends to focus conversation and learning on the actual intended learning rather than the activity or experience used to stimulate student thinking. If appropriate success criteria for the learning are co-constructed the learning will be even greater.

As mentioned earlier in this chapter, modelling and scaffolding are a significant and critical aspect of teaching and learning. Dialogue about the knowledge students have and need assists this process. Teachers as "experts" assist and guide students to independence. This style of teaching raises significant challenges to teacher's management and organisation abilities. Student action plans assist teachers' awareness of the intended pathways of learning for each student and the degree and timing of the "just in time" or "just in case" teaching needed. Needs-based learning and skill development is more likely to ensure stronger motivation for students. Students play a significant role in the accomplishment of their dreams and aspirations. The will, drive or determination to achieve is called "conation", also known as self-actualisation, self-efficacy or individuation. Conation has two components, knowing what has to be done to achieve a special goal and then doing what has to be done to the best of ability to achieve the goal. Fundamental attributes of conation include belief, courage, energy, commitment, conviction and change. Interestingly, students involved in authentic learning are seldom motivated by any material rewards. Intrinsic motivation develops through the challenge, relevance, interest and involvement in the study. If students choose to learn they need courage. The choice is influenced by their perception of self, the world around them, beliefs and interpretations, what they know or think they know and how they choose to respond to those beliefs.

These characteristics of conative classrooms closely resemble the notions of authentic teaching and learning discussed in this book. Authentic teaching and learning using authentic experiences will foster learning and increase social wellness. Empowered students given choice, responsibility and encouragement will mostly flourish and develop the skills and frameworks needed for successful lifelong and authentic learning. For these students, motivation, drive and determination will not be problematic. They will learn effectively and successfully relate these connections to the real world in which they live. Learning focus should be on identity and "being" in a complex, rapidly changing and culturally diverse world. We can no longer simply "train" our future workers to be obedient, punctual and loyal. They must know how to be self-reliant, critical and creative thinkers. Students must manage the cognitive, metacognitive, affective and emotional aspects of their learning, understanding what constitutes good learning in a range of situations, when and how to seek help, when and how to collaborate with others. To assist students to take more responsibility for their own learning they must know how, when and why they learn best. Power structures in the classroom need to change. Teachers must empower students as they guide, coach, model, collaborate and give feedback, and share their expert

Rationale for and nature of technology education 59

knowledge. This works on the premise that the knowledge we have stored in our brains is worthless if it cannot be put to meaningful use so we need to enable students to use their existing knowledge to create new knowledge.

There are a number of design characteristics that make classroom activity authentic. These include a culmination of much of what we have said previously about authentic activity and also consider other aspects of classroom learning such as assessment. Authentic classroom activities:

1 have real-world relevance;
2 require defining and refining by the students;
3 are complex tasks investigated over a sustained period of time;
4 provide the opportunity to examine the task from different perspectives;
5 provide the opportunity to collaboration;
6 provide the opportunity for reflection;
7 can be integrated across different learning areas;
8 include seamlessly integrated assessment;
9 create polished products valuable in their own right;
10 allow for competing solutions and diversity of outcome.

What does this mean for those in the field of technology education and how does it contribute to enhancing students' ability to develop quality technological outcomes? We have looked at three dimensions of authenticity: Practice, Culture and Pedagogy and Teaching. These are woven together through a range of teaching approaches that are particularly suitable for both authentic learning and technology.

Teaching approaches

We are seeing a significant shift in teaching philosophy and approaches to learning. Views of learning in the current century are significantly different to that of the past, ensuring students are ready for their future lives in the information age. Teachers need to include development of skills and knowledge vital for 21st century living such as: collaboration, cooperation, critical thinking and problem-solving skills at the same time ensuring that curriculum content knowledge is not lost. Learning prior to and including the 20th century mainly focused on the predetermined learning of discipline-based facts, knowledge and skills, and sometimes the subsequent application of those facts. Learning was frequently contrived, unfamiliar or presented in outdated contexts. Typically, assessment occurred through the regurgitation of facts in tests or examinations. Educational achievement in the 21st century focuses on discipline content knowledge along with the development of appreciative dispositions (represented as key competencies in NZC) that enable people to react to situations they face for which they may not be specifically prepared.

The emergence of innovative learning environments (ILEs) in New Zealand has led to a focus on the ways in which teachers develop their pedagogical

60   *Rationale for and nature of technology education*

responses to accommodate students' learning needs. School structures are changing because new ways of designing and delivering a curriculum are needed. In this learning context, curriculum models can be integrated or interdisciplinary, responsive to students' interests or inquiry-based. The benefits of an integrated approach can include a more coherent education, where students are encouraged to make connections between different subjects and learning is negotiated to increase active involvement. Such an approach requires teachers to collaborate across curriculum areas. A correlation between the ILE model and improved student outcomes has been made in the literature, as the result of interdisciplinary, collaborative approaches to teaching, but only where there were sustained professional learning and supportive school structures.

The New Zealand Ministry of Education in NZC presents the notion of "effective pedagogy." It states, "there is no formula that will guarantee learning for every student in every context" (p. 34) that students learn best when they feel supported and safe in their school or classroom. Teachers are encouraged to reflect on and consider their own actions, understand the focus of the learning, support students' collaborative practices, recognise their experiences, and offer substantive learning opportunities.

Technology is particularly well suited to what is currently termed innovative/modern learning pedagogies because when fully implemented it uses a range of problem-centred, constructivist and sociocultural pedagogical approaches. When participating in technology, students are engaged in context-based problem solving to develop and understand products and systems. Students should have opportunities for classes to develop multiple outcomes as opposed to very similar, or the same, outcomes within and across a range of authentic contexts. Teachers facilitate learning, identify and teach generic and specific knowledge and skills when the need arises.

Learner-centred classrooms

Learner-centred approaches to pedagogy are identified in the NZC (p. 34–40). There has been considerable attention paid to this pedagogical approach internationally because it supports a democratic and responsive style that can recognise students' academic interests and needs. In addition, these approaches encourage students to take responsibility and engage in critical and authentic learning.

Self-regulated learners are confident, diligent and resourceful; they know what they can do and are proactive to seek support as they require it. They can problem-solve, take responsibility for their learning, plan, set goals, reflect and action the need to change thinking. The term "self-regulated learners" is applicable to research in relation to how adaptive professionals *think* and how their pedagogies foster students' agency in the classroom.

Self-regulating teachers (and students) often present as motivated learners, who have high self-efficacy and intrinsic motivation. With appropriate support, self-regulated students are likely to find a learner-centred approach to technology education an experience that affirms their confidence, but this will depend

Rationale for and nature of technology education   61

on the professional skill of the teacher to organise the learning process appropriately. Although adolescents are undoubtedly capable of innovative thought, they are less likely than their younger counterparts to volunteer or articulate their ideas unless the teacher fosters a classroom environment where they feel safe to engage and take risks in their learning. Inevitably, there are some students (and teachers) who engage with learning and intuitively work autonomously and without the need for systemic intervention.

Student engagement is a concept that has historically focused on teachers' need to increase achievement, encourage positive behaviour, and a sense of belonging within the classroom. Whilst important concepts, there has also been a focus in New Zealand on developing students' lifelong learning capabilities to support their ability to function in a knowledge-based society. Student engagement has evolved as a means to cater to students who may be "at risk" of underachieving or disengaging from school altogether. In technology education, this might equate to placing students in programmes to support "hands-on" learning facilitated through authentic contexts such as pathways into trades.

We do know that when students understand the place of their learning and why they are learning it they become more motivated and engaged. One approach to learning that aids situating learning within real-world contexts is subject integration.

Integration

Integration occurs when a number of different subjects are taught through a project or learning task that facilitates the development and use of knowledge from a range of disciplines through authentic contexts. The rationale for subject integration in schools is strong. It facilitates the development of meaningful programmes for students and increases the relevance of learning programmes and aims to reduce duplication, at the same time developing students' abilities in transferring knowledge and skills across learning contexts. When well executed, it assists teacher manageability addressing the age old challenge of lack of time and facilitates coverage of learning areas.

Imagine an integration continuum, comprising three stages from simple to complex. The three major forms of integration on this continuum are: multidisciplinary, interdisciplinary and transdisciplinary. The multidisciplinary approach is the lowest level of integration and typically involves teachers gathering resources, websites and books that they use to plan many activities that are fun for the children. Often called a thematic approach, units of work include a range of activities and learning in different discrete curriculum areas. An issue with this approach is that units often lack substance and are not based on major concepts providing little opportunity for transfer of skills and understandings between different curriculum areas.

At the other end of the curriculum integration continuum is the transdisciplinary approach within which students come across a range of curriculum areas appropriate to real-life contexts. Typically, the study begins with a real-life issue

62 *Rationale for and nature of technology education*

or interest, the community becomes the classroom and learning involves real-life problem solving. Students within these programmes are self-directed and often work as individuals of small interest groups. This approach is an example of full and more complex curriculum integration and underpins the philosophy of teaching in Christchurch's Ao Tawhiti Unlimited Discovery School. In the middle of the continuum, interdisciplinary integration is discussed in a separate section as it is most relevant to technology education in mainstream schools in New Zealand.

Innovative learning environments

ILEs have been proposed by the government as a means to develop a world-leading education system and to provide all New Zealanders with the knowledge, skills and values to be successful citizens in the 21st century. Future-focused practices are inclusive of digital pedagogies, learner-centred in nature, and designed to emphasise critical and creative thinking. The technology curriculum in New Zealand positions teachers to enable such approaches to learning if they are adaptive and reflexive practitioners who embrace a range of new or different resources. Such practices are dependent, however, on teachers having the knowledge, collegial support and motivation to mediate any necessary changes to their pedagogy.

Teachers in New Zealand are increasingly encouraged to adopt a future-focused approach to curriculum, using pedagogies which are sufficiently flexible to accommodate students' learning needs as situated within open and adaptable teaching spaces, and by using digital tools. Technology education is a subject that conceptually aligns with such practice. The emergence of ILE in New Zealand has led to an increased focus on how teachers respond to students' learning needs in flexible and responsive ways. Secondary schools are beginning to develop curriculum models that are integrated or interdisciplinary in nature, responsive to students' interests or inquiry-based. The benefits of an integrated approach to curriculum, when enacted effectively, include a more coherent education where students are encouraged to make connections between different subjects, and learning is negotiated to increase active involvement. A correlation between the ILE model and improved student outcomes has been found but only where there was sustained professional learning and supportive school structures facilitate interdisciplinary and collaborative approaches to teaching.

The recent revision of the technology curriculum in New Zealand emphasises the role of digital technology to meet the needs of a digital and fast-paced world. It aims to ensure students are job-ready on graduation and to make New Zealand global leaders in education. This change highlights the need for a future-focused approach for all educators in New Zealand. However, within technology education, there is the risk that misunderstandings of the nature of the subject are perpetuated and that the role of other technological areas, including processing (e.g. biotechnology, food), materials (e.g. wood, textiles), and design and visual

Rationale for and nature of technology education   63

communication (e.g. media design, graphics), could become marginalised. Chapter 4 provides more information about the technological areas.

Elizabeth Reinsfield conducted research during 2018, into this phenomenon, entitled Technology Education in New Zealand: Secondary school Innovative Learning Environments (TENZsILE) project. The project explored how teachers were using future-focused approaches to learning in culturally inclusive ways, to increase their students' engagement. The findings from two teachers were of particular interest. Imogen had been teaching for seven years and was qualified as a secondary teacher of Food Technology and Hospitality. Ngaire was co-teaching with Imogen on the "Kai and who am I?" project and was a teacher of languages – in this case, Te Reo Māori. When asked to explain how the integrated approach to curriculum was future-focused, Imogen indicated that:

> [the] whole module is culturally bounded. It is including the real-world experience – that is future-focused for me.

Associations with the cultural context in New Zealand, and an emphasis on students' use of Te Reo Māori, were cited by both teachers as being a priority within their future-focused approach to learning. Imogen also indicated that they felt that they must place:

> ... the student in the centre [of the learning] ... we plan the big idea, but go with our students... we check with students, looking for the naturally occurring aspects, rather than plan everything ahead. We show the students that life isn't in silos.

Imogen suggested that her teaching in this school differed from previous experiences and required a more fluid and responsive approach to planning. Ngaire also described a need to approach learning differently, stating:

> We collaborate with both students and teachers ... it is a different relationship you build for learning. We are also looking for integration. We find the future is integrated, we show that life is intertwined.

Ngaire explained that the learning module with the Year 7 and 8 students was taught over a six-week period, within the context of "Kai and Who am I?", and demonstrated:

> ... the integration of the two subjects in the first place ... By putting two subjects together students can see the inter-relationship between the two ... We often focus on the 'becoming a food technologist' part in this module and sell this as a genuine career path ... In terms of growing empathy and knowledge around Tikanga Māori, students become more aware and value our indigenous culture.

64   *Rationale for and nature of technology education*

In this instance, both teachers described a future-focused approach in a way that aligns with the revised technology curriculum (MoE, 2017a, 2017b), which outlines that students need to "learn that technology is the result of human activity by exploring stories and experiences from their heritage, from Aotearoa New Zealand's rich cultural environment, and from contemporary examples of technology" (p. 1). In this case, the integrated approach to learning provided opportunities for both teachers to reinforce the importance of New Zealand's bicultural heritage in contemporary and personally meaningful ways.

Imogen and Ngaire used a range of strategies to engage their learners. These included a visit to a local forest to meet a Kaumatua (Māori elder) and learn about the medicinal properties of indigenous ingredients. Afterwards, students were taken into the food classroom, to experiment and explore ways that indigenous ingredients reacted when processed. This knowledge was applied later when students worked collaboratively to develop food-based technological outcomes. The learning was organised so that at different times, either Imogen or Ngaire took the lead. For example, students were regularly exposed to games-based learning, to support the development of their own Pepeha (a way to introduce yourself in Māori). The aim was to encourage students' sustained engagement with one of New Zealand's official languages, and so that they could interact with their clients when they catered for a lunch at the end of the project. Structuring learning in this way is reflective of interdisciplinary integration.

Interdisciplinary integration

Interdisciplinary integration begins with a problem or issue that facilitates the linking of skills and understandings between different curriculum areas. There is an emphasis on children's needs and making meaningful connections between curriculum and children's lives. The inter-relationship of important concepts is explicit as too are the cross-curricula skills such as the curriculum key competencies and values. Units of work typically start with an issue for which the students design and develop a solution, often presented as the end of the units' "grand finale." When planning an interdisciplinary approach to curriculum integration, teachers consider the skills and knowledge from a range of disciplines needed by the students to successfully complete and present their project at the "grand finale." Students understand what and why they are learning, as it all relates to their current study.

Technology education lends itself to this approach as it makes enterprising use of its own academic and practical knowledge and skills, together with those of other learning areas. Graphics and other forms of visual representation offer important tools for exploration and communication of design ideas. Skills and knowledge from other areas such as maths, English, art and social studies are also authentically engaged. One approach that facilitates this approach to integration is inquiry learning.

Inquiry learning

Set within a socio-constructivist paradigm, inquiry learning encourages students to construct knowledge and understandings in their own cultural settings. It enables students to take greater ownership of, and responsibility for, their learning and encompasses a wide range of skills. Inquiry facilitates higher-level thinking and problem solving very successfully as it encompasses a wide range of skills and processes in active learning, leading to a much broader understanding of the world. This approach uses a student-centred approach that meets the needs of, and extends, learning for individuals. When learning through inquiry, students are encouraged to develop skills, knowledge and understandings within their own cultural framework, enabling them to take ownership of, and responsibility for, learning. Like integration, there are a variety of approaches to inquiry, from teacher directed very structured inquiry to open inquiry within which students are free to inquire about anything they are interested in. In the middle is Guided Inquiry.

Guided inquiry learning

Guided Inquiry focuses on the facilitation of independent knowledge-based learning. In order to stimulate and develop a child's curiosity and thinking, adults need to interact with the child at their potential level not at their actual level or as Vygotsky termed within their "Zone of Proximal Development" (ZPD). Guided Inquiry is one approach that teachers can use to enable them to plan and implement a constructivist classroom that meets the needs of, and extends, learning capacity for individual students. The Guided Inquiry approach reflects the belief that construction of knowledge and active involvement is essential for effective learning. Within this approach, inquiry is guided and systematic with learning proceeding through a number of teaching/learning phases. It is very different from "open" discovery learning as teachers have a major and continuing responsibility to structure activities sequenced to maximise skill development and thinking processes of their learners. Guided Inquiry uses a wide range of teaching approaches from teachers' exposition to independent student research. It involves students in developing deep learning through the process of self-motivated inquiry that strives towards development of "big understandings" and "rich concepts" about the world and how it functions. Like technology education, Guided Inquiry is centred on both process and content with students taking considerable ownership and responsibility for their learning and project.

The process defined by Kuhlthau moves through a number of phases as is outlined in Table 3.1. In the first phase, in most cases, the teacher announces a topic of study that requires thorough research, thus *initiating* the inquiry process. During this time, the students prepare to select a sub-topic of research through a variety of immersion activities. A range of strategies aim to motivate and engage students. During this phase, it is not unusual for students to feel

66 Rationale for and nature of technology education

Table 3.1 Information search process model

Phases	Feelings (affective)	Thoughts (cognitive)	Actions (physical)
Initiative	Uncertainty	Vague	Seeking
Selection	Optimism		relevant
Exploration	Confusion, Doubt		information
	Frustration		Exploring
Formulation	Clarity		
Collection	Sense of direction/		
	confidence		
Presentation	Satisfaction or disappointment		
		Focused	
			Seeking
			pertinent
			information
			Documenting
Assessment	Sense of achievement		
		Increased self-awareness	

Source: Adapted from Kuhlthau et al. (2007)

uncertain and perhaps "bogged down." The second phase involves the *selection* of a topic of study. The students then identify significant questions within the aspect of study they have elected to work on. Topics come with many parameters or points of interest for the students such as time available and resources or information available and assessment requirements. Students often feel optimistic about the journey ahead during this phase. *Exploration*, the third phase, involves sifting through information available to find a focus. Students need to be well informed about the general topic in order to find an area to focus on. The most difficult phase with an abundance of open-ended questions and wonderings means that confusion and doubt can set in. Students can become easily frustrated and discouraged with many dropping their projects as they come across inconsistencies within the information and across what they might already know. The fourth phase, *formulation*, is a time when students identify ways to focus and organise their topic which provides a degree of clarity. *Collection* follows naturally with an extended focus on how to present the new understandings. Students experience a sense of direction and increased confidence as they take ownership. Once all the required information is gathered,

Rationale for and nature of technology education 67

students consider the nature of the presentation considering a range of styles from informal to formal outcomes. Often these may become celebrations that can be shared with peers, parents or other stakeholders in the problem or issue. The *assessment* phase concludes the project as both teachers and students judge what has been learned about content and process. Critical reflection and evaluation into the inquiry process as a whole is critical; however, it is important not to confuse this phase with the ongoing formative assessment of content and process throughout the project.

During Guided Inquiry, students learn through instruction and experience. It offers them an opportunity to build on what they already know and to gain new knowledge through active engagement in, and reflecting on, experience and learning. Students develop and use higher-order thinking skills with teacher guidance at critical points in the learning. The Guided Inquiry process allows for different modes of learning to be catered for and facilitates learning through social interaction with others as seen in Table 3.1.

One issue with inquiry learning we have observed is that learning and activities are sometimes not structured nor targeted, in fact – too open. Students are left to their own devices, free to study or investigate what they wish with very little intervention and guidance from their teachers. When teachers do not have comprehensive curriculum and pedagogical content knowledge opportunities for the learning of specific skills and knowledge from some curriculum learning areas are not taught. Discrete curriculum knowledge disappears. In this situation, students are very busy; maybe having fun, but there is very little focus on curriculum content or process knowledge. Wendy has termed this "Mucky Brown Paint Syndrome." Let us explain. Imagine each curriculum learning area is a colour of the rainbow. When taught in a planned and structured manner, Guided Inquiry enables students to learn and deploy specific knowledge and skills from a range of curriculum learning areas to assist them with their research and solve identified problems and issues as an ongoing part of their inquiry. Imagine vibrant swirls of colour similar to that of a rainbow, each colour, or curriculum learning area, maintaining its integrity while enhancing and supporting its neighbour. However, if learning is not discrete and articulated to the students, colours blended together, lose identity and mucky brown paint emerges. In New Zealand primary schools, for a period of ten years from 2008 to 2018 there was considerable emphasis on literacy, numeracy and key competencies with other learning areas usually confined to afternoon "topic time," often taught through inquiry. As a result, student curriculum content knowledge has decreased in technology, science and social sciences among others. To avoid "Mucky Brown Paint Syndrome" we must maintain the integrity of each curriculum area within inquiry. Inquiry methodology and integrated curriculum support learning as the brain seeks patterns, meaning and connectedness – methods of meaning-centred learning.

Another of many challenges faced in the implementation of technology education in New Zealand is the development of a notion of authenticity that allows for full coverage of the curriculum in a way that is meaningful and useful to

68 *Rationale for and nature of technology education*

students. The Interdisciplinary Integration and Guided Inquiry approaches mentioned above facilitate authentic learning, another critical element in technology education. Let us now explore this further.

Implications for the classroom

Technology teachers and students need to act like technologists in their classrooms as much as is feasible. Teachers need to model the solving of unfamiliar technological problems for, and with, their students and not be afraid to make errors or have difficulties finding solutions. By serving as a role model, technology teachers can show students how to collect and use information to solve technological problems and help them realise that not all problems have straightforward and simple solutions, nor can some be solved.

We talk about the need for technology education to be holistic rather than fragmented. By holistic we mean the need for students to develop an understanding of the links in the design process rather than a fragmented view of each part in the process. For designing to be successful, the process should be a holistic experience that is the processing of information in whole rather than in parts. To develop this understanding, students need to be aware of the whole technology process and how the components are linked together. This is best done in situations authentic to practise so students are aware of what the technologist is involved in during the design process.

Our MoE has signalled very clearly that technological activities, including digital technologies, must occur in authentic situations. The government recently released new initiatives to strengthen digital technologies in the curriculum. This is to be done by embedding students in authentic technological practice to develop and practise skills and develop knowledge that is contextualised and integrated with a range of others, for reasons that are real and make sense to them. We believe there are implications here for the direction of professional development for our teachers. Teachers need to be informed about technological practice and the technological areas, and make links with authentic practice facilitating sound decision-making for their students. Let us now look at a technology activity that illustrates many of the key ideas mentioned so far in this chapter.

Authentic technology practice: a case study

An example of authentic technological practice was undertaken by initial teacher education students at the University of Canterbury with Wendy, one of the authors as lecturer. The study was presented at an international conference as an example of authentic technology activity. Students were members of the primary under-graduate programme in technology education. In the course, they undertook a collaborative exercise that involved considerable dialogue, inquiry and collaboration to design and develop a technological outcome to the high standard required.

An article in the local Newspaper identified an influx of immigrants into Christchurch region, also indicative of a wider trend in New Zealand. While New Zealand has a long history of colonial settlement, over more recent years the diversity of immigrating cultures has broadened. New Zealand is a very multicultural society. Some immigrants come as refugees, often having problems settling to their new home and integrating into the existing culture. The exercise undertaken by the students in this case was aimed at helping these people feel more welcomed, comfortable and settled in New Zealand. Figure 3.9 shows examples of the students' work. Using what is called a "company approach" students are grouped to produce, package and market a New Zealand styled biscuit that incorporates aspects of an immigrant culture. The student teachers work collaboratively in a "mock company" situation to produce and market to an aid agency supporting new immigrants to New Zealand. Collaboration between the teams was fundamental to the success of their final outcome, this authentic to technologists working in the real world. As part of their course assessment students individually developed a portfolio recording their research, planning, decision-making and outcome development with appropriate reflection on their understanding and knowledge of technological practice.

This task was authentic to technology practice because the design processes undertaken by the students aligned as closely as feasible to that of commercial or "real-world" technological practice. The company approach, although a mock situation, did facilitate authentic design and product development processes and facilitate authentic conversation and interaction across and between the three teams in each company. The task was culturally authentic because (i) students understood that being a food technologist developing new biscuits to meet specific needs is something that they or others they know could feasibly undertake at some stage in the future. The same for designing and making a package or marketing campaign. (ii) The task was culturally appropriate for New Zealand. Kiwis are known for their inclusive welcoming nature. Welcoming immigrant people to our country is something we pride ourselves on and therefore the required task was culturally authentic. Finally, the task involved authentic teaching because it involved the students in Guided Inquiry. The task was a rich task and although contrived by the staff it allowed students to move in multiple directions and to think and act in complex ways.

Let's now look closely at how this activity illustrates a rich task. As adult ITE students those who participated in this activity understood that cultural mobility is a real and current phenomenon and that in New Zealand multiculturalism is a local reality. The company approach to teaching leads to a variety of different outcomes, although all packaged biscuits students' outcomes were very different, each reflecting aspects of their immigrant group's culture, tastes, sights, sounds and images merged with a New Zealand welcome. During the activity students discovered that food production, packaging and marketing were heavily legislated to benefit the consumer. The NZC's key competencies and values were integrated throughout the activity. Cultural influences determine appropriate technological outcomes for each product, students were encouraged to research

70 *Rationale for and nature of technology education*

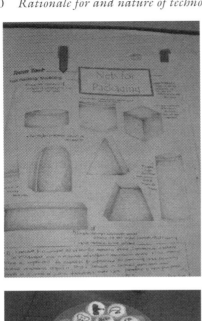

Figure 3.9   Examples of the students' "Immigrant biscuit" portfolios and outcomes

Rationale for and nature of technology education   71

the culture, and customs of their immigrant group to avoid stereotypes and generalisations. Depending on their team students researched existing biscuits, package and marketing outcomes. This investigation and critique of the physical and functional nature of existing biscuits, packaging or marketing techniques was a crucial component of their design process. Market research informed their design decision-making. Each "company" appointed a Chief Executive Officer (CEO) whose role was to facilitate communication between the team. Time and task management strategies determined important deadlines for each team within their company. Students were required to complete a list of tasks and critical path (Gantt chart) or herring-bone timeline to manage their own tasks in conjunction with team mates and fellow company members. The projects concluded with a CEO-organised product launch and presentation of processes undertaken by each team.

As the students worked through their technology practice they recorded their practice in a preprinted portfolio template. The portfolios included information on their brief development, planning for practice, and outcome development as well as research and reflection. This portfolio was used for assessment of technology but potentially could have been used to assess other curriculum areas as well, such as aspects of English, maths, science, art and social sciences. In their reflection section students made links between theory and practice, by referencing their practice against the models of technology practice. They also considered their practice in relation to key Māori values as well as discussing the implications of their practice on teaching and learning.

The practical nature of this task ensured active participation. Multiple solutions allowed the students the freedom to choose the "best fit for purpose" outcomes. Many identified with the reality of the context because of the multicultural nature of their peers and the students they teach when on practicum. The company approach allowed them the choice to work in areas of strength, thus gaining mana through the recognition for their skills. The students' technological practice incorporated many forms of modelling including: conversation about design ideas, sketching, graphical drawing, testing and trialling, product analysis tests. The final outcomes of each "company" included 6–12 biscuits with prototyped packages and advertising campaigns including posters. A range is shown in Figure 3.9.

Technology education programmes are rich sources for authentic teaching and learning. The illustrations demonstrate how a meaningful context such as the Immigrant Biscuit can integrate significant learning using activities from different learning areas and the wider curriculum. The opportunities for students to take on ownership, decide on potential pathways and achieve significant deeper learning are unbounded. In Table 3.2 we have taken criteria for authentic activity to illustrate how authentic practice can be used to make informative assessment decisions.

In summary authenticity, authentic pedagogy, teaching and learning and engaging authentic activities are all significant aspects relevant to and supportive of socio-constructivist learning theory in technology education. Authentic technology engages the 21st-century thinking through connections to real,

72 *Rationale for and nature of technology education*

Table 3.2 Authentic activities and pedagogy within the immigrant biscuit context

Authentic activities	Production team	Packaging team	Marketing team
Involved real-world issues	Biscuit needed to include the images, flavours and ingredients of the immigrant group merged with New Zealand concept of a biscuit	Biscuits needed to be legally packaged, and in a way protects the product	Products were market tested to ensure fitness for purpose. Advertised and marketed to promote the product to aid agencies, not directly to immigrants
Required clear definition *All students researched the immigrants' country. Identified important considerations including food preferences or restrictions, images, colours and sounds from that country*	Researched biscuit production, methods, equipment, health and safety issues, product testing, codes of practice	Researched packaging purposes, types, nets, product protection, vacuum forming, visual layouts	Researched marketing strategies, laws logos, presentation tools and techniques, poster layout, software and equipment, e.g. PowerPoint or use of video cameras
Were complex tasks *All students completed time management strategies including key task lists, critical paths and herringbone timelines*	Ideas for flavours are shared, recipes are trailed, testing, baking, icing or filling	Vacuum forming, package production, using a nutrition panel calculator, package production	Storyboards, PowerPoint production, video editing
Used different perspectives and a variety of resources	Food Technology Processed technologies Baking equipment, food hygiene	Digital Technologies; Materials Technologies Food safe materials Legal requirements Nutritional Panel calculator	Digital Technologies Design and Visual Communication (DVC) technologies
Involved working in collaboration *Each company has a Chief Executive Officer and each team has five or six members. Stakeholders perspectives are addressed*	Workload was shared, ideas pooled and debated, teams and company meetings, CEO's role was co-constructed and CEO appointed from within the company. Each team member undertook individual tasks and responsibilities in collaboration with team members and CEO. Each individual portfolio contained some unique aspects, some aspects shared with teammates only and some aspects common to the whole company		

(Continued)

Rationale for and nature of technology education 73

Table 3.2 (Continued)

Authentic activities	Production team	Packaging team	Marketing team
Required in-depth reflection *Part of technological practice, made connections to relevant literature and future classroom practice as a teacher*	Throughout their practice students reflected against five pre-determined aspects. These included making meaningful links to NZC, links between their technology practice and the theoretical models of technology practice, implications for them as a learner (Orange hat thinking), implications for them as a teacher (Brown hat thinking) and bicultural perspective – integration of Māori values, practices, knowledges and ti kanga		
Facilitated meaningful integration	Science, Social Sciences, Mathematics, Health – food and nutrition NZC Key competencies and values	English, DVC, Visual Art, Mathematics, Social Sciences NZC Key competencies and values	English, DVC, Visual Arts, Sound Arts, Social Sciences NZC Key competencies and values
Integrated assessment	Students maintained an individual portfolio of their practice and associated reflections with links to NZC and the Technology Curriculum. This document accounted for 50% of the total assessment value of the course. For this half of the course not other assessment tasks were required. Clear criteria were given to the students indicating expectations for A, B and C grades for each		
Involved the development of polished products and diverse outcomes *While portfolios were working documents students were expected to demonstrate good quality research and annotated conceptual drawings of final outcomes*	Some created specifically shaped biscuit cutters, biscuits produced for trialling and a final production run. Colour, size, shape, viscosity of icing and biscuit construction were among the multiple considerations for a quality biscuit	An authentic package with all details included – nutrition, ingredient list, graphic display, producers were required. Most biscuit packages needed an inner package as well. Some developed a vacuum formed tray to protect biscuits	Promotional video or PowerPoint and A3 promotional poster. Some groups also wrote and produced a jingle

meaningful and purposeful work. Students make sense of and interact with their world. An increasing number of school students in New Zealand primary schools are actively engaged in excellent and authentic learning programmes in technology, however many are not. There is still a huge need for professional development and in some cases, a shift away from past teaching practices to ensure all students are given the unique learning opportunities technology affords.

74 *Rationale for and nature of technology education*

Upon arrival at secondary schools, secondary technology teachers are faced with the dilemma that some of their students have had a range of authentic technology experiences and some none. Progression to secondary school often leaves students with feelings of frustration, tedium, disengagement and constraint as their teachers start all students on activity assuming their students' primary technology experiences are limited. We urge a more formative, needs-based approach, using diagnostic assessment activities to determine actual levels of achievement of each student. Secondary teachers must not treat new students as empty vessels and subjected to individualistic, assessment-based, text-oriented and content-driven courses. Secondary technology programmes should be based on authentic problems and be needs based. We need to promote the overcoming of inhibitors and constraints such as timetabling and assessment to allow for more stimulating, connected and meaningful programmes of learning promoting habits for lifelong learning and technologically literate students who develop quality technological outcomes. Another aspect important to technology teaching and learning is the role of talk.

Social interaction and talk in technology

Language and social interaction are vital components of working collaboratively and therefore fundamental components of learning in technology. Vygotsky suggested that there are two opposing tendencies always at work in social interaction – intersubjectivity and alterity. Intersubjective dialogue occurs between a novice and an expert and works towards shared definition and aims to move the novice to a state in which performance can be carried out independently. This means an expert is guiding the novice from the interpsychological plane of understanding to the intrapsychological plane. The idea of two planes of learning suggests that, initially, interaction appears between the child and another person on an interpsychological plane and then within the child on an intrapsychological plane. Marylin Fleer helps us understand the interpsychological and intrapsychological planes through the example below.

> Children participate in social activities without necessarily understanding what they mean. An example is that of a toddler participating in hand-washing after visiting the toilet or before eating. This ritual is practiced by the child's family and hence is a part of accepted behaviour patterns known to the child. However the child may not necessarily fully understand what this action means. Vygotsky termed this social behaviour as occurring at an *interpsychological* level of functioning – at a social level of functioning without understanding. It is when the child understands why she/he is washing her/his hands that the child is said to be operating at an *intrapsychological* level of functioning. Learning occurs when the child moves from one level of functioning to another.

Alterity occurs when discrepancy or conflict of opinion or perspective between one's own and another's view sparks cognitive development. Alterity is concerned

Rationale for and nature of technology education 75

with the distinction between self and others, within thought generation. The listener perceives and understands the meaning and simultaneously takes an active response to it, either agreeing or disagreeing, partially or completely. Understanding of speech is imbued with response. Within a constructivist paradigm, interaction between people is a central aspect of cognitive, social and cultural development. People interact, they construct their world. Joint problem solving uses debate as a major force in cognitive development. However, language is not a system of set meanings which everyone agrees with. Single statements can mean different things to different people, thus a potential for conflict and disagreement with the significance of each understood against the background of language and culture of giver and receiver. The discussion that takes place during the course of education activities is called dialogue. Within everyday dialogue the speaker regularly considers the listener's response giving insight into variability of meaning. When the response aligns with the speaker's understanding, the conversation is enriched. On the other hand, when the listener's understanding differs the speaker can sense resistance. Beliefs, values and attitudes inform the way people act, read, what they say and how they interact; however, these are not static and change as people read, experience, observe and adapt to new situations.

Dialogue is much more than talk; it is complex and dynamic and often involves very different cultures, perspectives, ideas and people. It generally involves the use of words and requires engagement with people. Dialogue can bring moments of intense connection with another person with feelings of remarkable openness, deeply affirming and highly exhilarating moments. It is critical in learning and considerably more important than has been demonstrated in schools in the past. Educational success and failure may be explained by the quality of educational dialogue, rather than by the capability of individual students or the skill of their teachers.

When people work together in problem-solving situations they do much more than just talk together. They "inter-think" by combining shared understandings, combining their intellects in creative ways often reaching outcomes that are well above the capability of each individual. Problem-solving situations involve a dynamic engagement of ideas with dialogue as the principle means used to establish a shared understanding, testing solutions and reaching agreement or compromise. Dialogue and thinking together are an important part of life and one that has long been ignored or actively discouraged in schools. There are very clear implications here for technology given the collaborative nature of problem solving required to develop technological outcomes.

Teachers need to engage in quality dialogue with students (and parents) to assist with cognitive and experiential understanding of the world in which they live. Teachers make powerful contributions to the way children think and talk and convey powerful messages about thinking by the way they structure classroom activity and talk. Students need to be engaged in thoughtful and reasoned dialogue. Teachers need to model and scaffold useful language strategies to extend thinking. Students need regular opportunity to practise using language to reflect, enquire and explain their thinking to others. This will enable them to seek and compare points of view, use language to compare, debate and reconcile questions taking

76 *Rationale for and nature of technology education*

learning beyond teachers' factual questions. Spoken language is one of the tools students use to make sense of the world and is a teacher's main pedagogical tool.

Many people have tried to describe quality interaction between adult and child, and there is no one ideal way of interacting with students. Interactions are context bound and specific to the immediate situation. Often students are not given time to think about what they are doing in relation to the wider situation or previous learning and experiences. They are not taught useful ways of using spoken language as a tool for learning and working collaboratively. Social construction theory suggests that high quality interaction is best exemplified when teachers engage the philosophy that all students are unique individuals with special interests and temperaments. Unfortunately, a great deal of adult interaction with students is about management rather than learning resulting in many lost learning opportunities.

Social Construction Theory Symbolic Interaction, Sociocultural Conflict Theory and Grounded Theory also give insight into interaction between teachers and students and between students. Symbolic Interactionism makes a significant contribution to the understanding that knowing, thinking, believing and notions of self have origins in social interaction and that the mind is inseparable from the social process. This theory suggests how an individual thinks and acts is determined by the actions of others. Sociocultural Conflict Theory sees conflict as an essential ingredient of any joint involvement involving cognitive change. Doise and colleagues have demonstrated that children working in pairs solve problems at a more advanced level than those working by themselves (regardless of the ability of the partner). These studies reveal that when coming up against an alternative point of view (not necessarily the correct one) forces the student to coordinate his or her own viewpoint with that of another. The conflict can only be resolved if cognitive restructuring takes place and therefore mental change occurs as a result of social interaction. Thus the social interaction stimulates cognitive development by permitting dyadic (people working in pairs) coordinations to facilitate inner coordinations. Technology education typically involves children in problem-solving situations which are done collaboratively and cooperatively with their peers and key adults and naturally involves the discussion of conflicting thoughts and ideas.

Grounding is defined as a collective process by which participants try to reach a mutual belief of understanding about the meaning of a conversation contribution For two people to communicate both need to contribute to the conversation and have common understanding of the exchange that is taking place or is about to take place. This common understanding is called *grounding* and ensures what is said is understood. Grounding is a basic component of and essential to communication. It is shaped by two main factors, *purpose* and *medium*. People engaged in conversation establish a collective purpose for it using a number of techniques, which typically change according to the purpose and content of conversations. Communication is constantly changing and differs according to the media used such as: mobile phone, texting, email, social media (Twitter, Snapchat and Facebook), post-it notes, personal face-to-face communication, digital face-to-face communication (Zoom, Hangouts, Facetime, Messenger,

Rationale for and nature of technology education   77

Skype). Techniques for establishing a clear conversation purpose differ according to the media used. One technique, commonly used on social media but elsewhere too, is called "least collective effort" suggesting people prefer to use the least amount of effort in their communication, thus exchanges are brief and with communication short cuts, for example the use of the term "okay" is a technique often employed in "face-to-face" and phone conversations to ensure the speaker does not say more than necessary. Symbols and abbreviations are often used in texting and within social media to decrease the need for further communication.

Intercognitive conversations

Having considered theory that contributes to our understanding of why dialogue is so important to learning, we would like to introduce you to the notion of Intercognitive Conversation. Intercognitive conversations are conversations within which all participants learn through the talk and associated reflections. Working within a common context and engaged in constructive talk or dialogue students assisted each other and advanced their own knowledge and understanding in their given context. Debate, argument and disagreement assist students' understanding and assist them to reposition new information. However, this cognitive growth only occurs if and when participants are open to change and new ideas.

There are two types of intercognitive conversation. The first is when cognitive growth occurs in the same field of learning or within the same context, we call this type of conversation Convergent Growth Conversation (CGC). This is exemplified when two students have a conversation each contributing what they know. Through the conversation both participants combine their existing knowledge and skills subsequently expanding their own understanding.

The second is when conversation participants learn new knowledge in different fields and for different purposes. This often occurs in teachers' conversations with students. Teacher questions assist the student to make new connections about their current context of learning. At the same time through the same dialogue with the same students teachers also gain new knowledge about students' learning strategies and successful pedagogical approaches. This type of conversation is characterised by divergent cognitive growth for all participants and is called Divergent Growth Conversation (DGC).

Understanding the importance of, and facilitating, student-teacher and student-student dialogue is particularly relevant to technology education because of the hands-on practical nature of many of the lessons, teachers are easily distracted by organisation of activities and management of the children's behaviour. Teachers need to be disciplined to ensure these things do not distract them from engaging the children in conversation about their learning and practice. Technology education allows children to use creativity and innovative thinking, to move in directions very different from current thinking or thinking of their peers, offering teachers unique opportunities and insight into their students' thinking. This was illustrated when one of the authors Wendy was working with a group of six-year olds who were asked to design a car for their future. Issy, a

78 *Rationale for and nature of technology education*

very quiet classroom member, who rarely contributed orally, designed a car that had wings rather than wheels. Dialogue between the author and Issy allowed insight into her forward thinking and understanding that previously has not been identified by the classroom teacher. She had identified that cars in the future might have wings instead of wheels. During the same conversations Issy was able to reflect on some of the issues associated with flying cars such as flying over people's houses and stopping for other "cars."

Intercognitive talk is particularly relevant to technology because students are often asked to work collaboratively in groups to work on a technological issue and develop a single technological outcome. In order to develop a single solution members of the group must listen to and accept others' ideas, clearly articulate their own thinking and reasoning behind that thinking or make a shift in their own thinking to find a compromise. It is during these often meaningful conversations that students often draw on their cultural FOK, as they may have cultural experience, skills and knowledge that other group members do not have and thus giving value to often undervalued cultural knowledge and skills or FOK.

Technology observations and conversation framework

The technology observations conversation framework (TOCF) was developed to assist teachers' facilitation of quality conversations with students while they work in technology. The framework offers a large number of questions teachers can select from to initiate conversations with students, it gives suggestions as to the types of comments that might be useful and makes suggestions for behaviours to observe. The TOCF has a dual role, also assisting to develop teachers' understanding of technology.

The framework identifies five behaviours considered as desirable for success in learning and living in the 21st century: resilience, transference, flexibility, reflection and socialisation. These behaviours were selected as being particularly relevant to technology and come from the work of Claxton and colleagues. The first behaviour "resilience" includes capabilities of perseverance especially after initial failure, managing distractions from peers, other activities and people around them, and absorption in any given task. Absorption, likened to Csikszentmihalyi's state of "flow," is described as a state of deep absorption in an activity that is intrinsically enjoyable, as when artists and athletes are focused on their play or performance. Its relevance to technology is clear. Students must be able to fail repeatedly during their design processes and testing phases. Modelling is all about discovering what will and will not work. In technology mistakes are celebrated, each identifying something that does not work "yet" and that that a solution may lie elsewhere or indeed does not exist. A favourite quote from Thomas Edison comes to mind when considering resilience:

> I have not failed. I've just found 10,000 ways that won't work. Our greatest weakness lies in giving up. …. The most certain way to succeed is always to try just one more time.

Rationale for and nature of technology education   79

The transference of knowledge occurs when students develop understanding in one context and are able to use this knowledge in another context. This does not always occur naturally for students but is something that teachers can enhance with awareness and good understanding of content knowledge and the ability to make authentic connections. Transference includes making links to technologies experienced or seen, and experiences undertaken previously and drawing on existing FOK. It also includes students reflecting on and questioning the relevance of previous experiences and knowledge and skills, imaging how if and how it is relevant to and be transferred to new situations to assist and or improve performance. Again, the relevance to technology is clear. As students design and develop their technological outcomes they will automatically be given opportunities to deploy knowledge and skills from other learning areas. The domains of mathematics, writing, reading, social studies and science are significant contributors to technology; however, teachers frequently need to bridge the learning between the learning areas, as students do not always recognise these opportunities. The need for bridging transference was clearly illustrated for Wendy a number of years ago. She was teaching a "foods" unit to a group of Year 7 and 8 students. An aspect of the brief given to the students was that they needed to design and develop a food package 1000cc in volume. During the unit planning process Wendy checked with the students' maths teacher to ensure finding the volume of a container was some the students were familiar with. She found that they had recently completed a unit on measurement including volume. During class a group of students asked Wendy how to design a package of the required volume (1000cc). She replied, "I know you know how to do this because Miss Tomms [not her real name] told me that you have just done this in mathematics – finding volume and creating nets for 3D cuboids of specific volumes. One student looked at Wendy and said, "Oh, but that is maths, can we use that?" "Yes" Wendy answered. Away the students went to complete their task successfully.

Of course there are times when students can and do deploy prior knowledge and skills when immersed in technology, thus transferring skills and knowledge learning from school, home and within their community to their technology projects. Wendy has observed students can and do deploy home and cultural funds and knowledge to their technology projects as well as some aspects of learning from other learning areas, especially the skills and knowledge they are very familiar with. We suggest this is most likely to occur when the students are fully engaged in their project and motivated to do a good job.

Flexibility and sophistication indicate a depth to understanding as well as an openness to new and potentially strange ideas. They involve the use of reasoning to evaluate and distil information in order to understand what is learned from an experience. The ability to think flexibly and sophisticatedly includes the questioning of relevance and asking questions of others to learn more by getting below the surface of ideas and artefacts. Planning ideas and actions and capitalising or making the best use of resources also characterise this behaviour. There is an intuitive connection between creativity and cognition. Increased sophistication of ideas is linked to thinking creatively and flexibly. In technology David

80   *Rationale for and nature of technology education*

Spendlove identifies strong societal benefits of being creative within technology education. There are two important documents that assist teachers' understanding of how technology knowledge and understanding develops in sophistication and flexibility as students move through the achievement levels in technology. These are the achievement objects and their associated indicators of progression. The indicators of progression in the NZC sit alongside the achievement objectives to guide teachers in teaching technology and identify what students are able to do when achieving at each of the curriculum learning levels 1–8. They can be found in Technology Online. Table 3.3 illustrates increased sophistication and flexibility of thinking across two achievement objectives: brief development and characteristics of technology, guided by the indicators. The third column in Table 3.3 explicitly identifies ideas that are developed between levels 1 and 4 of the curriculum.

Reflection describes the strategic and self-managing aspect of learning and includes the planning and anticipating of needs and potential issues and distilling information for potential or future use. Reflection includes the revision of prior learning and its evaluation as a part of the distilling process. It assists with the identification of relevant learning that is transferrable to new contexts. It also involves self-generated questioning and self-monitoring of progress through being cognisant of what, how and why learning is taking place. Technology practice is a highly reflective process, as we saw in Kimbell's APU Model of technology practice. In order to design and develop successful technological outcomes reflection must be continuous and active. In other words, students need to understand their thinking, being engaged in metacognitive thinking and be informed by their insights.

Socialisation identifies with the inherently social nature of being human. Technology is a human activity and there are huge physical, social and environmental impacts of technology. Whether engaging in the use or the development of technology students will be interacting in a social manner. They may be collaborating with others to develop single or parallel technologies, they will experience interdependence, or the balancing of self-reliance and socialisation, as the need for resources and skills arise. Even when interacting with technology in a solitary manner children are still engaging with people. Their evaluation of the technology and decisions about whether to come back for further engagement or not will impact other people in the long term if not sooner, for example teachers will not purchase a technological device, toy or piece of equipment that their children choose not to engage with.

The behaviours identified above, incorporating cognitive, social and physical behaviours, are a modified and blended version of the domains and capabilities identified by Guy Claxton and colleagues. Within each behaviour, sit a number of capabilities. The behaviours and capabilities are outlined in Table 3.4.

TOCF uses the above behaviours and capabilities coupled with the components of technology to create sets of questions to facilitate teacher conversation with students to assist learning in technology. It is aimed at both improving learning for students and to develop teachers' understanding of technology

Rationale for and nature of technology education 81

Table 3.3 Sophistication and flexibility of thinking across two achievement objectives

Achievement objective	Indicators of progression	Increased sophistication and flexibility
Brief Development		
The students will describe the outcome they are developing and identify the attributes it should have, taking account of the need or opportunity and the resources available. Level 1	*Students can ...* • communicate the outcome to be produced • identify attributes for an outcome	The students develop sophistication and flexibility by progressing *from* the ability to ... • articulate what they are developing *to* identifying a need or opportunity within a given context • identify some attributes for their intended outcome *to* writing of a conceptual statement that describes and justifies their outcome
Justify the nature of an intended outcome in relation to the need or opportunity. Describe the key attributes identified in stakeholder feedback, which will inform the development of an outcome and its evaluation. Level 4	• identify a need or opportunity from the given context and issue • establish a conceptual statement that communicates the nature of the outcome and why such an outcome should be developed • establish the key attributes for an outcome informed by stakeholder considerations • communicate key attributes that allow an outcome to be evaluated as fit for purpose	• identify list of attributes *to* establish and justify key attributes developed from stakeholder's needs and feedback
Characteristics of Technology		
The students will understand that technology is purposeful intervention through design. Level 1	*Students can ....* • identify that technology helps to create the made world • identify that technology involves people designing and making technological outcomes for an identified purpose • identify that technological practice involves knowing what you are making and why, planning what to do and what resources are needed, and making and evaluating an outcome	The students develop sophistication and flexibility by progressing *from* the ability to... • identify that technology creates the 'made-world' *to* understanding that technology changes people's abilities, perceptions and experiences of the world • understand that technology is around us *to* understanding technology has short- and long-term impacts on the world

(*Continued*)

82 Rationale for and nature of technology education

Table 3.3 (Continued)

Achievement objective	Indicators of progression	Increased sophistication and flexibility
Understand how technological development expands human possibilities and how technology draws on knowledge from a wide range of disciplines. Level 4	• identify examples where technology has changed people's sensory perception and/or physical abilities and discuss the potential short- and long-term impacts of these • identify examples of creative and critical thinking in technological practice • identify and categorise knowledge and skills from technology and other disciplines that have informed decisions in technological development and manufacture	• understanding people make technology for a reason or purpose *to* understand people think critically and creatively when developing technology to meet a need or opportunity • understanding the process of making technology involves knowing what is being made, the resources needed and why *to* understanding technology practice involves recognising and deploying skills and knowledge from technology and other disciplines • understand technology practice involves design and outcome evaluation *to* understand that evaluation of technology design and outcomes includes technological development and manufacture

content and pedagogical content knowledge. The framework was originally produced to work with students aged 4–6 years of age. This version was published in the *International Journal of Technology and Design Education* in 2019.

Parts of the Years 7–8 version based on NZC level 4 are included in this book (Table 3.5). It is recommended that when using the framework to assist conversations with students that teachers concentrate on one selected technology component or achievement objective. In this book, we have included the questions situated in the Nature of Technology for the AO CT and CTO.

Table 3.4 Potential behaviours underpinning success in technology

Behaviours: demonstration of:	Resilience	Transference	Flexibility and sophistication	Reflection	Socialisation
Capabilities	Perseverance Managing Distractions Absorption	Making links Imaging Noticing Questioning	Planning Distilling Reasoning Imagining Capitalising Evaluating	Questioning Distilling Revising Meta Learning Evaluating	Empathy and listening Collaboration Interdependence Imitating

Table 3.5 TOCF nature of technology level 4 NZC

		Desirable behaviours to support technology learning			
Strand and achievement objective	Resilience	Transference	Reflection	Sophistication and flexibility	Socialisation
	Look for … Evidence of understanding the developing technology may require repeated failure and modification Perseverance with and through issues Total absorption while others are working around them	Look for students drawing on knowledge from other learning areas and technology learning to enhance their understanding of technology and to inform their technology practice	Look for … Critical analysis of technologies from the past, present and future Questioning and critique of existing technologies Questioning and critique of their own design decisions	Look for advancement of key ideas and the ability to take thinking in different directions when considering past, present and future technologies	Look for understanding that …. Technology is for people Technology impacts and influences people People influence technological design and development Technology practice is a collaborative process Technologists rely on others even when working on an individual project
Characteristics of technology	How has repeated failure from the designer improved the functionality of this technology?	Tell me which knowledge and skills from other learning areas (e.g. maths, social sciences) assist the technologist as they design and make technology?	There are two ways of making a critical technology. One requires an extra month to manufacture it and the other requires extra material to manufacture. Either way the manufacturing cost is the same. Which way would you choose and why?	How has this example of a technology that has changed human physical limitations – either positively or negatively	Some technologies work but was not accepted by people? (Google Glasses, Segway are good examples.) Why do you think people did not accept some technology?

(Continued)

Table 3.5 *(Continued)*

	Desirable behaviours to support technology learning				
	Identify three potential negative impacts of technology. What causes this impact?	Tell me which knowledge and skills from other areas of technology (e.g. digital, foods technologies) assist the technologist as they design and make technology?	If everyone could have X technology, how would your life change?	Give example of features in technology that you think are creative and well thought. Why is it so?	How does the role of the society affect the way in which technology is used and produced?
	What could be done to prevent this impact or make the impact less severe?		How would your life change without technology?		
Characteristics of technological outcomes	Take any obsolete technology from the past (example typewriter, pagers). Why are they obsolete today? What has replaced this technology? Why?	In this product design, what knowledge has been used from other subjects or areas like science or maths?	What about this design that confuses you? What kind of knowledge do you think you might lack to understand this thoroughly?	What is the key or primary function of this *technology*? How do you know this?	How do you think people in a colder/ hotter/richer/poorer/ religious country would rate this product? Why? Do you think they would find it meets their needs in the same way?

Table 3.5 (Continued)

Desirable behaviours to support technology learning				
If you were a technologist, what steps would you take to make sure that your technology does not become obsolete?	In this product, how has the technologist used understanding of function and aesthetics to make their design better?	If it was your job to design this technology, what information do you think you would need to get a good outcome for your stakeholder?	Identify a technology that has alternative functions to that of its original design. What influenced/instigated this alternative use?	What kind of attributes do you think your parents/grandparents/ Captain Cook wanted for travel/ communication/food? How are your criteria for that different?
			Give an example of a technology from the past that we no longer use. Why do you think this technology was developed in that time and why is it not around now?	Think of your life without X (name a specific technology), how would your life change?

86 Rationale for and nature of technology education

Teachers' conversations with students are frequently about management or superficial features of design and technology practice. By drawing on questions from this framework, teachers are able to facilitate conversation and thinking about the deeper features of technology.

Sources of funds of knowledge (FOK)

As mentioned earlier in this chapter, one cultural rationale for the teaching of technology was that it gives students opportunities to draw on their cultural knowledge to enhance their own and possibly others' learning. It facilitates useful interaction between knowledge found inside and outside the classroom. González and her colleagues identified that the more teachers know about the home and cultural activities and experiences of their students the better informed they are to maximise learning opportunities, make the most of knowledge and skills already accessible to some students. Wendy Fox-Turnbull undertook research related to students' deployment of FOK in technology education identifying two sources, participatory enculturation and passive observation.

Participatory enculturation

When students gain knowledge and skills through active engagement in the activity resulting in transferable knowledge we call this participatory enculturation. This engagement includes active participation, where the student is involved in the activity, or peripheral participation where they are on the periphery of the activity but able to engage through questions and conversation. This might be a part of the gaining of knowledge and skills through the transfer of knowledge and skills from expert to novice as suggested in the apprenticeship model of learning discussed earlier in this chapter. Gaining knowledge through participatory enculturation provides students with opportunities to learn and share information their peers may be unfamiliar with and involve practices unique to their family and culture. Knowledge gained from these experiences can provide them status or mana within their peer group. There are a number of avenues from which students gain FOK from participatory enculturation: family activity, after-school activities, parents' occupation and interests, artefacts used at home, and family cultural, social and cooperative practices. Each is illustrated below with examples of a study within which primary students worked in groups of three or four to design and develop a prop for their school production.

Evidence of participatory enculturation through family activity occurred very early in the unit. As a part of the project, the students were given a disposable camera so that they could record their process of developing their prop. Their first task was to ask a friend to take their photograph so that the first photograph in each camera was that of its owner. Having just had her photo taken on her camera, Mim, aged six, was concerned that her camera was broken; this was her first experience with a non-digital camera. Duncan, who was talking to Wendy

Rationale for and nature of technology education 87

when Mim approached her, was able to reassure Mim as he had experienced how the photos were released. The conversation went as follows:

MIM: Wendy, my camera is broken
WENDY: What makes you say that Mim?
MIM: I cannot see the photograph inside the camera.
DUNCAN: Oh, it's okay. You just take them to 'The Warehouse' and they hit them with a hammer and the photos jump out
WENDY: How do you know that Duncan?
DUNCAN: My Dad had one and we went to The Warehouse and that's what they did

The knowledge Duncan gained through participatory enculturation with his Dad gave Duncan the confidence and status to reassure his classmate that her camera was not broken. It demonstrates that use and knowledge of technological devices gained from home and community assist students' confidence in their use.

Students also use knowledge and skills learned from after-school activities to assist them in understanding. After-school activities are defined as activities that students do independently of their family; typically going to external teachers for lessons or tutoring, playing sports or undertaking hobbies by themselves. When researching props, much of the information the students came across was from the United States of America. This is illustrated in the example below. Alan explained how he knew the symbol " stood for inches. He cited the reason for knowing about this symbol was through his active participation in gaming on the computer or that the knowledge may have come from his father.

WENDY: 13 and a half something. What does that mean? *Points at;*
ALAN: Inches
WENDY: How do you know that, Alan?
ALAN: It's like probably, I just know that from my father
WENDY: But, how did you know? You said inches. I can't see inches anywhere on that
ALAN: It's those two things. That's what inches is
WENDY: How do you know that? Alan Umm, because I do war gaming and that's what they use for inches.

Alan demonstrated his ability to interpret a symbol of measurement not used in his school environment but one used in his home environment. Drawing on the information gained through participation assisted Alan's understanding and interpretation of information relating to research in another area. It is a requirement in technology to interpret designs of others.

Students use FOK gained from parents' occupations to position themselves as an expert and to gain *mana* from their peers. This was illustrated by three Year 6 children developing a 1930s microphone as they discussed suitable materials.

88 *Rationale for and nature of technology education*

Alan mentioned his Dad was a racing car designer and had a workshop at home. David chipped into the conversation in a competitive manner explaining that his Dad has much more than blocks of wood because he worked in the construction industry. They had decided that the head of the microphone could be made from wood.

DAVID: My Dad owns a whole yard of everything. He's got lots of things, yeah. He's a drain layer. He's an excavation worker. He's a construction builder. He has a yard, a whole yard.

Students deploy knowledge gained through interaction with artefacts in their home environment. This was illustrated in the props study when Minnie and David were problem solving how to hold the microphone head at the correct angle before attaching it to the stand. Wendy asked what they were working on. When trying to explain David used an example from his home computer docking station. He deployed an idea of one thing slotting into a specific place designed to hold it, to assist his design concepts and his explanation of his and Minnie's design.

WENDY: How are you going to attach, so what is this going to be?
DAVID: The base)
MINNIE: It's the base) [together]
WENDY: I know it's the base and it's to make it stand up, but what does it actually do
DAVID: It's going to be like a [docking] station at the back and um it's like, it's going to have like glue around it to stand by itself

Students deploy FOK about not only artefact and process knowledge and skills directly linked to home and community culture, but they also deploy their community and family social skills and knowledge. This is relevant to working collaboratively in technology. Three Year 2 students Rex, Debbie and Issy who had to agree on one final design for their prop illustrate this. Issy and Debbie had a history of disagreeing with each other so Rex took on the role of peacemaker by deploying social FOK as he worked with the girls on the design drawing. Issy and Debby were having trouble deciding on the colours of their prop, and who decided what. Rex attempted peacemaking by deploying a strategy his father used at home.

DEBBIE: I like the blue one.
ISSY: I like the green one.
REX: You can have the blue wings, the one there. The one of yours but just the wings. What one do you like?
ISSY: I want the body ....
DEBBIE: But that one, yeah, have the body but not the face and I'll have the face and the ... .

ISSY:	But I'm drawing the face. I'm drawing the face
REX:	No, that one. That one, eh?
DEBBIE:	No
REX:	That one.
ISSY:	Yeah.
DEBBIE:	No.
ISSY:	Yes. We like it so there's cause ...
REX:	What I used to do is if there was two and there was one, so I did this, because my Dad always says, 'which one' and then the other two wanted two and then if there's one person who likes it, then we, we don't like it though.
ISSY:	[very softly] you just have to do it

Learning through participatory enculturation involves the students in interaction with the context of learning and involves dialogue with participants, active engagement with materials, activities and artefacts, and practices that are an integral part of living in a community. Conversations in participatory enculturation are interactive in nature.

Passive observation

When learning deploying passive observation FOK the students are non-participatory observers, for example, through watching movies, television or reading books then apply it in their classroom. This includes the location of technology in historical and cultural contexts. Gaining knowledge through historical location is illustrated below. The Year 6 students understood props assisted in the historical location of a play or setting. In an activity aimed at understanding the role of props in a play the students were given a range of photographs of play props. Minnie recognises a cart and knows they are from the past. She heard about them in the song Little House on the Prairie – set in pioneer times in the Midwest of the United States of America. Minnie used prior observation to assist her personal construct of an object from a different era. In Year 2, they students listened to Julian, the props manager from the local Court Theatre explain the purpose and function of props. He illustrated his talk with a range of props his company used in the past. He discussed how each was used in situ. Issy was reminded of a show she has seen in the previous school holidays. As an audience member she observed one particular prop used in a variety of ways, using knowledge gained from attending the theatre to assist her understanding of the definition of a technological outcome. Issy's input into the conversation indicates that she understands that the truck, as a prop, had multiple purposes.

| ISSY: | I saw a show about a magic truck in the holidays and it changed [voice trails off] |
| JULIAN: | Ohh, *Auntie McDuff's Magical Trunk*. That was the show that we did in the last school holidays. Yeah, so what they did was they had this big |

90 *Rationale for and nature of technology education*

> box and they opened up bits of the box and when they opened up the front bit of the box, they put umm, a, a, they used a blackboard and they put a little drawing of some wheels at the bottom of the box and then that prop became a train or a car and then they'd close another bit and they'd open another bit and they'd put umm, a flag on it and it would become a boat. So sometimes ...
>
> ISSY: and a dog
>
> JULIAN: and it became a dog at the end. Yeah. So sometimes you can use a prop a lot, lots and lots of different ways.

At the time of actual learning for these students, the context was not embedded in authentic meaningful activity; however, the students later deployed knowledge gained through these means to inform their practice, thus authenticating its deployment rather than the actual learning. Teachers need to engage in quality dialogue with students and parents to help them make sense both cognitively and experientially of the world in which they live and work. By doing this, teachers facilitate deployment of knowledge and skills learning through passive observation. Teachers need to know and understand the communities and cultural practices of their students to maximise learning opportunities in the classroom by making explicit connections. This can occur through a range of methods: anecdotal conversations with students before and after school about their interests and hobbies, a formal survey of students or the undertaking of a "talents" unit early in the year in which students demonstrate their outside interests and talents to other class members. Clear articulation from the teacher to the students about the purpose of this information gathering, whatever form it takes, may enhance student participation in all the ideas above.

Summary

It is imperative for teachers of technology to have thorough content knowledge and pedagogical content knowledge (PCK) and understand the values of teaching technology. This chapter began by considering a rationale for teaching technology in primary and secondary schools in New Zealand. Given technology's recency and connections to former skill-based programmes such as manual, cooking, sewing, woodwork and metalwork, this is critical. The chapter outlined a number of models of technology practice and then identified and discussed pedagogical approaches along with a number of pertinent learning theories.

Technology has the potential to become an excellent model or vehicle for the learning of other curriculum areas. Within integrated programmes centred on solving technological issues and the development of technological outcomes, students are given authentic opportunities to measure, speak, write reports, discuss and consider social, environmental and health issues, making other curriculum more accessible. When participating in holistic technological practice,

Rationale for and nature of technology education 91

students require a range of academic, social, cultural and physical skills in order to collaboratively develop technological solutions to meet identified needs or opportunities.

Bibliography

Alcorn, N., & Thrupp, M. (2012). Uncovering meanings: The discourses of New Zealand secondary teachers in context. *New Zealand Journal of Educational Studies*, *47*(1), 107–121. https://search.informit.com.au/documentSummary;dn=671428728522989;res=IELHSS.

Alton-Lee, A., & Densem, P. (1992). Towards gender-inclusive school curriculum, changing educational practice. In S. Middleton & A. Jones (Eds.), *Women and education in Aotearoa 2*. Bridget Williams Books.

Apple, M. W. (1988). *Teachers and texts: A political economy of class and gender relations in education*. Routledge.

Association, I. T. E. (2007). *Standards for technological literacy: Content for the study of technology*. International Technology Education Association [ITEA]. https://www.iteea.org/File.aspx?id=67767.

Atkinson, S. (1999, Spring). Key factors influencing pupil motivation in design and technology. *Journal of Technology Education*, *10*(2).

Bell, B., & Reinsfield, E. (2012, November). *Becoming a culturally responsive teacher*. New Zealand Association for Research in Education Conference and Annual Conference.

Bereiter, C. (1992). Referent-centred and problem-centred knowledge: Elements of an educational epistemology. *Interchange*, *23*(4), 337–361.

Bishop, R., Berryman, M., Cavanagh, T., & Teddy, L. (2007). *Te Kōtahitanga Phase 3 Whānaungatanga: Establishing a culturally responsive pedagogy of relations in mainstream secondary school classrooms*. Ministry of Education.

Black, P., & Wiliam, D. (1998). *Inside the black box – raising standards through classroom assessment* (1st ed.). King's College.

Blythe, T. (1998). *The teaching for understanding guide*. Jossy-Bass.

Bourdieu, P., (1986). The Forms of Capital (in The Sociology of Cultural Life, pp. 78–92). Routledge.

Brown, J., Collins, A., & Duguid, P. (1989). Situated cognition and the culture of learning. *Education Researcher*, *18*(1), 32–42.

Brown, M., Benson, S., & Ferguson, D. (1999). *Development of technology education in New Zealand* [Unpublished paper].

Clark, H., & Brennan, S. (1991). Grounding in communication. In L. Resnick, J. Levine, & S. Teasley (Eds.), *Perspectives on social shared cognition* (pp. 127–149). American Psychological Association.

Clarke, S. (2008). *Active learning through formative assessment*. Hodder Education.

Clarke, S. (2014). *Outstanding formative assessment: Culture and practice*. Hodder Education.

Clarke, S., Hattie, J., & Timperley, H. (2003). *Unlocking formative assessment – practical strategies for enhancing learning in the primary and intermediate classroom* (New Zealand edition ed.). Hodder Moa Beckett.

Claxton, G. (2007). Expanding young people's capacity to learn. *British Journal of Educational Studies*, *55*(2), 115–134.

Claxton, G., Chambers, M., Powell, G., & Lucas, B. (2013). *The learning powered school: Pioneering 21st century education*. TLO Limited.

92 Rationale for and nature of technology education

Counts, E. (2017). *Teaching staff*. https://www.educationcounts.govt.nz/statistics/schooling/teaching_staff.

Cowie, B., & McNae, R. (Eds.). (2017). *Partnership research: A relational practice* (Vol. 1). Brill. https://doi.org/https://doi.org/10.1007/978-94-6351-062-2.

Csikszentmihalyi, M. (1990). *Flow: The psychology of optimal experience*. Harper-Perennial.

Dakers, J. (Ed.). (2016). *New frontiers in technological literacy: Breaking with the past*. Palgrave Macmillan.

Daniels, H. (Ed.). (1996). *The genesis of higher mental functions*. Routledge.

Doise, W., & Mugny, G. (1984). *The social development of intellect*. Pergamon Press.

Feenburg, A. (2009). What is the philosophy of technology? In A. Jones & M. de Vries (Eds.), *International handbook of research and development in technology education* (pp. 159–166). Sense Publishers.

Ferguson, D. (1991). *Discussion papers* [Papers for circulation within the Ministry of Education and beyond, unpublished].

Fleer, M. (1995). *Staff-child interactions – a Vygotskian perspective*, Vol. 1. Canberra: Australian Early Childhood Association Inc.

Fleer, M., & Quinones, G. (2009). Assessment of children's technological funds of knowledge as embedded community practices. In A. Jones & M. de Vries (Eds.), *International handbook of research and development in technology education*. Sense Publishers.

Fox-Turnbull, W. (2006). The influences of teacher knowledge and authentic formative assessment on student learning in technology education. *International Journal of Technology and Design Education, 16* (Springer), 53–77.

Fox-Turnbull, W. (2013). *The nature of conversation of primary students in technology education: Implications for teaching and learning* [University of Waikato]. University of Waikato.

Fox-Turnbull, W. (2019). Assisting teachers' understanding of student learning in technology. *International Journal of Technology and Design Education, 29*(29), 1133–1152. https://doi.org/doi.org.10.007/s10798-018-9484-x.

Gawith, J. (2000). Technology practice: A structure for developing technological capability and knowledge in schools. IDATER Loughborough University, Loughborough.

Gay, G. (2010). *Culturally responsive teaching: Theory, research, and practice*. Teachers' College Press.

Gilbert, J. (2007). Knowledge, the disciplines, and learning in the digital age. *Educational Research for Policy and Practice, 6*(2), 115–122. https://doi.org/doi.org/10.1007/s10671-007-9022-1.

González, N. (2005). Beyond culture: The hybridity of funds of knowledge. In N. Gonzalez, L. C. Moll, & C. Amanti (Eds.), *Funds of knowledge* (1st ed., Vol. 2009 reprint, pp. 29–46). Routledge.

González, N., Moll, L. C., & Amanti, C. (Eds.). (2005). *Funds of knowledge* (1st ed., Vol. 2009 reprint). Routledge.

Guy, T. (1992). *Resources and facilities for technology education* [Unpublished paper].

Hennessy, S. (1993). Situated cognition and cognition apprenticeship: Implications for classroom learning. *Studies in Science Education, 22*, 1–41.

Hennessy, S., & Murphy, P. (1999). The potential for collaborative problem solving in design and technology. *International Journal of Technology and Design Education, 9*(1), 1–36.

Johnson, S. D. (1992, Spring). A framework for technology education curricula which emphasises intellectual processes. *Journal of Technology Education, 3*(2).

Jones, A., & Carr, M. (1993). *Towards technology education Vol. 1, working papers from the first phase of the learning in technology education project*.

Rationale for and nature of technology education   93

Jones, A., & Compton, V. (2009). Reviewing the field of technology education in New Zealand. In A. Jones & M. de Vries (Eds.), *International handbook of research and development in technology education* (pp. 93–104). Sense Publishers.

Kadi-Hanifi, K., & Keenan, J. (2016). Finding the "A-ha" moment: An exploration into higher education in further education teacher self-concept. *Research in Post-Compulsory Education, 21*(1), 73–85. https://doi.org/doi.org/10.1080/13596748.2015.1125672.

Kimbell, R. (1997). *Assessing technology international trends in curriculum and assessment.* Open University Press.

Kuhlthau, C., Maniotes, K., & Caspari, A. (2007). *Guided inquiry: Learning in the 21st century.* Libraries Unlimited Inc.

Lave, J. (1992). Word problems: A microcosm of theories of learning. In P. Light & G. Butterworth (Eds.), *Context and cognition: Ways of learning and knowing* (pp. 74–91). Harvester Wheatsheaf.

Le Métais, J. (2002). *New Zealand stocktake: An international critique: Report presented to the Minister of Education.* https://www.educationcounts.govt.nz/publications/curriculum/5815/.

Lewis, T. (1999, Spring). Research in technology education: Some areas of need. *Journal of Technology Education, 10*(2).

Lopez, J. K. (2010). Funds of Knowledge. *Learn NC.* Retrieved 9 March 2010 from www.learnnc.org.

MacGregor, D. (2017). Exploring the role of professional learning communities in supporting the identify transition of beginning design and technology teachers. In J. Williams & D. Barlex (Eds.), *Contemporary research in technology education* (pp. 143–159). Springer.

McCormick, R. (1997). Conceptual and procedural knowledge. *International Journal of Technology and Design Education, 7,* 141–159.

McLachlan-Smith, C. (1998). Designing for dialogue at a distance: Reflections on how to create and maintain an effective teaching-learning relationship with students. *Journal of Distance Learning, 4*(1), 11–22.

Medway, P. (1989). Issues in the theory and practice of technology education. *Studies in Science Education, 16,* 1–24.

Mercer, N., & Hodgkinson, S. (Eds.). (2008). *Exploring talk in school.* Sage Publications Ltd.

Mercer, N., & Littleton, K. (2007). *Dialogue and the development of children's thinking – a sociocultural approach.* Routledge.

Minister of Education (MoE). (1988). *Tomorrow's schools: The reform of education administration in New Zealand.* G. Printer.

Ministry of Education (MoE). (1993a). *The New Zealand curriculum framework.* Learning Media.

Ministry of Education (MoE). (1993b). *Technology in the New Zealand curriculum – draft for consultation.* Learning Media.

Ministry of Education (MoE). (1995). *Technology in the New Zealand curriculum.* Learning Media.

Ministry of Education (MoE). (2007). *The New Zealand curriculum.* Learning Media.

Ministry of Education (MoE). (2017a). *Te marautanga o Aotearoa.* Ministry of Education.

Ministry of Education (MoE). (2017b). *Technology in the New Zealand curriculum.* Ministry of Education. Retrieved 20 February from http://nzcurriculum.tki.org.nz/The-New-Zealand-Curriculum/Technology.

Mumtaz, S. (2000). Factors affecting teachers' use of information and communications technology: A review of the literature. *Journal of information technology for teacher education, 9*(3), 319–342. https://doi.org/doi.org/10.1080/14759390000200096.

94 Rationale for and nature of technology education

Murdoch, K., & Hornsby, D. (2003). *Planning curriculum connections whole school planning for integrated curriculum.* Eleanor Curtain Publishing.

Newmann, F. M., & Wehlage, G. G. (1993, April). Educational leadership: Five standards of authentic instruction. *Educational Leadership, 50*(7), 8–12.

Nikirk, M. (2009). Today's millennial generation: A look ahead to the future they create. *Techniques: Connecting Education and Careers, 84*(5), 20–23.

Novak, G. M. (2011). Just-in-time teaching. *New Directions for Teaching and Learning, 128*, 63–73. https://doi.org/doi.org/10.1002/tl.469.

Onchwari, G., Onchwari, J., & Keengwe, J. (2009). Technology and student learning: Toward a learner centered teaching mode. *Association for the Advancement of Computing in Education Journal, 17*(1), 11–22.

Organisation for Economic Co-operation and Development. (2002). *Definition and selection of competences (DeSeCo): Theoretical and conceptual foundations: strategy paper.* http://hdl.voced.edu.au/10707/156754.

Osmond, P., & Goodnough, K. (2011). Adopting just-in-time teaching in the context of an elementary science education methodology course. *Studying Teacher Education, 7*(1), 77–91. https://www.learntechlib.org/p/52280/.

Pacey, A. (1983). *The culture of technology.* Blackwell.

Paechter, C. (1995). Sub-cultural retreat: Negotiating the design and technology curriculum. *British Educational Research Journal, 21*(1), 75–87. http://www.jstor.org.ezproxy.waikato.ac.nz/stable/1501284.

Parsons, J., & Taylor, L. (2011). Improving student engagement. *Current Issues in Education, 14*(1), 1–33. https://cie.asu.edu/ojs/index.php/cieatasu/article/viewFile/745/162.

Perkins, D. (1999). The many faces of constructivism. *Educational Leadership, 57*(3), 6–11.

Prensky, M. (2008). Turning on the lights. *Reaching the Reluctant Learner, 65*(6), 40–45. http://www.ascd.org/publications/educational-leadership/mar08/vol65/num06/Turning-On-the-Lights.aspx.

Reinsfield, E. (2019, 27 March). A future-focused conception of the New Zealand curriculum: Culturally responsive approaches to technology education. *International Journal of Technology and Design Education.* https://doi.org/doi.org/10.1007/s10798-019-09510-y.

Reinsfield, E., & Williams, P. J. (2017). New Zealand secondary technology teachers' perceptions: "Technological" or "technical" thinking? *International Journal of Technology and Design Education*, 1–13. https://doi.org/doi.org/10.1007/s10798-017-9418-z.

Renzulli, J. S., Gentry, M., & Reis, S. M. (2004). A time and a place for authentic high-end learning. *Educational Leadership, 62*(1), 7377.

Riggs, E. G., & Gholar, C. R. (2009). *Strategies that promote students engagement* (2nd ed.). Thousand Oaks, CA: Corwin Press.

Rogoff, B. (1990). *Apprenticeship in thinking: Cognitive development in social context.* Oxford University Press.

Rogoff, B., & Lave, J. (1999). *Everyday cognition: Development in social context.* Harvard University Press.

Seemann, K., & Talbot, R. (1995). Technacy: Towards a holistic understanding of technology teaching and learning among Aboriginal Australians. *Prospects, 25*(4), 14.

Shields, C., & Edwards, M. (2005). *Dialogue is not just talk – a new ground for educational leadership.* Peter Lang Publishing Inc.

Skills, T. P. C. (2009). *A framework for 21st century skills.* Retrieved 21 January from www.p21.org.

Rationale for and nature of technology education 95

Slavkin, M. L. (2004). *Authentic learning: How learning about the brain can shape the development of students*. Scarecrow Education.

Snape, P., & Fox-Turnbull, W. (2011). Perspectives of authenticity: Implementation in technology education. *International Journal of Technology and Design Education* (early access online). http://link.springer.com/article/10.1007%2Fs10798-011-9168-2.

Sullivan, A. (2001). Cultural Capital and Educational Attainment. *Sociology 35*(4), 893–912. https://doi.org/10.1177/0038038501035004006

The Taskforce to Review Education. (1988). *Administering for excellence. Effective administration in education [The Picot Report]*. G. Printer.

Turnbull, W. (2002). The place of authenticity in technology in the New Zealand curriculum. *International Journal of Technology and Design Education, 12*, 23–40.

Vygotsky, L. S. (1978). In M. Cole, V. John-Steiner, & E. Souberman (Eds.), *Mind in society: The development of higher psychological processes*. Harvard University Press.

Wagner, T. (2008). *The global achievement gap: Why even our best schools don't teach the new survival skills our children need – and what we can do about it*. Basic Books.

Wallace, J., & Hasse, C. (2014). Situating technological literacy in the workplace. In J. Dakers (Ed.), *New frontiers in technological literacy* (pp. 134–164). Palgrave Macmillan.

Wertsch, J., Minick, N., & Arns, F. (Eds.). (1999). *The creation of context in joint problem-solving*. Harvard University Press.

Williams, P. J. (2015). Vocational and general technology education. In A. Jones, C. Buntting, & P. J. Williams (Eds.), *The future of technology education* (1st ed.) (pp. 201–216). Springer.

Williamson, J. G. (2013). *Did British capitalism breed inequality*. Routledge.

Zimmerman, B. J. (1990). Self-regulated learning and academic achievement: An overview. *Educational Psychologist, 25*(1), 3–17. https://doi.org/doi.org/10.1207/s15326985ep2501_2.

Zlatković, B., Stojiljković, S., Djigić, G., & Todorović, J. (2012). Self-concept and teachers' professional roles. *Procedia-Social and Behavioral Sciences, 69*, 377–384. https://doi.org/doi.org/10.1016/j.sbspro.2012.11.423.

Zuga, K. (1999, Spring). Addressing women's ways of knowing to improve technology education environment for all students. *Journal of Technology Education, 10*(2).

4 Implementing the technology curriculum in New Zealand

Introduction

This chapter outlines the framework and all components of technology education in New Zealand. The first section of this chapter focuses on the current situation in technology education in New Zealand. Our aim is to explain the intent and structure of the various ways that curriculum in New Zealand situate technology. The intent is that this will assist those new to teaching technology to understand the structure and implementation of the curriculum. There is a particular focus on the structure of the New Zealand curriculum (NZC) (Ministry of Education, 2007, 2017a, 2017b, 2017c, 2017d), which is conceptualised as three strands – the nature of technology (NT), technological practice (TP) and technological knowledge (TK). There are components within each of these strands, as illustrated in Table 4.1. The second half of this chapter discusses these technological areas and provides examples.

Technology in NZC is taught through five technological areas, including

1 computational thinking (CT);
2 designing and developing digital outcomes (DDDO);
3 designing and developing materials outcomes (DDMO);
4 designing and developing processed outcomes (DDPO);
5 design and visual communication (DVC).

Technology in the New Zealand curriculum

Technology was first included as a learning area with the publication of *Technology in the New Zealand Curriculum* released in draft in 1993 with the final document published in 1997 with full implementation from 1999. The arrival of *The New Zealand Curriculum* saw major changes in the structure of technology education from its predecessor *Technology in The New Zealand Curriculum*. In July 2016, the Minister of Education announced that digital technologies needed to have greater focus and be more explicit in the NZC and would be introduced into *The New Zealand Curriculum*, coming under the umbrella of technology education. The web-based *Technology in*

Implementing the technology curriculum 97

Table 4.1 Technology components and levels adapted from NZC

Strand	Technological practice	Technological knowledge	The nature of technology
Components	Planning for practice	Technological modelling	Characteristics of technology
	Brief development	Technological products	Characteristics of technological outcomes
	Outcome development and evaluation	Technological systems	
← Achievement objectives at Levels 1–8 of the curriculum →			
1	2	3	4	5	6	7	8

the New Zealand Curriculum was released online in 2017 to be fully implemented by 2020 (retrieved from http://technology.tki.org.nz/Technology-in-the-NZC).

Hangarau

The first iteration of the Hangarau curriculum was developed between 1996 and 1999, the second between 2006 and 2008, which was gazetted as a compulsory part of the national curriculum in 2011. In Māori medium settings, a focus on Hangarau Wāhanga Ako (technological understanding) enables learners to determine learning relevance from their worldview.

The Hangarau curriculum (Te Tāhuhu O Te Mātauranga, 2008) is conceptualised in similar ways to the technology learning area of the NZC (MoE, 2007) to allow children to engage in purposeful problem-solving and address an identified need. The Hangarau curriculum emphasises the importance of Māori values, beliefs and language, and includes two strands (whenu):

1 the Nature of Hangarau (Ngā Āhuatanga o Te Hangarau);
2 technological practice (Te Whakaharatau Hangarau), which focuses on the development of learners' knowledge and skills.

Hangarau has five learning contexts (aho) to enable students' learning. These include:

1 information communication technology (Te Tuku Mōhiohio);
2 food technology (Hangarau Kai);
3 biotechnology (Hangarau Koiora);
4 structures (Ngā Hanga me Ngā Pūhanga Manawa);
5 electronics and control (Te Tāhiko me te Hangarau Whakatina).

As with the new technological areas of CT and DDDO (in the NZC), the Hangarau Matahiko content was updated for implementation in 2020. In Hangarau Matahiko, the two concepts are called CT (Te Whakaaro Rorohiko), and people and computers (Tangata me Te Rorohiko) (Te Tāhuhu O Te Mātauranga, 2017).

Te whariki

The 2017 edition of Te Whariki is currently New Zealand's early childhood education (ECE) curriculum. Although the word technology is only mentioned twice in this document the curriculum offers ample opportunity for students to build key dispositions, skills and knowledge to support technology. This occurs through suggestions that opportunities be given to students to explore their world and develop an ability to build, create and construct using different techniques, materials and tools. The below extracts from Te Whariki below illustrate the presence of technology as a critical learning area in New Zealand ECE.

> A curriculum must speak to our past, present and future. As global citizens in a rapidly changing and increasingly connected world, children need to be adaptive, creative and resilient (p. 7).
> They learn by engaging in meaningful interactions with people, places and things – a process that continues throughout their lifetimes (p. 12).

In Strand 5 Exploration:

The students will demonstrate:

- curiosity and the ability to inquire into, research, explore, generate and modify working theories about the natural, social, physical, spiritual and human-made worlds (p. 47)
- ability and inclination to cope with uncertainty, imagine alternatives, make decisions, choose materials and devise their own problems (p. 47)
- recognition of different domains of knowledge and how they relate to understanding people, places and things (p. 47)

Students learn:

- to be innovative developers of products and systems and discerning consumers who will make a difference in the world. Students will explore and investigate properties of materials within each context of learning. They will also consider processes and production systems within technologies. These are reflected in the designs and plans produced by students (p. 57)
- curiosity and the ability to inquire into, research, explore, generate and modify working theories about the natural, social, physical, spiritual and human-made worlds (p. 57).

Although we wish for a stronger more explicit presence of technology in Te Whariki it is present. Children today are born into technologically complex worlds. They interact and engage with technology from before birth. Many are in the world with considerable assistance from technology. We believe that developing an understanding of the "made-world" is vital for students as they develop into culturally, spiritually, socially and technologically capable citizens of the future.

Technology as a learning area in *The New Zealand Curriculum*

This chapter focuses on aspects of technology as a learning area in *The New Zealand Curriculum*. As with all learning areas in NZC, technology is divided into eight achievement objectives (AOs) for students from Years 1 to 13. In technology education, the AOs are formulated at each level from the components of technology, outlined in Table 4.1. For example, the component of brief development has an AO at each level from Levels 1 to 8. The three strands situate the components of technology within broader categories. These three strands are: the NT, TK and TP. In the updated 2017 version of Technology in the NZC is defined as

Technology is intervention by design. It uses intellectual and practical resources to create technological outcomes, which expand human possibilities by addressing needs and realising opportunities.

Design is characterised by innovation and adaptation and is at the heart of technological practice. It is informed by critical and creative thinking and specific design processes. Effective and ethical design respects the unique relationship that New Zealanders have with their physical environment and embraces the significance of Māori culture and world views in its practice and innovation.

Technology makes enterprising use of knowledge, skills and practices for exploration and communication, some specific to areas within technology and some from other disciplines. These include digitally-aided design, programming, software development, various forms of technological modelling, and visual literacy – the ability to make sense of images and the ability to make images that make sense.

Achievement in the three strands leads to the development of technological literacy for students, with an aim to not only survive but also flourish in our current and future technological world. This includes being critical consumers of technology as well as critical and informed developers of technological outcomes. The three strands, TP, TK and NT, are equally important and occur in teaching and learning in no particular order and sometimes not even discreetly. As mentioned, components are extrapolated into the AOs at each level of achievement, which progress in both sophistication and complexity as students work through their education. All AOs are taught within a given context, never in isolation.

The technology curriculum statement was modified to emphasise the role of digital technologies within the NZC in 2017. To reflect this, changes were made to the technological areas. The existing ones were condensed into three: DDMO, DDPO, and DVC. Two more added: CT and DDDO. More about these technological areas are discussed later in this chapter. However, they are worth mentioning here because of the associated progress outcomes (POs). To assist teachers in their understanding and delivery of the new digital technological area content, a number of POs signal progression and specificity in content

100 *Implementing the technology curriculum*

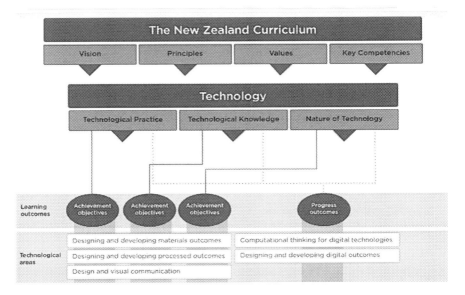

Figure 4.1 The organising structure of technology in the NZC

knowledge. The organisational structure of the technology learning area is outlined in Figure 4.1.

The POs sit alongside but are separate to the AOs. It is envisaged that the POs assist teachers to understand and teach the new content knowledge related to digital technologies. They are not to be used as a set of skills to be "ticked off" as they are learned, rather they are designed to inform quality technology practice to enable students to design and develop digital technological outcomes within authentic contexts. It is therefore important that students are engaged in holistic TP, thus they use digital technologies through the components of technology – as outlined in Table 4.1.

Technology education differs from other curriculum areas because most units of work cover learning from all three strands, especially at primary and lower secondary school. Often units of work in the primary and lower secondary schools will include the design and development of a technological outcome or system, designed to meet a recognised need or opportunity within an authentic context. In technology, some units of work will conclude for students with the development of detailed drawings of intended designs for their technological outcomes. Some will progress to 3D model or mock-up stage. These outcomes can be described as intermediate outcomes and model design ideas. Sometimes students develop a prototype or a fully realised technological product or system. These technological outcomes are fully functional. Over their time in technology at school, students should experience all alternatives mentioned above – multiple times.

In Chapter 3 we explored Kimbell's APU model of technology design process. The design and development of technological outcomes is an iterative process of

Implementing the technology curriculum 101

thought and action. Through interactions between the mind such as imaging and modelling and the practical ideas and designs are formulated, tested and reformulated. Through their stages of their TP students use guided inquiry to explore authentic and meaningful problems either individually or collaboratively with peers. They initially aim to develop accurate knowledge of the issue or situation and its effects on the various stakeholders. Up to and including Level 5 of NZC, technology practice is initiated with a given brief from the teacher. Students research and gather important information necessary to consider what direction they will take to meet the "given" brief. The initial brief, a modified, more specific version of the "given brief" will lead into planning for practice considering a range of time and task management strategies to identify steps in the process, key stages and resources required.

During their technology practice, students move from hazy impressions of their intended technological outcome to a formulation of a much clearer sense of direction as they progress towards their goal. These steps involve all aspects of the NZC's key competencies and values. With increased clarity, conceptual drawings, sketches and discussions further their brief development and intermediate outcomes may be produced in various forms – including functional modelling.

Students' design briefs change and evolve as they progress through the exploration and modelling phases of their technology practice. The brief concludes as the final brief is generated and either just before or when the technological outcome is completed. This brief can then be used to evaluate the new product or system against the attributes and specification identified within the final brief to assist in determining fitness-for-purpose of the final technological outcome. It is an accepted part of TP that technologists (designers) present their final designs or outcomes. This can be done using a range of information, media or technology skills, with a sense of achievement being developed as students meet the needs of their stakeholders. A broad range of skills, content knowledge and processes are deployed and integrated in students' technology practice through the use of an inquiry learning approach. Rich contexts for study, practical construction of outcomes, social connections, cooperation and collaboration with others and practical engagement in worthwhile and real-world activities merge. Such approaches ensure students in primary, intermediate and lower secondary school experience a wide range of technological experiences and are given opportunities to develop a variety of skills and knowledge. There is also a need to enable senior secondary students with the opportunity to specialise – this is often motivated when students have positive experiences in a range of technological areas.

Technological areas

The areas of technology guide primary schools in their programme planning. Teachers of students up to Year 10 use the technological areas to plan programmes of work and ensure their students experience a range of technologies

102 *Implementing the technology curriculum*

and develop a range of skills across differing contexts, whilst using materials and extending their exposure to diverse techniques.

There are five areas of technology including CT, DDDO, DDMO, DDPO, and DVC. Despite the changes that have occurred in the structure of the technological areas, there is an enduring understanding of the need for different areas of technology.

Designing and developing a new food product is very different to designing and developing a new toy or game, which is very different to developing a computer programme to assist in the collation of statistical data. However, exactly what these divisions are and how they are organised do not appear to be so easy. It is our view that to fully understand the scope of the current technological areas, we need to look back at the previous iterations of technological areas in the NZC. Table 4.2 shows the links between the three iterations of technological areas in New Zealand.

In the sections below, we explore the scope and key ideas for each of the 2017 technological areas, incorporating ideas for previous iterations to ensure a full

Table 4.2 Links between the 1995, 2007 and 2017 technological areas

Technological areas		
2017	*2007*	*1995*
CT for digital technologies	Not included	Not included
Designing and developing digital outcomes	Aspects of information and communication technologies	Aspects of electronics and control technology Information and communication technologies – also included information technologies that are not digital in nature such as posters, puppets, games, instruction manuals, etc.
Designing and developing materials outcomes	Structural technology including: resistant materials (wood, plastic, metal, resin) garment and fashion design Aspects of control technology, e-textiles	Structures and mechanisms Materials technology Soft and resistant materials Aspects of electronics and control technology such as: hydraulics, pneumatics
Designing and developing processed outcomes	Food technology Biotechnology Textile design (new materials and fabrics)	Production and process technology Food technology Biotechnology
Design and visual communication	Previously an aspect of all design and situated across all technological areas with DVC specialism at senior secondary school	Aspects of information and communication technologies Previously across all technological areas with graphics specialism at senior secondary school

Implementing the technology curriculum 103

understanding of the scope and depth of the technological areas. Each technological area is discussed in the following section.

Digital technologies

When we tell people that we are technology teachers, most want us to fix their computer or discuss the latest digital device. When talking about technology many people default to recent information and communication inventions – usually digital technologies such as computers, iPad, cell phones, etc. However, digital technologies, as an area in technology education, is much more than this – the aim is to enable students to be designers and developers of digital technologies rather than only users and consumers. In Years 1–8, the two areas can be implemented within other learning areas, integrating technology outcomes with the learning area (such as learning languages) outcomes and providing opportunities to further develop students' key competencies.

By the end of Year 10, students' TK and skills (in digital) enable them to follow a predetermined process to design, develop, store, test and evaluate digital content to address a given issue. Throughout this process, students consider social and end-user considerations. They can independently decompose computational problems into an algorithm used to create a programme incorporating inputs, outputs, sequence, selection and iteration. They understand the role of systems in managing digital devices, security and application software, and they are able to apply file management conventions using a range of storage devices. By the end of Year 13, students who have specialised in digital technologies will design and develop fit-for-purpose digital outcomes, drawing on their knowledge of a range of digital applications and systems and taking into account a synthesis of social, ethical and end-user considerations. They understand how areas of computer science such as network communication protocols and artificial intelligence are underpinned by algorithms, data representation and programming, and they analyse how these are synthesised in real-world applications. They use accepted software engineering methodologies to design, develop, document and test complex computer programs.

Short history of digital technologies

In 2015, due to concern from the Information Technology (IT) sector, the Ministry of Education undertook to review the place of digital technologies in the NZC. Concerns were voiced about the lack of people moving into the IT sector and the lack of skills and knowledge of those who do. Another apparent concern was the invisibility of digital technologies in primary schools. One of the difficulties of the review was to define what was talked about when people referred to digital technologies. There was uncertainty about whether society understood the difference between the everyday use of digital technology, the need to develop digital citizens or the skills required to work with digital technology. It was clear that there needed to be a distinction made between learning about digital technology and the use of e-learning in education.

104 *Implementing the technology curriculum*

The decision to situate digital technologies within the technology education curriculum was somewhat controversial. It was welcomed by most in the technology education sector as digital technologies is fundamentally about design and development of digital outcomes and therefore aligns with the philosophy of technology education. This was the outcome lobbied for by Technology Education New Zealand (TENZ), during the initial consultation phase. TENZ (a Subject Association) felt that if situated elsewhere a number of problems could emerge. For example, if digital technology were to become its own learning area, there were concerns that learning would become a series of skills and knowledge-based activities rather than learning built on a holistic constructivist model of learning. Another potential concern was that, where some educators perceived there was a crowded curriculum, they might replace technology education with digital technology. The decision was made after an 18-month consultation period with a range of interested sectors and is described below.

New Zealand was an early adopter of computer science in secondary schools. In the early 2000s, national assessment for senior secondary students was available through unit standards in computer science. Unit standards were not a popular choice with "academic" students as unlike achievement standards (AS) they were not able to gain "merit" or "excellence" grades. Unit standards were only assessed as "achieved" or "not achieved." Digital technologies became a technology subject in the National Certificate in Educational Achievement (NCEA) qualification beginning with Year 11 in 2011 with Level 1 AS and rolling out to Year 13 in 2013 at Level 3. This change was a part of the NZC/NCEA alignment project, which aimed to align the 2007 curriculum with NCEA assessment standards. At this time, no change was made to the NZC. The emphasis was on breadth of learning rather than depth, and exposure to digital technologies had aimed to assist students with informed career choices. This change meant considerable up-skilling for teachers to enable coverage of a range of computer science related topics including programming, algorithms, computer-human interaction, encryption, artificial intelligence, formal programming languages, and computer graphics, among others. Prior to this, there had been some initial teaching of computer programming as a part of the mathematics curriculum from 1974 to 1985. Between 1985 and 2011, as school computers became more mainstream, the teaching and learning focus shifted to teaching students how to learn to use computers.

When technology education was introduced into *The New Zealand Curriculum* in 1995, electronics and control technologies was one of the then seven technological areas, Information and Communication technologies (ICT) was another. ICT was a very broad area that included digital technologies and much more. Broadly speaking, ICT is the development of systems and products that manage, manipulate and communicate information. This includes a wide range of products and systems. It began 1000s of years ago with communicating technologies such as cave paintings and smoke signals. In early times, Egyptians and Greeks began writing – another technological innovation. In more recent history semaphore,

Implementing the technology curriculum   105

Morse code, postal systems and telephones are devices and systems often forgotten about. More recently, our televisions, computers, digital phones, iPods, tablets, video and cameras are reflective of our technologically mediated world.

The year 2007 saw the revised *New Zealand Curriculum* released. The technological areas of Information and Communication Technology and Control Technology were retained; however, there were concerns that many schools did not engage with topics situated within these technological areas, despite some attempts to guide teachers into deeper and richer approaches to computing education.

Issues were raised by the IT industry in a report released by the New Zealand Computer Society (now known as The Institute of IT Professionals – IITP) in 2008. The main concern was that the generic AS of technology did not obviously relate to digital technology. This led to a call for the separation of Computer Science from the technology education curriculum and for it to have its own learning area within the NZC. This opinion was not unanimous. Many in the technology education sector disagreed with the perspective presented in the report and felt that it was based on a narrow and technicist view of learning for technology education.

In 2015, the Education Minister undertook a systematic approach to examine the place of digital technologies within the NZC, undertaking a number of steps recommended for curriculum change and enabling both scholars and practitioners to reach independent conclusions about their preferred options. Throughout 2015 the Ministry of Education called a series of three meetings. Attendees included a panel of experts from a range of relevant sectors to debate the place of digital technologies in the curriculum. At the first meeting, with Wendy in attendance, the Associate Deputy Secretary indicated the Ministry was using a new approach to curriculum review and development. Previous consultation processes involved approaching and consulting with each sector individually. This approach included all interested parties to debate the issues and develop a recommendation for the Minister of Education to consider. The sectors and organisations represented at the meetings included:

- teacher education providers;
- early childhood providers, primary schools, secondary schools (including Māori medium);
- computer science researchers;
- three teacher subject associations (Technology Education New Zealand, TENZ; New Zealand Graphics and Technology Teachers Association, NZGTTA; New Zealand Association of Computer and Digital and Information Technology Teachers, DTTA)
- information technologies industries;
- the New Zealand Qualifications Authority (NZQA);
- the Education Review Office (ERO);
- the primary and secondary teacher unions (NZEI and PPTA);
- the Eureka trust;
- the Royal Society;

106 *Implementing the technology curriculum*

- the Schools' Trustees Association (NZSTA);
- Kia Ata Mai Educational Trust;
- Education Council;
- Kura Kia Kohe.

A wide range of views were vigorously debated in the first of the three meetings. It became obvious that a research-informed framework would be required for further discussion. Some participants presented views from their organisations, these included Professor Tim Bell (University of Canterbury computer science department), Julie McMahon (NZACDITT), Dr Wendy Fox-Turnbull (TENZ) and Paul Matthews (IITP). The Institute for IT Professionals advocated strongly for a separate curriculum area. TENZ strongly advocated for digital technology to remain within technology. NZACDITT offered a balanced argument for staying within technology, with a number of cautions noted, and Professor Bell indicated that staying within the technology curriculum was a possibility, but not necessarily the most desirable outcome, as digital technologies needed a much stronger presence in the technology curriculum.

Ultimately, the recommendation to the Minister of Education in December 2015 suggested that digital technologies remain situated within the technology learning area, but that it receives a far greater presence. The Ministry planned a development process to ensure a multi-pronged approach to the development and implementation of digital technologies. Five working groups identified the nature and format of the new look technology curriculum as an overall plan for implementation. Undertaking a similar and parallel process, our Māori medium colleagues developed Hangarau Matihiko. Five working groups facilitated the meeting of the five elements key to curriculum change: enablement and change, implementation and support in learning and teaching, partnerships for curriculum intentions and content, learning and teaching and NCEA, the intentions, evaluation and teaching. On 12 July 2016, the Minister announced a strengthening of digital technologies within NZC situated under the umbrella of technology education coming into effect in 2018.

This work culminated in the launch of the Digital Technologies/Hangarau Matihiko: Draft for Consultation curriculum document in June 2017. The new content included the two new technological areas of *CT* and *DDDO*, each containing unique Māori content. At its launch, the Minister of Education with the Prime Minister also announced that the government would spend $40 million on developing teachers' knowledge to deliver the new aspects of the curriculum and to enable all learners from Years 1 to 10 to take part in digital technologies education.

The Ministry of Education established a curriculum advisory group (CAG) as an independent panel of experts commissioned to advise the Ministry on the draft curriculum content. This advice was to include input from the working groups and provide recommendations on feedback received during consultation. This work was collated in the *Curriculum Advisory Group Report*. Significant projects undertaken by the working parties included a drafting of the proposed new structure of Technology/Hangarau, the first and final drafts (see

Implementing the technology curriculum 107

Figures 4.2 and 4.3). The rewritten technology essence statement provided an overview of the curriculum area, reflecting the inclusion of digital technologies and learning progression for Years 1–10 students with new content. The New Zealand Qualifications Authority also modified NCEA AS for senior secondary assessment.

A carefully planned and delivered consultation process followed to ensure both the English and Māori medium sectors could respond to the proposed changes to the curriculum. The Ministry of Education commissioned a process to include questionnaires, workshops, written submissions, analysis and collation of all feedback. This work culminated in the release of a report in November 2017 (Jenkins, 2017). This report indicated that the proposed changes were seen as a positive move, although questions were raised about progressions, implementation at Years 9 and 10, links to Te Whāriki (early childhood curriculum), and applications in partnership schools and other alternative schools – such as Steiner schools.

Another project undertaken by the working parties was the trialling of aspects of the new technological areas. These trials were performed with the help of commissioned progress experts in Educational Technologies. Key features of CT for digital technologies and DDDO were put to the test, resulting in the writing of eight draft POs for each new technological area. These proposed outcomes were published in the draft curriculum.

In 2017 the CAG made 43 recommendations offering useful comments for the Ministry of Education. A number of these recommendations are worth mentioning as they illustrate the iterative and consultative nature of the process. These were that consultation needed to continue alongside research, piloting and implementation, that there was need for greater visibility of Te Ao Māori and Te Tiriti in the learning area essence statement and POs but warned against the shallow, decontextualised inclusion of Māori concepts. The danger of confused implementation and reporting, and unintended future consequences was signalled. They also suggested that the other three technological areas replace the AOs with PO or that the language of PO/AO be clarified to reduce confusion for teachers and recommended that all time bound language (PC, tablet for example) be removed to future proof the document and prevent dating.

A dedicated Professional learning and development (PLD) plan in consultation with the Education Council of New Zealand was recommended to update current and newly qualified teachers. They recommended digital technology as part of a curriculum area in its own right with its own content, understanding and capabilities, and not just a pedagogical vehicle/tool for delivering the whole curriculum. Finally, they suggested a new name for technology to incorporate the word "Digital" in the title suggesting Digital and Materials Technology as one possibility. PLD began in Term 1 2018, with full implementation of the Digital Technologies/Hangarau Matihiko curriculum planned for Term 1 2020. Although this process began, the 2020 school year was interrupted with the COVID-19 pandemic – likely delaying full implementation for many schools.

Education in digital technologies involves applying and knowing about computer science and electronic and digital applications with the aim of designing

108 *Implementing the technology curriculum*

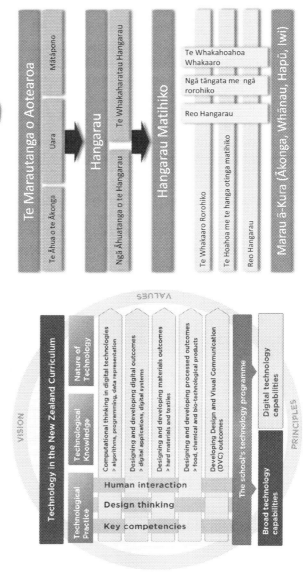

Figure 4.2 Ministry of Education's first draft proposed models for technology education and Hangarau Matihiko published 2017

Implementing the technology curriculum 109

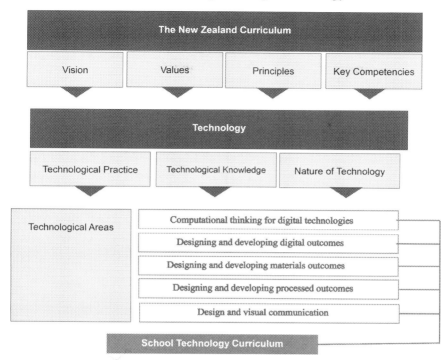

Figure 4.3 Ministry of Education's released draft technology education and Hangarau Matihiko published later in 2017

and developing quality digital technologies within authentic contexts. These objectives can translate to learning in a range of sub-areas, focused on computing, digital media, information management and electronics. Two technological areas deal with digital technologies in NZC, CT and DDDO.

Computational thinking (CT)

Enabling people to take advantage of computing technology in the digital age is one of the most cited benefits of CT education. CT can be characterised by the notions of decomposition (breaking concepts down into easier, manageable parts), pattern representation (such as the use of a character to represent a piece of data), abstraction (ideas) and algorithms (rules used during problem-solving operations). Learning in this technological area will support students to understand the principles from computer science that underpin all digital technologies, such as programming concepts. CT enables students to express problems and formulate solutions in ways that means a computer (an information processing agent) can be used to solve them. Students develop algorithmic thinking skills and an understanding of the computer science principles that underpin all digital technologies. They become aware of what is and isn't possible with

110 *Implementing the technology curriculum*

computing, allowing them to make judgments and informed decisions as citizens of the digital world. Students learn core programming concepts and how to take advantage of the capabilities of computers, so that they can become creators of digital technologies, not just users. They develop an understanding of how computer data is stored, how all the information within a computer system is presented using digits, and the impact that different data representations have on the nature and use of this information.

Much of the emphasis in CT is incorporated into other subjects and aspects of life. Importantly, when a student implements a concept on a computer, the device is an unforgiving judge of how well they have articulated their understanding. The practical element of CT is core to successful application in digital technologies. Situating CT within computing effectively distinguishes it from other already established problem-solving methods used in education.

In NZC the POs describe the significant learning steps that students take as they develop their expertise in CT for digital technologies. In CT there are eight POs. Looking at POs 1 and 8 gives us an idea of the scope and range of learning undertaken by our students. Students work in authentic contexts and take account of end users. At PO1 in Levels 1–2 "students use their decomposition skills to break down simple non-computerised tasks into precise, unambiguous, step-by-step instructions (algorithmic thinking). They give these instructions, identify any errors in them as they are followed, and correct them (simple debugging)." At PO8 in Level 8 "students evaluate concepts in digital technologies (for example, formal languages, network communication protocols, artificial intelligence, graphics and visual computing, big data, social algorithms) in relation to how key mechanisms underpin them and how they are applied in different scenarios when developing real world applications. Students understand accepted software engineering methodologies and user experience design processes and apply their key concepts to design, develop, document and test complex computer programs."

CT is partnered with, and aimed to develop, students' skills and knowledge therefore enabling success in the next technological area DDDO.

Designing and developing digital outcomes (DDDO)

The second of the new technological areas aimed to increase the presence of digital technologies in NZC is DDDO. In this technological area, students learn how to develop *fit-for-purpose* digital solutions. Students develop understandings of the relationship between people and digital technology and how this facilitates the location, analysis, evaluation, and presentation and manipulation of information. Ethical issues, such as intellectual property, copyright and patents, are pertinent to their learning, as is an understanding of electronic components, networks and systems, and their impact on the effectiveness of digital solutions. Students engage with a range of technologies to create digital content for a range of interactive digital platforms.

DDDO also has POs to assist teachers' understanding of the key learning steps in this technological area. DDDO has six POs. PO1 is situated at Level 2

Implementing the technology curriculum   111

NZC, PO2 at Level 4, PO3 at Level 5 and PO4–6 across Levels 6–8. Let's take a look at PO1 and 6 to gain an indication of the scope of learning within this technological area. In authentic contexts and taking account of end users in PO1 "students participate in teacher-led activities to develop, manipulate, store, retrieve, and share digital content in order to meet technological challenges. In doing so, they identify digital devices and their purposes and understand that humans make them. They know how to use some applications, they can identify the inputs and outputs of a system, and they understand that digital devices store content, which can be retrieved later." In PO6 "students independently investigate a specialised digital technologies area and propose possible solutions to issues they identify. They work independently or within collaborative, cross-functional teams to apply an iterative development process to plan, design, develop, test and create quality, fit-for-purpose digital outcomes that enable their solutions, synthesising relevant social, ethical and end-user considerations as they develop digital content."

Students integrate in the outcomes they develop specialised knowledge of digital applications and systems from a range of areas, including: network architecture; complex electronics environments and embedded systems; interrelated computing devices, hardware and applications; digital information systems; user experience design; complex management of digital information; and creative digital media. In both CT and DDDO, exemplars at the junior levels and Snapshots at senior levels have been produced to illustrate students' learning. These are situated in the Ministry of Education's website Technology Online.

Designing and developing materials outcomes (DDMO)

In this area, students develop skills and knowledge to facilitate the transformation of, and work with, resistant materials, textiles and fashion. Through the NZC levels, students become increasingly skilled in applying their knowledge of design principles to create innovative outcomes that realise opportunities and solve authentic problems and satisfy needs. Students create technological outcomes, including conceptual designs, prototypes and batches of a product using manufacturing and quality assurance processes. They develop knowledge about the systems, structures, machines and techniques used in the manufacture of products. Through the levels, students' thinking becomes more and more reflective, critical and creative as they assess and critique material outcomes in terms of quality of design, fitness-for-purpose, and impact and influence on society and the environment.

Materials technology focuses on designing and making products and devices. There are two main classifications of materials: resistant and textile materials. Resistant materials include woods, metals, plastics, glass and acrylics incorporating studies in mechanics, engineering and aspects of electronics. It can include the design and development of large structures such as bridges, large vehicles, and buildings, or smaller structures and mechanisms such as toys, mousetraps, small engines, garden structures and many, many more. Textiles materials include the

112 *Implementing the technology curriculum*

full range of clothing fabrics as well as materials such as nylon, canvas, leather and materials used in making sports equipment such as balls. Increasingly e-textiles are also making an appearance in this area. These objectives can translate to school courses such as textiles and fashion, resistant materials, product development, automotive, and furniture designing and making. Increasingly, computer-aided design and manufacture (CAD/CAM) and 3D printing are being used as a means to model outcomes and facilitate the realisation of outcomes.

Control

Although not now an official technological area, non-electronic control technology is still used every day and worth considering in DDMO. Control technologies can be defined as systems that control, monitor and automate specific functions. Control technologies connect well with CT and DDDO. Control is the manipulation of an input to get a desired output and therefore is very closely related to technological systems (TSs) that control flow. Examples of this can include the flow of water, people, cars, electrons, water, oil, air and many more. Apart from electronic systems, covered in digital technologies, other everyday examples of control technology include traffic systems, household electrical systems, water and waste systems, crowd control at popular tourist attractions, pneumatic and hydraulic systems.

Designing and developing processed outcomes (DDPO)

Humans have been using organisms to make products for more than 10,000 years. Processing technologies focuses on formulating and knowing how to formulate processed products, as conceptualised in biotechnology, chemical technology, agriculture and horticulture (and systems control), food technology, product development, and sometimes new textiles. Process technologies differ from materials technologies in that the technological outcomes are chemically and structurally different from the original materials or ingredients used. For example, a cake is structurally and chemically different from the flour and eggs that form it. Students develop understandings of the systems, processes and techniques used in manufacturing products and gain experience from using these, along with related quality assurance procedures, to produce prototypes or multiple copies of a product. They also explore the impact of different economic and cultural concepts on the development of processed products, including their application in product preservation, packaging and storage. Biotechnology and food technology are explained below.

Biotechnology

Biotechnology has a range of definitions according to its context or purpose. In the NZC the definition is broad and includes both modern and ancient biotechnologies. Technology in the NZC (Ministry of Education, 1995) defined biotechnology as "The use of living systems, organisms, or parts of organisms to manipulate natural processes in order to develop products, systems, or environments to benefit people." We redefine biotechnology as "The use of living systems, organisms, or parts of organisms to manipulate natural processes in order to develop products or systems to benefit people." This definition is inclusive of both products and systems. Biotechnology began with the domestication of animals and growing of crops for food, both of which instigated a fundamental societal change from hunting and gathering to farming and raising livestock. Humans began using microorganisms to make products like beer, wine, yoghurt, cheese and bread somewhere between 4,000 and 8,000 years ago. At this time, they were also beginning to use organisms or the products of organisms in medicine. In recent history, the rate of development in biotechnology has accelerated with the increased understanding of organisms and cells based on the comparatively recent discovery of DNA in 1953 that has subsequently led to DNA sequencing of the human genome, gene cloning and genetic modification. These discoveries in biotechnology's use of organisms or parts of organisms has raised a number of ethical and legal concerns such as the use of embryonic stem cells to treat disease, transplant of organs from pigs to humans and the use of donor mitochondrial DNA in IVF conceptions.

Biotechnology products can be food based, such as bread and other yeast-based foods or pharmaceuticals, nutraceuticals, genetically improved and modified crops. Systems can include compost, agriculture, horticulture, water purification, hydroponics, biocontrol, genetic or biomedical engineering, and waste management.

In primary schools, learning about biotechnology typically involves the development of products and systems that can easily be developed in a general classroom such as bread, ginger beer, composting, worm farming, organic and traditional garden design and construction as well as very simple pharmaceuticals such as hand cream. For secondary students, learning about biotechnology can often be situated within science programmes rather than technology programmes. It is not unknown for teachers and schools to develop biotechnology courses within technology for the purposes of senior secondary assessment. Understanding the ethical and legal implications of particular biotechnological processes is an excellent example of learning as conceptualised in the NT strand. In this area, there are often connections made to the systems that can control and monitor outcomes.

Food technology

In New Zealand, food technology tends to focus on the development of new products and systems to enhance food production and safety. It is usually informed by food science and can include food processing, preservation, packaging, labelling, and health and safety practices. Food technology has been conducted for well over 100 years. For example, Pasteur's research on the spoilage of wine and his description of how to avoid spoilage in 1864 was an early attempt

114 *Implementing the technology curriculum*

to situate food technology as a scientific endeavour. Pasteur conducted research on the production of alcohol, vinegar, wines and beer, and the souring of milk. He developed the process of pasteurisation – heating milk and milk products to destroy disease-producing organisms. Appert's development of the canning process in 1810 was also a significant step in preservation.

Currently in intermediate and secondary schools, food technology and food and nutrition (as a part of home economics) are often either confused or combined, although they have very different purposes and practices. Food and nutrition has its roots in the health and physical education learning area of the curriculum and aims to teach students about nutrition. When embedded in home economics programmes, the learning focuses on students' making informed food choices, by understanding their nutritional needs for growth and development. There is also a focus on the development of students' food preparation and life skills and, when taught as food technology in the senior secondary school, food technology programmes have the potential for students to work in authentic contexts. As an agricultural and horticultural rich nation, New Zealand offers ample opportunity for students and in Years 11 and 13 in food technology there should be an emphasis on innovation and the development of new food products in response to an identified issue. For example, a Year 13 student may work directly with research and development staff of a local dairy company to assist in the generation of a new heat reactive, dairy-based sauce.

Design and visual communication (DVC)

In DVC, students can focus explicitly on their visual literacy and creative thinking is developed using visual communication techniques the application of designerly thinking. Students develop a range of drawing skills, including computer assisted drawings and make informed decisions about the aesthetic and functional aspects of design. Design skills taught are manual, digital, two dimensional and three dimensional. There are three aspects including graphics practice, design and visual communication. In Years 1–6, students are taught the value of drawing their intended outcomes. More formal instruction in drawing and design is not likely to happen before Years 7 and 8, and more likely to begin at Year 9. A DVC focus can translate into programmes which centre on graphics and product design. Students apply their visual literacy through using sketching, digital modes and other modelling techniques to effectively represent and develop their design solutions.

Fox's Model – positioning senior secondary specialist areas

Once students transition into the secondary school context, programmes usually focus on one specialist area or domain of learning within the technological areas (such as DVC formally Graphics). The learning should still consider the generic concepts from the technology curriculum, like brief development, as well as the specialist understandings and skills underpinning the particular

Implementing the technology curriculum 115

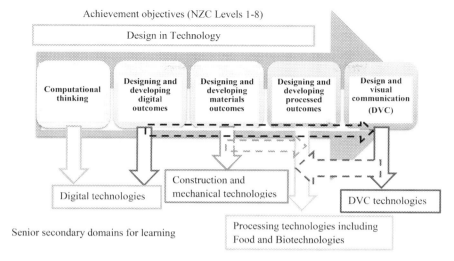

Figure 4.4 The relationship between the technological areas and the domain-specific specialist areas in senior secondary

domain or context for learning. Indicators of progression for the specialist areas (Levels 6–8) can be found in Technology Online.

The relationship between the technological areas and the specialist knowledge and skills within each domain of learning is represented in Figure 4.4. Fox's model demonstrates the connections between the technological areas (the coloured squares) and the specialist domains of learning (rectangles). All technological areas and domains are connected though the AOs as they are represented within the NZC. This is depicted by an arrow.

The specialist domains of learning are only usually assessed formally from Years 11 to 13 and are situated as being outside of the curriculum. Domain-specific knowledge and skills are situated outside of the curriculum content because they provide a means to facilitate understanding of technology education, and are identified through the domain-specific learning objectives (LOs), and assessed as part of the senior secondary NCEA Assessment framework.

In senior secondary schools, Levels 6–8 students' learning is assessed through ASs. There are two types of ASs – generic and domain specific. The generic AS are directly linked to NZC AOs and also include some standards, focused on design. The domain specific AS are divided into four: Construction and Mechanical (includes technological areas of structural, some aspects of control and uses resistant and soft materials (textiles); DVC formally known as graphics (includes visual communication techniques); Digital Technologies (includes electronics, computing, computer science, digital media and information management); Processing Technologies (includes food technology, biotechnology, agriculture, horticulture, and product and textile development).

LOs determine learning in each domain. Each domain has a set of AS which are used to assess students' specific skills and knowledge in each domain. The

116 *Implementing the technology curriculum*

LOs are located in the Ministry of Education's website *TKI* – Technology Online in the section "What does Learning in Technology look like?"

In May 2019, the Government announced a package with seven changes to strengthen NCEA and help maintain the trust and confidence in New Zealand qualifications. The rhetoric indicated that the planned changes would support young New Zealanders and international students to develop the appropriate skills and knowledge for further education or employment, either in New Zealand or overseas. A number of meetings were held for academics and teachers to review and redevelop the ASs in all subjects. This work was postponed as the result of the COVID-19 pandemic.

Transformations

The NZC outlines TSs as sets of interconnected components that transform, store, transport, or control materials, energy, and/or information for particular purposes. In fact, all technological development transforms materials, energy and/or information. We refer to these processes as *transformations* and consider them useful when identifying processes involving technological development. This notion enables students to consider the changes that need to occur within their TP and may give some insight into how such changes may occur. Although not necessarily directly taught through the AOs, understanding of transformations can assist students' thinking in terms of the breadth and depth of technological outcomes. They help to explain the important role that systems and products play in the modern age. Let us look at these one at a time.

Transforming materials

During technological product development, materials can be formed and/ or manipulated. To do this, they must be evaluated and eventually selected. *Forming* involves bringing two or more materials together to create a new material that has a different chemical composition and structure with different performance properties. For example, mixing flour, water and salt to make dough; mixing wood fibres, resin and wax to make fibreboard; combining glass fibre and a polymer resin to form fibreglass or fibre-reinforced polymer (FRP). DDPO looks at the design and development of newly formed materials. DDMO uses a wide range of natural and formed materials to create technological outcomes.

Manipulating materials involves working with existing materials in ways that do not change their composition and structure, or their properties. Rather, manipulation allows the material to be incorporated into a product in ways that maximise its contribution to the overall performance of the product. It can involve icing, coating with chocolate, laminating, changing shape or joining materials such as fabric, wood, metal or glass. Cutting, folding, piping, moulding, spooning, bending, jointing, gluing and painting are examples of manipulative operations.

For all technological development, materials are selected because their performance properties will help ensure that the outcome meets the required

Implementing the technology curriculum 117

performance criteria. Some properties may be valued for aesthetic reasons, others for functional reasons. Materials need to be properly evaluated so that those selected can be justified as optimal (not merely satisfactory), taking account of all the relevant factors. When evaluating the suitability of materials, it is important to understand their composition as well as the techniques and/or procedures used to form, manipulate and transform them. A material's composition is its nature, or what it is made from.

Transforming information

Information is transformed through control, storage and retrieval, manipulation and transportation. During the process of developing technological outcomes, transformation of information is frequently the central purpose of the technological development, such as in the case of software development or computer development – when making storage and retrieval easy. Information is controlled through storage, when it is able to be retrieved in its original form or manipulated into another form, such as when tables are converted to graphs or spreadsheets to show trends. Obvious examples of technologies that store information include computers, cloud-based storage facilities, letters, databases, word files, books, digital video and audio recordings. The media just mentioned for storage can also be used to transport information, and Internet-based digital technologies such as email and social media have largely taken over from physical and analogue mail systems with their origins in smoke signals, semaphore, letters and Morse code. Carvings, painting, dance, song, myths and legends are also ways in which many cultures store, retrieve and transport information from one group to another or from one generation to another.

Transforming energy

Energy too is transformed through manipulation, storage, transportation, or control, within, and by, technological products and systems. Transformation of energy occurs through storage in the development of products such as batteries and fuel. These products, as well as electrical and power generation systems, fuel systems, electronic systems, and others, allow energy to be transformed, stored and transported. Natural resources containing energy can be manipulated to make it energy accessible and/or safer to use such as the change from crude oil to diesel and petrol, or sunlight to electricity, water flow to hydroelectricity and coal to gas and electricity.

Immediate contexts for learning

Students are able to study technology in a huge variety of large contexts, mentioned in Chapter 3, and immediate contexts that are either teacher or student determined. The immediate context studied by students in Years 1–10 should come from a range of areas of technology as can be seen in Table 4.3. In Years 11–13, students work with fewer immediate contexts in greater depth.

Table 4.3 Immediate contexts of learning for technological areas at each NCZ level

Technological areas	Designing and developing processed outcomes		Designing and developing materials outcomes			Designing and developing digital outcomes		Design and visual communication (DVC)
NZC levels	Food	Biotech	Soft	Resistant	Non-digital control		Computational thinking	
1	Toast for my friend	Bread for staff lunch	Flugs [fluffy, funny ugly monster] to cuddle us at school	Pull-along toy	Moving around the classroom	Class newsletter	PO1: Task sequencing. Collecting Pollen with Beebot then opening a word document	Drawing our Flugs
2	Healthy hamburgers	Worm farms for school	Keeping safe sock puppets	Let's attract native birds to school	System for getting our school lunches off	PO1: Robots for the dance off	Writing a basic programme for dancing robot	3D drawing of our bird environment/ structure
3	Berry ice cream for sale	Savoury yoghurt	Gift for mother's day	Bridge for local park	Safe traffic flow outside our school	Animated video about our school	PO2: Debugging programmes	Intro to CAD for bridge drawing
4	Biscuits of welcome for immigrants	Medicinal drinks	New school sports shirts	Scooter racks for schools	Watering our plants. Irrigation PO2:		PO3: Creating programme for irrigation system using comparative operators, and iteration	Using CAD for scooter rack
5	Fit for Kai	Multilayered jams	Upcycling denim	New school playground for local primary school	Lifting heavy stuff hydraulic and pneumatic systems	Keyless entry for elderly	Programming remote control keys	Eco design
6 NCEA L1	Non-caffeinated drinks	Organic cosmetics	Dog outdoor carry bag	Composite materials	Means of motion	Website design	Career game: planning for the future	Charity marketing
7 NCEA L2	Alternate healthy pies	Cheese please	Ball gowns	Electronically activated gadgets	Smart design			
8 NCEA L3	Contexts and outcomes to be determined in consultation with identified companies							

Implementing the technology curriculum 119

Technology also requires students to draw fully on learning from other disciplines. For example, students working with food technology may need to refer to chemistry, and students working on an architectural project will find that an understanding of art history is invaluable. Learning for senior students opens up pathways that can lead to technology-related careers. Students may access the workplace learning opportunities available in a range of industries or move on to further specialised tertiary study.

Identification and selection of immediate contexts from Year 1–1 when made by teachers, should take into consideration the students' interests, cultural, geographical and economic backgrounds, the school and local communities, as well as prior learning activities and experiences in technology. What is paramount is that selected contexts offer students authentic opportunities to engage in TP.

Technology education should be delivered holistically. Students design and develop outcomes to meet needs and opportunities. From Levels 1 to 4, contexts are frequently determined by teachers in consultation with students to ensure a range of contexts are covered and that opportunities for a wide range of skill development occur. By Level 5 students may identify their own contexts in consultation with their teachers. Technology units and programmes of work should be holistic to encompass multiple strands and AOs as well as progress learning outcomes in the digital space. Let us now look at the strands and components in depth.

Strands and components

Within Technology in the NZC, students work within authentic immediate contexts across three strands. Located within the strands, components of technology guide teaching and learning. These are outlined in the following sections.

The nature of technology (NT)

The NT strand provides an overarching intent for technology education and situates students' understanding of technology as a discipline so they know how it differs from other disciplines. The NT strand acknowledges the conceptual understandings required for students to critique the impact of technology on societies and the environment and to explore how developments and outcomes are valued by different people in different times and places. To address the *NT* strand, teachers are required to foster students' critical thinking and encourage discussion about past and future technological responses with a view to supporting them to become informed consumers who can think creatively or "outside of the box."

Learning to critique the impact of technology on societies and the environment, and to explore how developments and outcomes are valued by different peoples in different times and places, is at the core of this strand. Students should come to appreciate the socially and culturally embedded NT to become increasingly able to engage with current and historical issues and explore future scenarios. There are two components in this strand, the characteristics of technology (CT) and the characteristics of technological outcomes (CTO).

120   *Implementing the technology curriculum*

Characteristics of technology (CT)

In this component, students develop an understanding of what technology is – human activity that is purposeful intervention by design resulting in technological outcomes that have an impact in the world. They also develop an understanding of the relationship and the increasingly permeable boundaries between the made and natural worlds. At Level 1, students will understand that technology is made by people for a purpose and at Level 8, students will understand the implications of technology, including the potential for intended and unintended consequences.

Characteristics of technological outcomes (CTO)

In this component students will understand that technology can be represented as either systems or products that are then evaluated in terms of their *fitness-for-purpose*. Students should also understand that outcomes can be described by their physical and functional properties and they can only be successfully critiqued within their social, historical, cultural and geographical contexts. At Level 1 students recognise technology as either systems or products both of which have physical and functional natures. At Level 8 students will understand how technological outcomes can be critiqued and justified as fit for purpose in their historical, cultural, social, and geographical locations.

An example to consider is the much loved food product, the meat pie. The CTO component would be addressed if there were discussion about the pie as a technological outcome, how and why pies have evolved over time to become popular in the New Zealand context. The nature of the pie, including physical and functional features such as why it had developed to have pastry outside and had different types of meat inside it, could relate to the CTO component because this concept addresses fitness-for-purpose.

Technological knowledge (TK)

In the TK strand, students develop knowledge particular to technological enterprises and environments and understandings of how and why things work. There are three components in this strand: technological modelling (TM), technological products (Tp) and. We consider this strand to be more theoretically based, in which students should understand why they are making specific design decisions and undertaking specific tasks within their own practice. For example, students learn what modelling is and why modelling is an important aspect of developing technological outcomes, rather than undertaking the actual modelling which occurs in ODE.

Technological modelling (TM)

TM is the testing of design ideas. There are two types of TM, functional modelling and prototyping. In this component, students learn the theory of modelling rather than undertaking modelling for their own technological outcomes, which occurs in technological practice. Students learn that the purpose of modelling is to increase the likelihood of a technological outcome being successful when

Implementing the technology curriculum 121

fully deployed and develop understanding of the role of modelling in TP. This understanding helps them develop confidence in the success of their outcomes.

Students learn to undertake functional modelling to evaluate design ideas and prototyping to evaluate the fitness-for-purpose of systems and products. Functional modelling includes very sketching, drawing, 2D and 3D representations of designs. It involves students' understanding that modelling represents reality and is used to test design concepts. Students also learn that functional modelling includes brainstorming, team discussions about design ideas as well as the construction of small components of a design to test functionality. Three-dimensional modelling can also occur in a virtual environment. A commonly used term in functional modelling is a "Mock-up" three-dimensional, non-working model, usually made to scale but in cheaper materials, used to assess the physical features of a design. For example, a toile is a term used in the fashion industry for a mocked-up garment made in a cheap poly-cotton or calico.

A prototype is a "to scale," fully functional model usually developed before the final outcome. By the time a prototype is built, the technologist would normally have very little impact on the design at this late stage in the development process. Only small changes would be needed if effective functional modelling had occurred previously.

Technological products (Tp)

Technology products are often material products. An understanding of material properties, uses and development is essential to understanding how and why products work the way they do. This component has a main learning focus on materials and their suitability for an intended outcome. Students learn that materials have performance properties that affect function, physical appearance and desirability. They also learn that materials can be formed, manipulated or transformed, and that, when developing technological products, techniques and operations can involve a combination of forming, manipulation and/or transformation. Understanding in this component goes from understanding, at Level 1, that many technological products are made of materials to, at Level 8, understanding concepts and processes employed in the development and evaluation of products with associated implications for construction and waste disposal.

Technological systems (TSs)

This component includes an understanding of the constituent parts of systems and how these work together, combined with understanding how and why systems operate in the way they do. A system is a set of interconnected parts, or modules, each with its own function involved in the overall purpose of the system. In general, systems have a set of inputs that are processed in some way to create desired outputs. Inputs can be materials, energy or information that are transformed, stored, manipulated or transported in carefully controlled ways to produce the desired outcomes (outputs).

122 Implementing the technology curriculum

The concept of a system helps us understand complex, interconnected operations and includes the notion of modularisation. Using the concept of a system, modern manufacturing can be seen as a system in which raw materials "flow" into one end of a factory are then processed and new products emerge from the other end. At this level of modularisation, we can analyse the manufacturing in three parts, inputs, processes and outputs. At a more detailed level, we can consider the subsystems within the manufacturing process by which materials are manipulated and transformed into the final product. In any system, how the parts, or subsystems, work together is as important as their individual characteristics.

At Level 1, learning about TSs would include students' understanding that systems have inputs and outputs and that something is transformed in a controlled way. At Level 8, sophistication increases to students understanding operational parameters impacting on design and maintenance of systems and the products they produce.

Many systems are designed to control and manipulate the flow of something. For example:

- digital information such as in computer systems and other digital outcomes;
- information such as enrolment systems in schools and universities, library catalogues, retail stocktaking (today most systems of this nature are digital in nature, however previously systems were mechanical or manual in nature);
- water such as in irrigation, sewage and plumbing;
- people such as in air, sea and road traffic; crowd control in shops, stadia and tourist attractions;
- oil as in hydraulics, air as in pneumatics;
- energy as in wind, hydro and solar power generation, transportation and distribution.

This list is by no means exhaustive but hopefully gives an idea of the scope and variety of systems we use in everyday life.

Technological practice (TP)

This strand is the practical strand of the curriculum, which enables students to design, develop and evaluate technological products or systems. In this strand, students study the practice of others and undertake their own TP in a way that mirrors that of existing technologists as closely as possible (depending on the age of the student). Students develop a range of technological outcomes that can be products or systems, and include concepts, plans, briefs, technological models, prototypes and fully realised products or systems.

In order to increase the likelihood of developing successful outcomes, students investigate issues and existing outcomes within authentic contexts. Students need to interact with their clients and other stakeholders and then use their new findings and understandings, together with design principles, to inform their own practice. They also learn to consider ethics, legal requirements, protocols,

Implementing the technology curriculum 123

codes of practice, and the needs of, and potential impacts on, their key stakeholder/s (or client), other stakeholders, and the environment. Some technology teachers find it challenging to make a distinction between students' TP and the skills needed to enact it. For example, one teacher reflected:

> With their technological practice, they were Emergent because they had no idea how to put a drill bit in, the fundamental understanding that you've got materials and you can add to them or subtract from them, they've never made anything.
>
> So when it came to them making a movie, they were taught how to use a proper [computer] package and they managed to work their way through that and they were manipulating data and taking images and adding special effects and that was awesome.

In this strand, there are three major components: brief development (BD), planning for practice (PP), and outcome development and evaluation (ODE).

Brief development (BD)

When learning about brief development, students are establishing the problem or recognising the opportunity (issue) for investigation. A technological brief is a statement given to or written by a technologist (the student) outlining the project. Typically, it consists of a *conceptual statement* which includes an overview of the situation that leads to the technological need or opportunity. The brief also includes a list of desirable characteristics of the intended outcome, characterised by attributes or a list of specifications. *Attributes* can be thought of both in the physical and functional sense. These might include such things as durability, reliability, looking good, ergonomics or attractiveness to the target audience. *Specifications* are the actual details that enable the attributes to be met and include such things as details on measurements, materials, colours, layout, fonts and textures. We like to think of specifications as the physical and functional properties that enable the attributes to be met. For example, a brief for the design of an armchair may have durability as an attribute. A resulting specification may be that it is to be covered in leather.

In NZC there are three major types of brief which students engage with throughout their TP: A given brief → Initial Brief → and Final Brief. Each is illustrated in Figure 4.5. Students studying in achievement Levels 1–4 are usually given the brief by their teachers. A given brief will consist of a conceptual statement, key attributes and maybe some basic specifications. Having received the given brief, either individually or in groups, students will research, investigate and generally immerse themselves in the immediate learning context to identify some initial ideas for their own technological outcome. The given brief should be flexible enough for students to develop their own solutions, different from those of their peers but limiting enough to ensure the scope of the project can be completed within the typical budget and time constraints that are

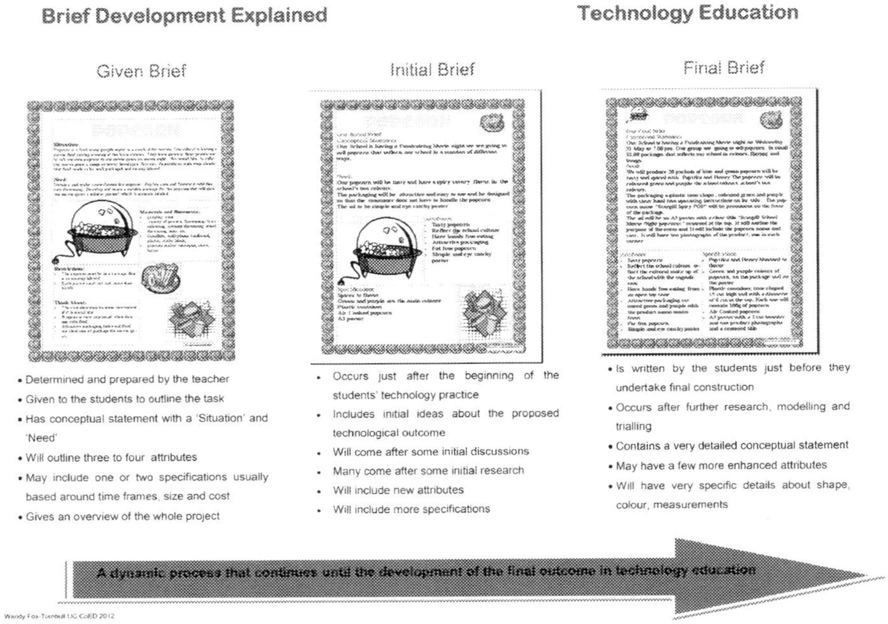

124 *Implementing the technology curriculum*

Brief Development Explained   **Technology Education**

Figure 4.5 The brief development process

a reality in the school and classroom environment. Initially students undertake research and critique of past and existing technological outcomes from their own and other cultures. At this stage, they should also identify the proposed physical and functional features. Students may also interview clients and other stakeholders before sketching some initial ideas. During this process they begin to form ideas about their own solutions, refining their teacher's given brief and therefore creating their own initial brief which will now differ from those in other groups.

In Levels 7 and 8, senior secondary students will not receive a given brief from their teachers. They are expected to find their own client and work with them to develop an initial brief. At this level of learning, students should be encouraged to contribute to their local communities by identifying authentic needs of local groups or individuals such as local business people, elderly, early childhood centres, schools, or interests groups. Senior students write their initial brief in the early stages of developing their technological outcome. Just before the final construction of their intended outcome, but after all of their functional modelling, students develop a final brief that details all the desirable attributes and specifications needed for the development of their design.

Within this strand, students should be learning about the ongoing nature of brief development to understand that a brief is not a static document. It evolves as they work through their TP by researching, interacting with stakeholders, and undertaking physical and functional modelling. Such actions lead to the development of deliberate attributes and detailed specifications. In reality, a final

Implementing the technology curriculum   125

brief is not completed until the actual technological outcome is realised. It is not uncommon for attributes and specifications to emerge, or change, during the construction process. Figure 4.7 shows a brief development process. This given brief outlines to the students that they are required to develop a new flavour of popcorn to attract people to a fundraising movie night in their school.

At the various stages of development, the briefs contain each of the following:

1   The conceptual statement, which outlines the project and comes in two parts:

- the situation or context – outlines or explains the situation that has led to the technological need or opportunity;
- the need or opportunity – in broad terms for the given brief and in detail for the final brief.

2   The attributes and specifications:

- An attribute can be a property, quality, or feature of a person or thing, thought of as the desirable characteristics for the intended outcome.
- A specification is a detailed description of the criteria for the construction, appearance or performance of a material or product and must be *measurable*.

An initial brief is likely to have more attributes than specifications and the level that the student is working at also has differing expectations. Specification usually increases as the design gets closer to the development of the final outcome. Table 4.4 provides a range of ideas for thinking about the differences between attributes and specifications.

Specifications facilitate the achievement of the attributes, for example "colourful" may be an attribute for a brochure to promote the school fair. Poppy red background with sunshine yellow font might be related to colour specifications.

Table 4.4 Potential attributes and related specifications

Attributes	Specifications
Colourful	Cobalt Blue and Cerise Moon acrylic paint
Wooden	$1300 \times 100 \times 12$ mm MDF
Textured	Cream brick cladding
Durable	Silicone
User-friendly	100 g butter, ergonomic keyboard
Patterned	Grey concrete hexagonal paving stones
Fit for purpose	600 mm high, 400 mm wide
Adjustable	$2000 \times 200 \times 50 \times 1.6$ mm tube
Absorbent	1×500 g sponge
Ethical design	Use recycled materials such as wood, fabric from clothing, etc.
Large/roomy	Dimensions, e.g. $5 \text{ m} \times 3 \text{ m} \times 10 \text{ m}$
Neutral tones	Actual colours, such as:
	"Sandy Day" beige acrylic paint
	"Weka Pass" Dulux green acrylic paint
	"Sand-fly Point" Resene brown stain

126 *Implementing the technology curriculum*

Planning for practice (PP)

Planning for practice is often confused with outcome planning; however, it is *not* students' planning or drawing their technological solutions. It is planning to ensure their own practice is completed within the given time frames. Planning for practice techniques ensures:

- efficient resource management – materials, time, money, people;
- appropriate planning tools are used – brainstorms, mind-maps, idea banks, journals, action plans, critical paths such as Gantt charts, herringbone time-lines, flow diagrams, graphic organisers, etc.;
- past and present experiences – own and others;
- existing ideas are considered;
- clear guidance of "where to next?"

Planning for practice also involves the studying of other technologists' practice in order to gain a better understanding of what TP entails. It involves the consideration of a number of key factors which contribute to better knowledge and understanding of their own practice. These include:

- task identification and sequencing;
- management of resources;
  - resource identification and sourcing;
  - quantifying (how much they need) and costing.

At NZC Level 1, this starts with the students identifying some of the tasks they need to do and in what order. At Level 8 students are identifying and employing project management practices. It also includes knowledge, critique and selection, with justification of practice planning tools.

In this section, we introduce four tools that students (depending on their ages) are able to complete as a part of the planning of their TP. These include examples of

1 key task lists;
2 critical paths;
3 herringbone timeline;
4 flow charts.

Key task lists

This is a detailed sequential list of the key tasks that need to be completed. They are noted in logical order of undertaking. The list can also identify who has been delegated to different tasks if students are working in a cooperative situation. It may also show when the task must be completed. A slightly advanced example for developing a new biscuit for to welcome immigrants to New Zealand is shown in Figure 4.6. Imagine this biscuit development is to be undertaken by a team of three: Wendy, Liz and Mike.

Implementing the technology curriculum 127

Technology Planning for Practice Key Task List

Biscuit Production Team

TASKS	COMPLETED BY (WHOM)	COMPLETED BY (WHEN)	COMPLETED
Discuss the given brief ad identify target market	Whole team	2 July	
Identify and allocate tasks	Whole team	3 July	
Research immigrant culture each team member taking a different aspect of: culturally relevant sights, sounds, tastes, flavours, images, shapes, colours, symbols,	Whole team	4 July-6 July	
Research existing recipes and historical recipes	Wendy	7July	
Interview immigrants to identify likes and dislikes	Liz	7 July	
Research biscuit shapes and colours	Mike	7 July	
Report findings	Whole team	8 July	
Brainstorm potential recipes	Whole team	8 July	
Test a range of flavour combinations	Wendy	15July	
Test a range of biscuit types and colours	Liz	15 July	
Select colour and type	Liz	15 July	
Test a range of shapes and thicknesses	Mike	15 July	
Seek client and stakeholder feedback on flavours, shapes, colour and biscuit types	Wendy, Mike and Liz	16-22 July	
Research potential ingredient availability and pricing	Mike	16-22 July	
Select two shapes to trial	Liz	23 July	
Select two flavour combinations to trial	Wendy	23 July	
Trial two options to bake with different combinations of flavour shape and type A &B	Mike A Wendy B	23 July	
Obtain client/ stakeholder feedback on both types	Mike A Wendy B	24 July	
Research and trial icing types, viscosity, colours	Liz	24 July	
Select final shape for biscuit	Mike and Liz	30 July	
Select final flavour for biscuit	Wendy	30 July	
Select icing	Liz	30 July	
Write final recipe	Wendy & Liz	31 July	
Liaise with tool/ cutter makers to develop or modify biscuit cutters	Liz	1-5 August	
Undertake cost analysis	Mike	1-5 August	
Bake final recipe trial batch	Wendy	6 August	
Evaluate and modify recipe if needed	Whole team	6 August	
Bake final Biscuits	Wendy	7 August	
Make icing and ice cooled biscuits	Liz	7 August	
Clean equipment and kitchen	Whole team	7.August	
Present final biscuits to client	Whole team	7 August	

Figure 4.6 An example of a key task list

128   *Implementing the technology curriculum*

To Do List

Make a bed for my cat

Order	What	When	Done ✓
1	Learn about what cats need in a bed	today	
2	Learn about cats' sleeping behaviour	tomorrow	
3	Look ata a range of cat beds	Wednesday	
4	Draw a picture of my cat's bed will be like	5 March	
5	Make a model of my design	6 March	
6	Think about all that I now about cats and change my design if needed	10 March	
7	Make a mock-up of my final design	11 March	
8	Think about how good my design is.	14 March	

Your name is :_____

My cat's name is _____

Draw a picture of your cat.

Figure 4.7 A simple task list for junior students

Obviously, for five- and six-year olds, this would be much less complex and may use a simple list of the tasks to be done such as in Figure 4.7.

Critical path

A critical path (which can be found in a Gantt chart) is the thread or pathway of time and tasks that runs through a plan of action in the development of a technological outcome. It shows the key tasks that are critical, i.e. the tasks that have to be completed on time and within projected costs, for the project to finish on time and within budget. It shows when tasks must happen for the continuous flow in the development or production process. For example, there is a logical sequence of activities when building a house, e.g. an electrician must wire the framed house before the "Gib" lining is attached. A critical path is used to let people who are contributing to a large project know the best or critical time for them to complete their specific task or tasks.

Implementing the technology curriculum   129

It may also offer other alternative, slightly less desirable times for some tasks. A Gantt chart is a project management tool and is frequently used in secondary schools. During TP, timelines and timeframes are critical. Therefore, tasks must be identified and then sequenced in the order they have to be performed. On a critical path, tasks are listed in sequence of completion from the top of the table. The other major decision to be made is what time intervals are to be used. For example in Table 4.4, we have used one-day intervals for developing new muffin types, with four days a week available. Obviously this interval would not be suitable for building a house. Time intervals for this might be one week. Tasks are allotted a best or optimal time slot to be completed by shading the corresponding cell on a critical path in a dark shade. Critical paths may also give possible alternative slots for a specific task identified by a lighter shade as seen in Table 4.5.

Although, in the above example, all the tasks are frequently carried out by one person, more complex critical paths can indicate tasks of multiple people. For example, in a kitchen renovation, the project manager may complete a critical path for the main and all the sub-contractors. In an example shown to me by a friend who is a painter, the critical path indicated that he needed to undercoat the kitchen in the fourth week in August and do the final coating in the second week in September. In between, the new kitchen cabinets are fitted and, after the final coat of paint, the electrician added final light fittings and the flooring was laid.

Herringbone timeline

The herringbone timeline is another method of communicating an intended timeline for TP in which there are different teams of people working on the one bigger project. The method allows us to put tasks of an individual or subgroup in the context of the big picture or whole project and it allows individuals to monitor their practice against others also working on the same project but in a different team. The herringbone timeline has a simple X/Y graph, with time indicated by an arrow from bottom left to top right. Tasks are placed on the timeline with distance between tasks indicating time passed. The task written on top of the timeline indicates the key or major task of the project (top tasks) and underneath shows individual's allocated key tasks broken into minor or sub-tasks (bottom tasks). This means that unlike both the key task list and the critical path, everyone's herringbone timeline will look different from others in the team or bigger group, sometimes called a company. This is because tasks on the bottom are individualised when working on a collaborative project.

Figure 4.8 illustrates this in a different context. This is the herringbone for a small "company" with two main teams, product and packing, each with three people. The context is the development of a legally packaged and labelled savoury flavoured yoghurt. The tasks on the top of the Herringbone are the main tasks for the project or "company" sequenced and placed on the timeline from "START" to "FINISH." The lower half of the timeline is that for one

Table 4.5 Critical path example for making a developing a new muffin type showing optimal and alternative time interval allocations

Tasks
Identify opportunity for a new type of muffin
Develop initial brief
Complete critical path for developing muffins
Investigate existing muffins
Identify base recipe to be modified to suit identified needs
Experiment with individual ingredients
List key attributes for high quality muffins *ATB*
Trial/model a range of options and select three for taste testing
Produce three options for further trialling and taste testing
Test trials on panel of experts

Table 4.5 (Continued)

Implementing the technology curriculum   131

Tasks	5/6	6/6	7/6	8/6	12/6	13/6	14/6	15/6	19/6	20/6	21/6	22/6	23/6	27/6	28/6	29/6	30/6	3/7
Gather and assessment feedback																		
Select one recipe to take further																		
Make modifications to selected recipe *ATB*																		
Investigate optimum colour and size for muffins *ATB*																		
Select size and optimum colour *ATB*																		
Write final brief																		
Produce batch of six final muffins																		
Evaluate against key attributes and final brief specifications																		
Time intervals by day/date	5/6	6/6	7/6	8/6	12/6	13/6	14/6	15/6	19/6	20/6	21/6	22/6	23/6	27/6	28/6	29/6	30/6	3/7

Time

Key

ATB = add to brief

Possible earlier alternative time. Optimal Time to perform task but still acceptable if pushed for time

132 *Implementing the technology curriculum*

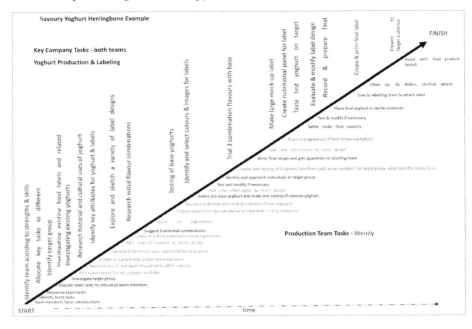

Figure 4.8 Savoury Yoghurt Herringbone example

individual in the product team, in this case Wendy. Other members of this team may have similar "bottom tasks" while the packaging teams' bottom tasks would look considerably different. You will see that the tasks from the top that Wendy is involved in are italicised on her Herringbone as opposed to those for the other team in the company which are not. Each of these main tasks is then expanded and colour coded to assist Wendy to complete her aspects of the product tasks.

This method of planning for practice is particularly suitable when the "Company Approach" is used for the development of technology products. When using a "Company Approach" teachers divide the class into two or three competing companies who appoint a Chief Executive Officer (CEO) and delegate company members to one of three teams: production, packaging and marketing (or similar). With the advice and guidance of their CEO each company works towards developing, packaging and marketing their product. Obviously this approach needs a high level of collaboration and cooperation between the teams within each "company." The unit concludes with each company launching their competing products to a group of potential clients.

Flow charting

A flow chart is often used in industry to record processes so that others can set up and follow it. Flow charts are often used in troubleshooting if there are difficulties within a process. A series of standard symbols (Figure 4.9) are used. An

Implementing the technology curriculum 133

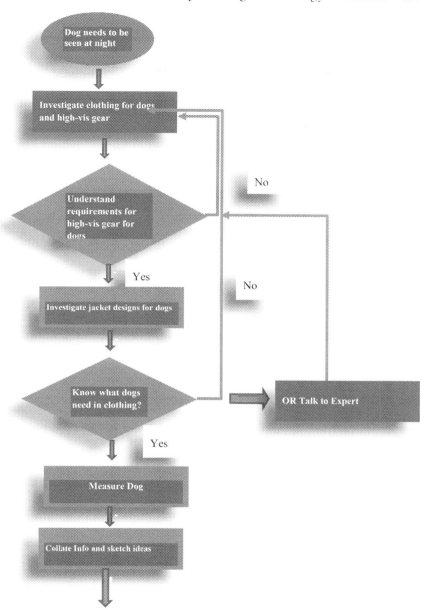

Figure 4.9 "High vis for dogs" an example of a simple flow chart

134 *Implementing the technology curriculum*

advantage of flow charts over the other planning for practice tools mentioned above is that, in a flow chart, decisions can be indicated and optional pathways taken with provision to make feedback loops. In flow charts, questions or decisions are differentiated from tasks.

One of the hardest parts of flow charting is to identify the decisions to be made because, at times, we make very many decisions so quickly that we are unaware that we have made them. This is particularly true for students who choose to develop a technological product where they are the key stakeholder. One of the challenges with technology education is that we need to make our decision-making explicit. This is especially true for experts. For example, think about driving. When we first learn to drive we are very conscious of all the decisions we make when turning a corner – Do I need to brake, indicate and put my foot on the clutch? Are there cars coming behind me, in front of me? But after a considerable time we become experts and make decisions automatically without being conscious that we are doing so.

Flow charting is particularly useful when DDDO. The technique can be used to assist understanding and portraying sequencing, a critical aspect of CT needed for the development of computer programming. For example, at progress outcome (PO) 3 in CT, students are required to break down problems into step-by-step instructions to create algorithms for computer programmes. They use logical thinking to predict the behaviour of the programs, and they understand that there can be more than one algorithm for the same problem. They develop and debug simple programs that use inputs, outputs, sequence and iterations (repeating part of the algorithm with a loop). These are easily depicted in a flow chart format.

Obviously in real life and authentic technology practice, flow charts are usually complex with multiple decisions and actions to be made or taken. Figure 4.10 demonstrates how a flow chart might look like at the beginning of technology practice. Obviously there is still a lot to add.

Figure 4.9 shows an example of the beginning of a flow chart of a task to design and develop a "high viz" vest for dogs. It illustrates two unique features of the flow chart. The first is the first *decision*, the identification of the initiating issue. The *No* direction arrow directs us back to the top. This is called a *feedback loop* and can be enacted as many times as desired. The second decision about understanding the regulations shows two alternative pathways of action. Feedback loops in flow charts depicting TP are particularly useful in the modelling and trialling stages as the loop can be repeated as many times as it takes to get the design right. This is an important aspect of product evaluation.

Let us now think about how the concept of flow charting can be transferred into computer programming. Figure 4.10 is a tiny segment of a computer programme using Scratch taken from Technology Online PO3, exemplar Climbing the Stairs. We suggest that before attempting to design and create a programme in Scratch, teaching students a simple flow chart will assist them to understand the sequence of tasks and feedback loop. Understanding tasks to be completed and the correct sequencing of those tasks is a key component of CT.

Implementing the technology curriculum 135

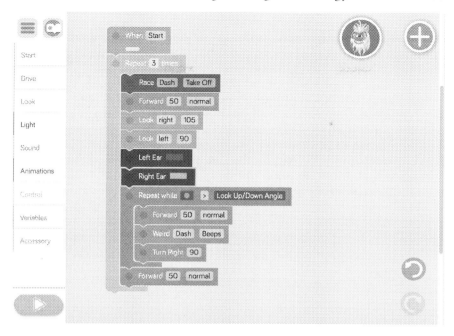

Figure 4.10 An example Scratch-like code computer programme

Outcome development and evaluation (ODE)

When working in this component, students are designing, developing and evaluating their own technological outcomes. This process is iterative and practical. It includes a range of tasks all working towards the development of successful technological outcomes. It usually occurs after considerable initial research and investigation. Below is a list of activities students may undertake when undertaking ODE:

- brainstorming initial ideas;
- sketching a range of design ideas;
- selection appropriate options for testing and trialling;
- relevant skill development;
- detailed design concept and working drawings;
- understanding and undertaking safe practice;
- modelling components or whole outcomes;
- regular consultation with clients and other stakeholders;
- ongoing critique of own designs informed by trialling, testing and modelling;
- design modifications resulting from the above;
- development of prototypes;
- final construction of quality outcomes;
- evaluation of technological outcomes with identification of potential improvements.

136 *Implementing the technology curriculum*

This list is not exhaustive and engagement in these tasks and activities will depend on the age and achievement levels of the students. The nature of the tasks will also vary depending on the technological areas in which students are working. For example, modelling design ideas looks completely different in DDMO (materials outcomes) to that of DDDO (digital outcomes). Students do not always develop a final outcome but may terminate their project after the development of "intermediate outcomes" such as a detailed drawing (plan) or 3D model. When this occurs, it is vital that students know this. Particularly in early years of learning where students are more likely to be making a model, it is important that they understand that they are making a model of a car, rather than an actual car.

A critical component of ODE is evaluation. In technology practice, when designing and developing their technological outcomes, evaluation is not a solely summative tool but also assists formative evaluation as outcomes develop. Students and teachers can use the final brief to evaluate outcomes as they develop by using the attributes and specifications outlined in the brief to evaluate the developing outcome. There are clear links here to Kimbell's Active Reflective Capability Model. As students work through their practice, they need to continually reflect on their practice and product to ensure issues are solved and the brief is met. When things are not as they should be, or could be better, feedback loops can be enacted with other options explored.

One of the goals of the technology practice strand is to get students undertaking authentic TP similar to that of those in the real world. Students' TP should mirror authentic TP as much as possible, but exact replication is not possible because there are constraints within which teachers have to work. The next section explores the nature of students' technology practice.

Students' technological practice

Within authentic contexts it is important that students behave as closely as possible as technologists do. This is why understanding technology practice is so important for student teachers and teachers. The technology they plan and implement for their students should mirror authentic technology practice as much as possible. However, we know that our students are not trained technologists and therefore their technology practice will differ to a degree. We also know that the facilities, machines and equipment available to our students in schools often differ from those in industry. Therefore, for a number of reasons including safety, physical and cognitive development and physical environment, student TP will look different to that of experienced technologists. Fox-Turnbull has identified a number of additional constraints within the school environment that also shape students' TP (Figure 4.11). This model is a merger and extension of Gawith's and, to a lesser degree, Pacey's model of technology practice. Although student TP should mirror authentic TP, the reality is that exact replication is not possible. There are constraints within which teachers

Implementing the technology curriculum 137

Fox-Turnbull Model of Student Technological Practice

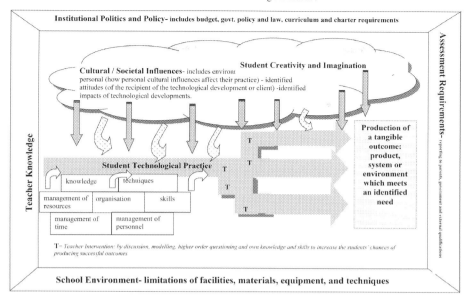

Figure 4.11 Fox-Turnbull model of student TP

and schools have to work; these are represented as a frame within which student TP occurs.

The first of these constraints is "institutional politics and policy." This influences classroom practice by imposing requirements on teachers and students. These include such things as curriculum requirements, school charter and policy, timetable and budget. The second constraint is the "school environment." The nature of the facilities available in schools will limit processes available to the students and therefore affect student TP. It is neither practical nor feasible for schools to have very expensive and complex facilities, machines or equipment that would allow students to undertake specialised TP. Some machines and equipment students are not physically capable of using safely or, to do so, are too risky. As a part of authentic student practice, however, students should be able to recognise which process could be best used to produce the final outcome. The third constraint is "teacher knowledge." To allow students to mirror TP, teachers need to be aware of the knowledge and skills needed by technologists in the field of practice being studied. This does not mean that teachers need to be skilled in all required procedures. Appropriate knowledge will allow them to direct students to experts in the field who are able to guide and assist them. Teachers also need to be aware of the logical sequences of the learning. When planning learning experiences, teachers need to take these into account thereby allowing students to experience practice that is as authentic as possible. Teacher knowledge is critical here. Without

138   *Implementing the technology curriculum*

sound knowledge, teachers are unable to identify and plan logical and relevantly sequenced learning experiences each with clearly focused intended learning. It will also affect the quality of guidance given to students. Teacher content knowledge and pedagogical content knowledge are pivotal for effective teaching in technology.

The fourth constraint is the assessment requirements and procedures imposed on schools and students. It has long been known that external assessment requirements influence classroom practice. In New Zealand secondary schools, technology education is included in the NCEA. It is inevitable that the structure of the qualification influences the practice of students and teachers. In the primary sector, literacy and numeracy national standards were implemented for nine years from 2008 to 2017. Although officially these should not have influenced the teaching of technology, they were disastrous. School programmes were driven by reading, writing and numeracy. Very little time was given to "topic" subjects, of which technology was one. Much technology that was undertaken was done so students could "write" about it. With National Standards removed in 2017 and the introduction of digital technologies in the technology curriculum, we are slowly seeing increased teaching of technology. However, the damage done will continue to constrain technology for many years to come.

The centre of the model in Figure 4.12 illustrates the position of TP for students. It acknowledges that social and cultural values and beliefs, creativity and imagination influence all TP. It also suggests that existing knowledge, skills and techniques, along with management of resources, personnel and time, are elements of TP. Student TP is represented as purposeful action through the centre of Fox-Turnbull's model of students' technology practice in a similar fashion to that presented by Gawith.

Unlike real TP, teacher intervention in the form of formative assessment and advice occurs regularly for students. This does not mean that students are not given the opportunity to fail and make mistakes. Failure and failure analysis are important components of TP. Teachers must allow students to make and learn from their mistakes; however, there will be an optimal time for teacher intervention, before frustration or boredom set in. As students become aware of new learning, the likelihood of producing a successful outcome increases. Figure 4.11 indicates how students' practice can be altered by teacher intervention through formative assessment opportunities by using open-ended or higher-level questions to extend and challenge thinking, suggesting techniques and ultimately influencing and altering students' practice. Teachers need to catch the "teachable moment" to maximise learning. Too much teacher intervention or inappropriate intervention will make any summative assessment judgments invalid, as they would not reflect the technology practice of the student but of the teacher. Formative assessment should be an integral part of student practice, involving feedback on knowledge and skills to enable students to move on safely. This formative assessment process will affect and possibly change the direction the students move within their practice, thus altering the final technological outcome.

Implementing the technology curriculum 139

Characteristics of Learning in Technology

To achieve the best possible learning outcomes in technology, programmes should reflect the following characteristics of technology education.

- *Technology education builds on students' existing knowledge and skills, values, interests, and aspirations. All students will be familiar with many technologies, but may not have articulated their understandings, nor recognised their own skills.*

- *Technology education deals with real, identified needs or problems, and with multiple solutions. There is no single "right answer"—lateral thinking and willingness to test divergent options are to be encouraged—although some solutions will be more successful than others.*

- *Further learning in technology occurs through failure analysis, recognising the value of alternative and unexpected outcomes.*

- *Technological activities usually lead to a tangible outcome: a product, a model, a modified environment, or a system. All students should experience the satisfaction of developing a range of outcomes.*

- *Technological developments are advanced by sharing ideas, presenting concepts, and evaluating possible solutions.*

- *The teacher's knowledge, experience, and skills provide input to assist in refining ideas, selecting resources, and achieving quality in products, as well as guiding students towards viable solutions.*

- *The teacher supports, guides, challenges, and learns with the students, interacting with their thinking and helping to clarify ideas.*

- *Technology education encourages risk taking: students' ideas should be accepted and valued, and students challenged to realise their aspirations. It provides opportunities for students to show initiative, make choices, and take more responsibility for their own work.*

- *Technological activities often require students to work co-operatively and collaboratively—with each other, their teachers, and other adults.*

- *Technology education recognises that students have different starting points and will progress at different rates: the teacher's role is to motivate, encourage, support, and provide feedback to students.*

- *Technology education gives opportunities for a wide range of people in the community to provide specialist input.*

Figure 4.12 Characteristics of technology (Ministry of Education, 1995, p. 16)

In student technology practice, it is also important to acknowledge that students' own culture and beliefs will influence their practice. They will deploy their own funds of knowledge to assist their own, and their peers', technology practice. They must also consider the values and culture of those for whom they are developing their technological outcomes. It is also critical that students consider likely possible impacts and influences of their intended outcomes. Research and planning needs to be thorough and implemented when relevant. Students will not always produce a "successful outcome"; however, a failed outcome does not mean failed TP. We might say to our students, yes this outcome is not successful but it has not failed, it is just not right YET.

140 *Implementing the technology curriculum*

In this model, teacher intervention is a vital part of students' TP. Teachers need to consider very carefully when to intervene in their students' TP. Too soon, and the students lose ownership of their designs. Too late, and they become disengaged through frustration or dissatisfaction with the quality or nature of their outcome. Teacher intervention should be timed to allow students to learn from their mistakes and continue through their technology practice in a timely fashion with increased chances of developing a successful outcome relative to their age and ability. The timing of teacher intervention can be judged through formative assessment. Failure and failure analysis are a very important part of the technological process. Teachers should allow students to make and learn from their mistakes. Figure 4.12 also illustrates how students' practice can be altered by teacher intervention (T) and is represented by the changed direction of the central arrows representing students' purposeful action through their technology practice.

In the end, not all students will succeed in producing a "successful outcome." This, in itself, is reflective of authentic practice and not necessarily a bad thing as long as reflective evaluation leads students to consider, and potentially identify, a possible way forward if they were to continue development of their "not successful yet" outcome. So how do teachers prepare for such complex practice and uncertain and varied technological outcomes? By careful and thorough programme and unit planning. Now let us think about how we might go about planning for teaching and learning to ensure the authentic technology practice as represented above can be implemented.

Planning units of work in technology

There are various approaches you could follow when planning for technology but there are certain elements or key ideas that are essential to the unit planning process in technology.

a Technology is taught holistically with units of work typically incorporating all three strands and multiple AOs although there are exceptions to this at senior secondary school where students may undertake research projects related to the NT; however, these are likely to be more successful if they too are contextualised within the students' technology practice.
b All technology units must reflect the characteristics of learning (Figure 4.12) from *Technology in the New Zealand Curriculum*.
c When planning for technology, teachers start with considering what the students need to know and be able to do to undertake successful technology practice within the given context. AOs are subsequently matched to the planned practice. Do not start planning lessons with the identification of an AO. For those in primary teacher education this is a significant difference from other learning areas.
d It is ok for teachers not to know everything about students' intended outcomes. What teachers do need to know and understand is TP, the

Implementing the technology curriculum 141

associated skills and knowledge applicable to the level of students they teach, and where to go to get their students assistance if needed and when to do this.

e   At senior secondary school, students are taught and undertake technology practice with the AOs guiding progression in complexity and sophistication of ideas. Students' work is subsequently assessed using AS. Ideally, they should be part of the conversation as to what aspects of their work are assessed. We acknowledge in the current climate that this is no easy feat. **We do not teach AS.** We teach the AO and assess using the AS.

f   Up to Year 10 separate assessment tasks such as tests do not have a place in technology. Students' holistic TP should evidence their learning. A portfolio approach is a good approach for students to evidence their practice and reflections.

g   Digital platforms (e.g. Google Sites, Google Slides, My Portfolio) are excellent tools for students to record the research evidence of their TP and associated reflections. They also enable varied ways of evidencing practice. It is critical for students to understand that writing is only one tool to evidence practice research and thinking. Drawings, brainstorms, mind mapping, concept maps and videos are some others. It is important that students who might struggle to write, or write well, are not excluded from achieving in technology, especially in NCEA ASs.

Unit preparation and preplanning

Before the unit planning process can begin, teachers need to be well prepared. This will involve research. First they must consider their students, understand their likes and dislikes, strengths and weaknesses, cultural background and other significant factors that may impact on their learning. They must also consider ways to honour the Treaty of Waitangi by incorporating bicultural practices and understanding into, and through, their planned programme and everyday teaching.

Bicultural perspectives and considerations

> *He oranga ngākau*
> *He pikinga wairora*
> *Positive feelings in your heart will raise your sense of self worth*

The Treaty of Waitangi informs and guides teaching practices in New Zealand. The inclusion of a bicultural perspective in lessons, units and programmes ensures consideration is given to the Treaty and its underpinning beliefs and understandings. Bicultural considerations in classroom practice and programmes should be a purposeful but natural aspect of teachers' planning and teaching. This can occur through a range of ideas and practices, some of which are outlined below. It should not be restricted to using Te Reo but includes such things as:

142 *Implementing the technology curriculum*

1 Looking at curriculum through Māori cultural perspectives such as: understanding the physical and spiritual nature of all artefacts, plants and animals; using native plants-fruits and vegetables; Matariki; patterns in a wharenui, tukutuku, kowhaiwhai; Māori artefacts, technological processes and practices such as food reservation, wood, stone and bone preparation and carving, preparation of harakeke, and traditional games, dances and musical instruments.

2 Selecting/using Māori role models to study or talk to students such as: carvers; artists; athletes for commonwealth and Olympic games; community leaders; health professionals; youth leaders; and sports players.

3 When exemplifying technologies from historical and contemporary settings, use Māori technological artefacts and processes. Food preservation, defence, food gathering and hunting, clothing and fabrics, information and communication (carving and patterns) are all well exemplified in Māori culture and practices.

4 Explicit links and integrated practices associated with Tātaiako competencies:

- Wānanga: participating with learners and communities in robust dialogue for the benefit of Māori learners' achievement
- Whanaungatanga: actively engaging in respectful working relationships with Māori learners, parents and whanau, hapu, iwi and the Māori community
- Manaakitanga: showing integrity, sincerity and respect towards Maori beliefs, language and culture
- Tangata Whenuatanga: affirming Māori learners as Māori Providing contexts for learning where the language, identity and culture of Māori learners and their whānau is affirmed
- Ako: taking responsibility for their own learning and that of Māori learners

5 Identifying and demonstrating relevant Māori values, some of which include:

- aroha (love and feelings for others, caring, compassion);
- āwhina (helping, assisting, befriending);
- haumāuiui (pride and achievement);
- kotahitanga (doing things together, everyone is brought together, all personal differences aired and, even if they cannot be incorporated, respect is still given);
- mahaki (finding ways to share knowledge whilst being humble);
- manaakitanga (hospitality/generosity, in everything you do care for people – reciprocal unqualified caring);
- rangatiratanga (process of holding status);
- rangimārie (tolerance);
- tū pono (knowing one's self, one's own identify);

Implementing the technology curriculum 143

- wairua auaha, wairua uiui (innovation inquiry and curiosity);
- wairuatanga (everything has a spiritual dimension, spiritual dimensions are involved in all things);
- whakanui (respect);
- whanaungatanga (making connections/relationships, family and social integration through kinship ties).

6 Teach using Māori pedagogies (shared presentations/teaching approach) values and beliefs, working as a group, storytelling, addressing learning styles, use of cultural artefacts, use of whakatauäki (proverbs).
7 Teach and participate in Māori cultural activities: waiata, whanau groupings, start each day with a karakia or whakatauki, etc.
8 Considering Māori historical contexts as well as European when exemplifying ideas and technologies.
9 Emphasise the importance of oral tradition.

As well as everyday practices such as:

10 Taking care to pronounce Māori names and places correctly.
11 Using Te Reo Māori for instructions, greetings and praise as a natural part of the classroom programme such as:
    Ka pai – good/well done;
    He pai tau mahi – good work;
    Tau kē – you've done it;
    Ka mau te wehi – awesome.
12 Using Te Reo Māori days, dates, months and time.

Preparatory research

Before beginning the planning of technology, teachers need to undertake preparatory research. They must identify their students' needs and interests that will be taken into consideration when selecting the immediate context/issue. In Levels 1–5 of the curriculum, it is common for teachers to identify an immediate context but this does not mean that a student driven/identified issue could not be used. Teachers then research the context and content knowledge. While it is often not possible to know everything students might require or encounter, teachers need to know enough to know where and whom to turn to for assistance if required. Teachers must then be very aware of the technology content knowledge to be taught. As suggested in Fox-Turnbull's model of students' technology practice, teacher knowledge is an influencing factor on students' learning in technology. Teachers need to be aware of prior technology learning undertaken by their students and refer to the school's technology curriculum plan (if there is one) to identify AOs for focused learning.

144 *Implementing the technology curriculum*

We recommend that teachers actually undertake the task or design process they are asking of their students, especially in the lower secondary, intermediate and primary schools. This will assist teachers to identify potential problems that might be encountered and resources that may be needed during the students' technology practice. It also assists the teacher in the identification of the skills and knowledge they need to prepare for before teaching, and may assist in calculating timeframes for specific activities. Remember the 5Ps "Prior Preparation & Planning Prevents Problems."

Pre-unit planning steps

Once a teacher has completed the preparatory research, she/he then sets about brainstorming, scoping and writing a unit of work based on authentic TP. A technology unit is a sequenced plan of the learning intentions with associated learning experiences that students undertake to meet an identified technological need or opportunity. It also considers evidence of learning and the learning that students need to achieve in order to produce suitable solutions to previously identified needs or opportunities. There is almost always a tangible outcome to a technology unit. This tangible outcome may be a product or system. At times students will complete a prototype of their outcome or, at times, they may only complete intermediate outcomes such as detailed drawings, 3D models, or mock-ups. Outlined below are the steps that can be taken to thoroughly prepare for and plan a technology unit. The steps are exemplified through two examples, one a unit at Level 1 called "Flugs for Cuddles at School" in the technological areas of DDMO (Figure 4.14) and the other "Website for Hobbit Harriers" at Level 6 in DDDO (Figure 4.15).

Learning needs

Identify the *learning needs* of the students in the class. This may relate to individuals or groups within the class and/or the class as a whole, and the essential skills. Note the age, year group and curriculum achievement level of the children.

Immediate context

Select the immediate context (topic). Identify an authentic opportunity or technological need. At Years 12 and 13, these are likely to be identified by the students themselves. Describe the scenario leading to or outline the issue and the identified need or opportunity. This later becomes part of the conceptual statement in the teacher's given brief.

Immediate contexts are selected for a variety of reasons and based on:

- an identified community/business technological need or issue;
- a local or national environmental issue;

Implementing the technology curriculum   145

- the interests of the class;
- the learning needs of the class;
- a specific need identified within the class or school;
- the required technological area (for example if a group of Year 5 students have never experienced processed technologies (food technology) in their previous four years at school);
- identified long-term plan (LTP) or as a part of the school's programme of work.

Technological area

Identify the potential or likely "tangible outcome" of the unit and determine the technological area to be covered. A tangible outcome may be a number of different things. For example, a product, a plan or concept drawing of a product, modified environment or system, a functional model, template, mock-up, prototype, actual system or environment. Because of restraints in skills, time, resources, equipment, facilities or finances, it is NOT always possible to see all projects to their conclusion. Students should experience a range of "outcomes" over their time at school. As they get older, they may be more likely to develop quality prototype outcomes unless of course they are studying DVC, when all outcomes will be intermediate outcomes – skilled drawings and possibly models.

Brainstorm

With the above information in mind, along with the requirements of the curriculum and the key technological learning students need, brainstorm all the learning that could take place to allow the students to develop the skills, processes, knowledge and concepts needed to meet the identified need through their own TP. The brainstorm should include contextual and procedural knowledge and skills, the requirements of the curriculum and the technological area within which the unit is situated. Figures 4.13 and 4.14 model this process at Levels 1 and 4 of NZC, respectively.

Scoping

Scope by circling the learning that is most relevant and totally necessary and focused on the TP, technological area and relevant transformations. Then sequence the learning to indicate the teaching order. We have done this by numbering in teaching order. In any one topic there are always too many options for teaching all aspects of TP. Teachers need to select a way through the myriad of ideas and possibilities. In most units, there is no one right order to teach; however, common sense must prevail. Obviously research into existing outcomes and stakeholder views will come before detailed designs are drawn. Detailed planning of outcomes must precede

Flugs for Comfort – Brainstorm

Adding specifications to write the final brief	When and why people need things to comfort them	Best features of our cuddly toys
What is a flug?		Fluffy funny monster
Tasks to be completed before grandparents' day	Things that comfort us	What is a design brief?
Need for emotional support		Writing our initial brief
	Let's looks at flugs, what are they, what do they look like	
Attributes, the things we need		Flugs can be made of polar fleece, faux fur, upcycled blankets- investigate the characteristics of these materials
What is a mock-up? Made of cheap materials	What does the materials look and feel like? How well do they last	
		Using needles and thread safely
What makes the features buttons for eyes etc.		Sewing machine safety
	Best features of favourite soft toys	Drawing or pattern
Detailed drawing of individual flugs- add accessories needed		Make pattern
	Communicate our design ideas to our grandparents	Stuffing Flug and closing gap
Evaluate final designs	Cut out and sew flug body and head	
Add final details to our brief		Select materials to be used and items for features
	Making our own mock-up	
How are patterns made? Talking to the pattern maker		Sketch design ideas and select one
		Upcycling, what is it and why do we do it.
	What are accessories and what ones do our toys have?	

Figure 4.13 Flugs for Cuddles at School brainstorm

NZC L6 Brainstorm: Website for Hobbits' Harriers and Athletic

Learning Foci: Brief Development & Characteristics of Technological Outcomes
Tech Area: Designing and Developing Digital Technologies
LO: Implement basic procedures to create a digital information outcome

Existing website investigate and holders interviewed text types and sizes

Successful website attributes page layouts effective graphics and colours

Write an initial brief' attributes and conceptual statement justify specifications

Undertake testing procedures in a manner that economises the use of time in the outcome's use

Complete a detailed final brief with specifications mocking up each page

Structure & coding of websites evaluating existing website purpose of modelling

Inserting pictures, graphics and text Web designer in action

uses for critical paths key concepts in design generate 3 design ideas

Planning techniques for designing website function of website

features required by clients imaging mapping title tags

function versus aesthetics planning practice using a critical path

develop working prototype receive feedback from client specifications
make modifications according to feedback alter critical path when needed,

Justify specifications according to Client's needs websites as products and systems

write attributes for intended website research impacts website have had on retail
pros and cons of their website, justification

investigate how people's values influence their website behaviour

Figure 4.14 Website for Hobbit Harriers brainstorm

148 *Implementing the technology curriculum*

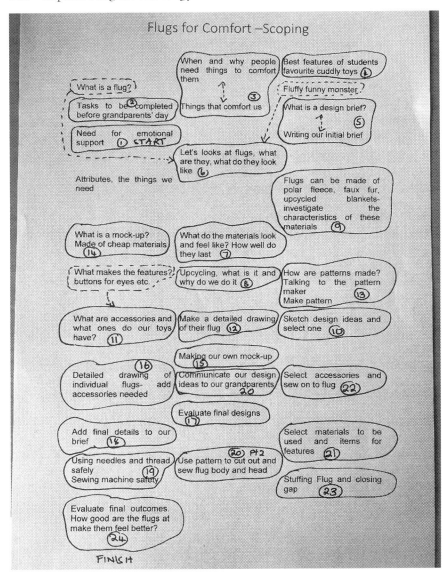

Figure 4.15 Flugs for Cuddles at School scoping

construction. Identification of key tasks and resources and practice planning should occur near the beginning of technology practice and an initial brief is begun as soon as enough information comes to light. Brief development continues throughout the students' practice as does evaluation of design ideas and outcomes. Figures 4.15 and 4.16 illustrate the scoping of our two units.

Implementing the technology curriculum 149

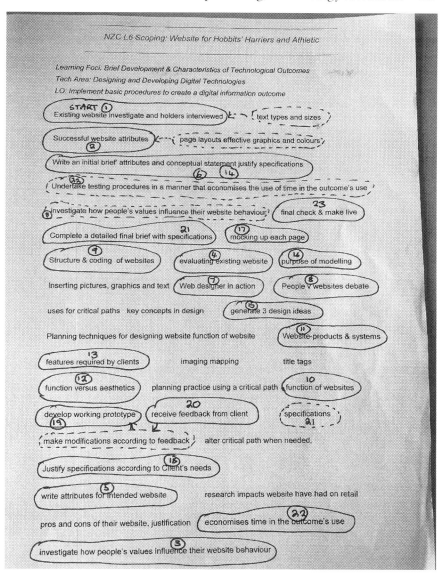

Figure 4.16 Website for Hobbit Harriers scoping

Pathway

Illustrated in Figures 4.17 and 4.18, the next step is to expand each aspect of the scoping into a detailed pathway of teaching episodes that will become lessons by adding detail such as what, how and where learning might occur. The pathway for each episode identifies the technology strands within which the teaching

150 *Implementing the technology curriculum*

Flugs for Comfort- Pathway

- Discuss the need to emotional support during difficult times Introduce given brief
- List the tasks that need to be completed before and during grandparent's day
- Identify things that comfort us when our parents, caregivers and whanau cannot be there with us
- Bring arrange of cuddly toys to school to identify best features to comfort us
- Write initial brief and identify 4-5 key attributes needed in a Flug
- Investigate a range of funny ugly monsters designs and ideas
- Research a range of possible fabrics that might be suitable,
- Investigate recycling or up-cycling fabric
- Select potential fabrics -add specifications to brief
- Draw a sketch of two or three design ideas, select one
- Go back to existing toys to identify accessories which give features such as eyes, mouths, teeth etc.
- Draw selected design idea in detail, annotate with fabric types, colours and items to make features and accessories
- Talk to a pattern maker, clothing designer to identify how to make a pattern for a stuffed toy, discuss the need for seams and sewing inside out
- Make the pattern for the Flug
- Make a mock-up of designed Flug with newsprint paper stapled and stuffed
- Evaluate design and make modifications to final pattern if needed
- Add to and write final brief with all specifications
- Lesson on needle safety
- With grandparents cut out and sew Flugs inside out, turn in right way and sew on accessories before stuffing and closing the gap.
- Place in class library corner and cuddle when needed.

Figure 4.17 Flugs for Cuddles at School pathway

episode is situated. Other additional information on the intended learning is added at this stage such as what and how the students will do to enable required learning.

Students will develop their own solution to the identified problem through investigation of existing TP and outcomes and immersion in their own TP. As a teacher, it is very important to understand where the brief (developed to give guidance when meeting a need) may take the students. Teachers frequently have to set restrictions; all technologists have to work within restrictions. As mentioned earlier, it is a very good idea for teachers to experience the practical activity first, before the students begin. This helps to up-skill the teacher if necessary and will identify potential problems and hiccups. It is also important to allow for learning and possible pathways that have not previously been identified by the teacher but identified by students. When the pathway is completed, the next step is to complete the unit planner using a template. Remember unit plans are professional documents and are evidence of your classroom programme. They may be read by multiple people for a range of purposes.

Implementing the technology curriculum   151

NZC L6 Pathway Sequenced for Teaching

> DDDO:PO4: In authentic contexts, students investigate and consider possible solutions for a given context or issue. With support, they use an iterative process to design, develop, store and test digital outcomes, identifying and evaluating relevant social, ethical and end-user considerations. They use information from testing and apply appropriate tools, techniques, procedures and protocols to improve the quality of the outcomes and to ensure they are fit-for-purpose and meet end-user requirements.

1. investigate a range existing of websites and holders interview for their views   NT:CTO
2. investigate page layouts, effective graphics and fonts, text types and sizes   TK:TP
3. investigate how people's values influence their website behaviour   NT:CT
4. evaluating existing website against established attributes NT:CTO & TP:BD
5. list 5-6 successful website attributes   NT:CTO &TP:BD
6. justify specifications according to Client's needs TP:BD
7. web designer in action   NT:CTO TP:TS
8. websites and people debate NT:CT
9. structure and coding of websites   NT:CTO
10. function of website   TK&TP
11. websites as products and systems   TK: TS & NT:CTO
12. function versus aesthetics TK TP
13. features required by clients   TP&BD
14. write an initial brief attributes and conceptual statement TP&BD
15. generate 3 design ideas TP&ODE
16. purpose of modelling   TK&TM
17. mocking up each page   TP&ODE
18. write attributes and specifications for intended website   TP:BD
19. develop working prototype   TP:ODE
20. receive feedback from client   TP ODE
21. complete a detailed final brief with specifications   TP BD
22. undertake testing procedures in a manner that economises the use of time in the outcome's use   NT:CTO
23. check final website and make live   TP:ODE

Figure 4.18 Website for Hobbit Harriers pathway

Unit planning steps

At the conclusion of the pre-planning exercises, teachers will now be ready to move onto the unit planner template. Planning and assessment must be flexible to allow for unexpected outcomes. Unit planner templates assist teachers to present their planning for intended learning in a succinct coherent manner. Some are generic in nature and used to plan all learning areas, others have been designed to meet the specific needs of each learning area, making unit planning easier for teachers as they provide prompts for a range of considerations necessary for quality unit planning within a specific learning area. The unit planner provided in this book (Figure 4.19 with guidelines to use it in Figure 4.20) is specific to technology. It is a planner that was originally developed by teachers in the first professional learning contract in technology undertaken by technology teachers in New Zealand in 1997 and has continually evolved over the last 23 years. Teachers frequently give us feedback about our planner. Recently we have made changes to align with formative assessment practices and the new curriculum. The planner includes space for predetermined learning intentions, learning experiences and evidence of learning (written sequentially for teaching), the identified technological need or opportunity, the technological areas to be covered and the strands and AOs linked to the intentions/experiences. Space on the front page is also allocated for the Health and Safety considerations which are very important. Teachers are responsible for the safety of their students. It is critical that hazards are identified and risk management considerations are signalled.

Also, on the front page of the planner template is a section for relevant resources for the unit, a space to list vocabulary that will be new to the students and to note the "big understanding." Think of this as the enduring learning or what you want the students to remember in 20 years' time. Careful consideration is also given to the AO to be covered and assessed. Not all AO covered will be assessed in any one unit. On the second and

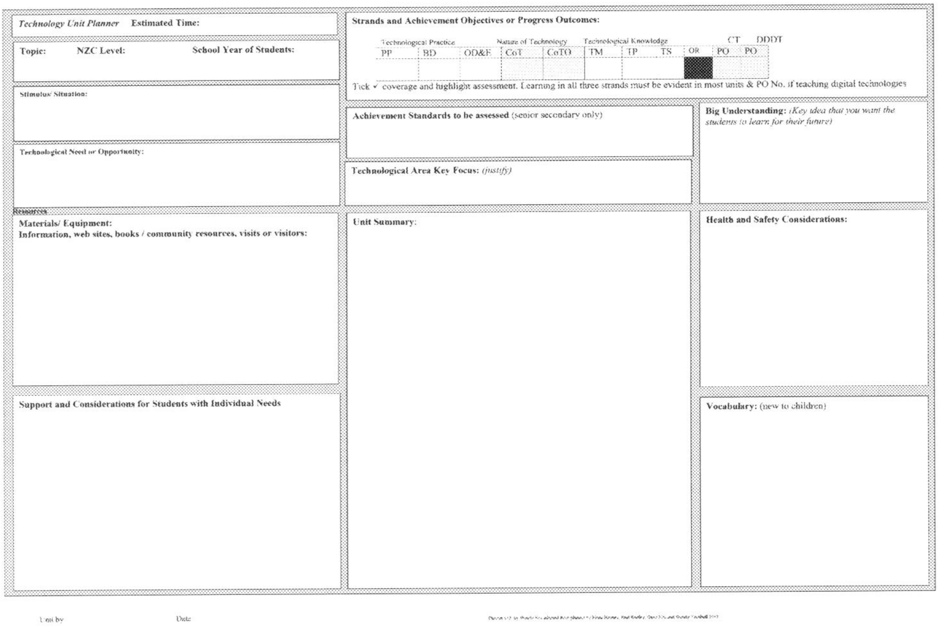
Technology Unit Planner **Estimated Time:**

Topic: **NZC Level:** **School Year of Students:**

Stimulus/ Situation:

Technological Need or Opportunity:

Resources

Materials/ Equipment:
Information, web sites, books / community resources, visits or visitors:

Support and Considerations for Students with Individual Needs

Strands and Achievement Objectives or Progress Outcomes:

Technological Practice			Nature of Technology		Technological Knowledge			CT	DDDT	
PP	BD	OD&E	CoT	CoTO	TM	TP	TS	OR	PO	PO

Tick ✓ coverage and highlight assessment. Learning in all three strands must be evident in most units & PO No. if teaching digital technologies

Achievement Standards to be assessed (senior secondary only)

Technological Area Key Focus: *(justify)*

Unit Summary:

Big Understanding: *(Key idea that you want the students to learn for their future)*

Health and Safety Considerations:

Vocabulary: (new to children)

Unit by Date

Figure 4.19 Technology unit planner template

Implementing the technology curriculum   153

Technology Learning Intentions LI *The students are learning to...*	Learning Experiences LE *The students will......*	Strand & AO/ PO (or Domain & LO or PO for sec)	Technological Learning Evidence TLE	Technology Success Criteria for Assessment at 3 or4 **Key Stages/ AS used for Assessment** *(L6-8 only)* *What are we looking for in the evidence?*

COPY THIS PAGE AS REQUIRED

Unit by: Date:

Technology Learning Intentions *The students are learning to...*	Learning Experiences *The students will......*	Strand & AO/ PO (or Domain & LO or PO for sec)	Technological Learning Evidence	Technology Success Criteria for Assessment at 3 or4 **Key Stages/ AS used for Assessment** *(L6-8 only)* *What are we looking for in the evidence?*

Unit by: Date:

Figure 4.19 (Continued)

154 *Implementing the technology curriculum*

Links to Key Competencies: *Highlight and explain* **Managing self** **Relating to others** **Participating and contributing** **Thinking** **Using language, symbols and text**	Links to Curriculum Areas: *Highlight and explain* **The Arts** **English** **Learning Languages** **Mathematics and Statistics** **Science** **Social Studies** **Health and Physical Education**	
Organisation of the students/class:	**Bicultural Focus including links to Tātaiako competencies:**	**Values:** Values: *highlight and justify* • Excellence • Innovation, inquiry, curiosity product • Diversity • Equity • Ecological Sustainability • Integrity
Unit Evaluation *(to be written post-teaching)* In this space identify the questions you would need to ask yourself.		

Unit by: Date:

Figure 4.19 (*Continued*)

University of Waikato Technology Education Unit Planner Template GUIDELINES

Topic/ Context State the topic. Link this to the tangible outcome **NZC Level** **Year Level** State the level of technology learning from NZC and the year level of the students undertaking the unit.	**Strands and Achievement Objectives or Progress Outcomes**							
	Technological Practice			**Nature of Technology**		**Technology**		
	PP	**BD**	**OD&E**	**CT**	**CTO**	**TM**	**TP**	**TS**

Remember you need to cover achievement objectives from all three strands in MOST units. In some units you will also include PO from Digital Technologies. Assessment in technology is holistic. The assessment should give you opportunity to assess at key stages during the unit. Highlight the achievement objects you plan to assess only. For these, PO you need to make sure you have success criteria noted in your unit plan. Digital technologies are included when students need the key ideas to enable them to develop their outcomes successfully.

Tick coverage and highlight assessment. Learning in all three strands must be evident in most units and some PO if teaching digital technologies.

Conceptual Statement: Situation How you will introduce or motivate the students. It should foster a student-centred approach and be exciting, authentic and possibly imaginative. **Need** State the need or opportunity for problem solving. This will form the focus of the unit. Outcomes developed meet this need or opportunity.	**Area of Technological Learning Focus (justify)** Name the technological area that is a focus in the unit. This focus should be evident in the learning intentions and experiences. Additional learning from other technological areas may occur incidentally. Justify the major by noting what the learning in this area.	**Big Understanding** What do you want the children to come away from the unit with? This may relate to processes, skills, understanding of social and environmental issues. It must be more than just content knowledge. What learning will endure?
Materials/ Equipment: Identifies the equipment and materials needed for the unit. Be as detailed as possible. This will help you with your organisation and planning. **Information, web sites, books / community resources, visits or visitors:** Also identifies information & resources needed for the unit. This needs to be detailed and specific where possible. Highlight organised visits /visitors & arrange early in the unit. Names, phone numbers and other details help planning and are a great reference for the future. Remember this is your idea. **Support and Considerations for Students with Special Needs** What pedagogical strategies are you going to undertake to ensure all students are catered for within the unit. This might include additional or alternative activities, assistance or more careful modelling and scaffolding of activities using shared, oral and written resources and instructions so ensure all students regardless of their needs are catered for.	**Unit Summary:** Provide an overview of the unit and the activities and learning that will occur during this unit. What are the students designing and developing and what activities will they undertake to ensure they have the required knowledge and skills to achieve their desired technological outcome OR intermediate outcome.	**Safety Considerations** Highlight the health and safety hazards and issues evident within the unit. This is very important, as it is proof that you have considered risks and risk. Do not forget them to teach safe practice as a part of the unit management. Use this URL to guide this section. https://education.govt.nz/assets/Documents/Ministry/Initiatives/Health-and-safety/NES-Safety-in-Technology-Education-AW.pdf For more hazardous unit also complete a Template for safety planning in technology education, found as Appendix 1 in the above document. **Literacy Links: New Vocabulary** The new words/term which the students have not come across before. They may include words from tech. areas, processes, principles etc. Introduce them to students.

Unit by: _____ Date: _____

Figure 4.20 Technology unit planner template guidelines

Implementing the technology curriculum 155

Technology Learning Intentions *The students are learning to...*	Learning Experiences *The students will...*	Strand & AO links	Technological Learning Evidence	Technology Success Criteria for Assessment at 2-3 Key Stages *What are we looking for in the evidence?*
Identify and note the learning needed. What you think, the students need to learn so that they can move on to the next step of their technological practice. Write them in sequential order for teaching. Make sure you are identifying the technological learning. Remember you need to cover learning from achievement objectives from all three strands in EVERY unit. Always cover learning from all of achievement objective ODE. Also some LI make come from the Digital technologies PO as well.	Consider what activities will allow the students to learn what you need them to learn. Write learning experiences that relate to the relevant technological practice to be covered. Write them in sequential order and make sure you have the students participating in learning experiences that relate to all three strands, and relates to their level of understanding. Make learning experiences varied and child centered.	Abbreviate the strands & AO to letters. Use upper case letters except for Technology Products which is Tp E.g. TP;PP, BB, OD&E TK-TM, Tp, TS NT-CI, CTO. State the level here only if it differs from what you have stated on Page 1	Identify what you think the students need to gain from the learning experience so that they can move on the next step of their technological practice. Then think about how you will know whether this learning has taken place. Evidence of learning is tangible evidence and something that can be used for assessment purposes when clear criteria for success have been established. Just state the actual evidence, do not repeat the learning experience. Bullet point and or a phrase is enough e.g.: list of ...... chart showing......, graph summarising	You need to identify two or three key stages in the unit when assessment will occur. For each identified key stage, write 3-4 specific success criteria. Ask yourself what successful learning would look like? The success criteria you write may allow for assessment of a number of different learning intentions. Can be used for self, peer and teacher assessment and are used in conjunction with the evidence of learning. Assessment in technology is holistic. The key stages you determine may allow for assessment of a number of different learning intentions.

COPY THIS PAGE AS REQUIRED

Unit by: _____ Date: _____

Planner v10 by Wendy Fox UW: adapted from planner by Fiona Havnes, Paul Rodley, Dave Sim and Wendy Turnbull UC 1997

Links to Key Competencies: *Highlight and explain*	Links to Curriculum Areas: *Highlight and explain*	
Managing self	The Arts	
Relating to others	English	
Participating and contributing	Learning Languages	
Thinking	Mathematics and Statistics	
Using language, symbols and text	Science	
	Social Studies	
Highlight and explain the KC threaded through all the teaching in the unit and justify why this is the case.	Health and Physical Education Highlight and explain how other learning areas will contribute to and enhance the students' technology practice in an authentic manner.	
Organisation of the students/class: Consider how the students and the physical space will be configured. Are the students working individually or in groups?	**Bicultural Focus including links to Tātaiako:** How will you engage all learners in understanding the obligations of all New Zealand citizens and schools to the TOW. Make use of Māori contexts, role models, examples, technologies, ways of knowing and understanding, especially with regards to the spiritual dimensions of technological outcomes. Make explicit links to Tātaiako competencies.	**Values:** *highlight and justify* • Excellence • Innovation, inquiry, curiosity product • Diversity • Equity • Ecological Sustainability • Integrity Highlight and explain the values threaded through all the teaching in the unit and justify why this is the case.
Unit Evaluation *(to be written post–teaching) In this space identify the questions you would need to ask yourself.*		
To be written post–teaching. In this space, identify the questions you would need to ask yourself to improve students learning and your teaching. What changes would you make next time you teaching this?		

Whanaungatanga: participating with learners and communities to extend dialogue for the benefit of Maori learners' poihi version. • Whanaungatanga: actively engaging in respectful working relationships with Maori learners, parents and whanau, hapu, iwi and the Maori community. • Manaakitanga: showing integrity, sincerity and respect towards Maori beliefs, language and culture. • Tangata Whenuatanga: affirming Maori learners as Maori. Providing contexts for learning where the language, identity and culture of Maori learners and their whanau is affirmed. • Ako: taking responsibility for their own learning and that of Maori learners.

Unit by: _____ Date: _____

Planner v10 by Wendy Fox UW: adapted from planner by Fiona Havnes, Paul Rodley, Dave Sim and Wendy Turnbull UC 1997

Figure 4.20 (Continued)

156 Implementing the technology curriculum

third pages, the last column on the right is for the identification of specific assessment criteria. These are identified at key stages in the students' practice. The successful meeting of these criteria allows the students to move to the next step to the development of a successful technological solution and make progress in their technological thinking. The final page of the planner has room for links to key competencies and curriculum areas, notes for classroom and student organisation and space for bicultural considerations with links to Tātaiako competencies and Māori practices, technologies and considerations.

Remember, when planning a unit of work in Technology, all three strands are integral to the students' practice. It is the teacher's responsibility, within the school setting, to ensure that coverage of all technological areas and strands are occurring multiple times as students' progress through their schooling. This is where technology programme planning is essential.

The following technology unit planner guidelines give instructions in italics on how to fill in each of the sections of the planner.

The completed units for Flugs and Hobbit Harriers (Figures 4.21 and 4.22) are included near the end of this section. To write your unit, use the above guidelines (Figure 4.20) to complete each section of the unit planner.

New Zealand curriculum learning level

The NZC level the unit is aimed at and the year level of the students.

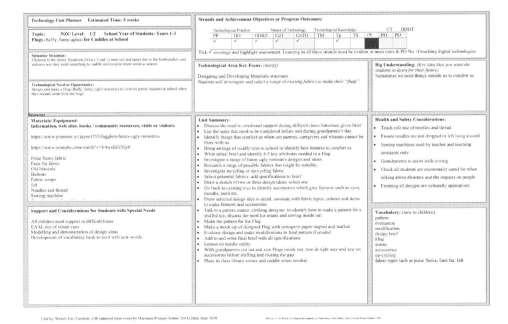

Figure 4.21 Level 1 Flugs for Cuddles technology unit plan

Implementing the technology curriculum 157

Technology Learning Intentions LI *The students are learning to ...*	Learning Experiences LE *The students will........*	Strand & AO/ PO	Technological Learning Evidence TLE	Technology Success Criteria for Assessment at 3 or4 Key Stages/ AS used for Assessment (L6-8 only) *What are we looking for in the evidence?*
discuss their emotional needs and consider how they might assist themselves Introduce given brief and identify key needs of students	discuss the need to emotional support during difficult times such as sickness or natural disasters. Read given brief to students and ask for additional information.	TP:BD	The given brief with student input	
list the tasks that need to be completed and the time lines for tasks	co-construct with their teacher a list the tasks that need to be completed before and during grandparent's day	TP:PP	List to tasks with timeframe	
identify out specific technologies have a role in comforting people	identify things that comfort us when our parents, caregivers and whanau cannot be there with us and that these things are technologies	NT:CT	Definition of comforting technologies	
investigate and deconstruct a range of technology outcomes to determine the materials they are made of and key attributes for a specific purpose	bring arrange of cuddly toys including an old one to school. Deconstruct and tryout to identify best features to comfort us. the materials to create these characteristics and how they are put together	NT:CTO	List of best features- attributes	
write initial brief and identify 4-5 key attributes needed in their technological outcome	write initial brief and identify 4-5 key attributes needed in their Flug	TP:BD	Initial Brief	
investigate a range of technological outcome designs and ideas to understand key features needed	investigate a range of funny ugly monsters designs and ideas to identify key features needed	TP:BD	List of key feature for their Flug	*Key stage 1 Technological Products
research a range of possible materials that might be suitable for their technological outcome and consider recycling or up-cycling options	research a range of possible fabrics that might be suitable for their Flug. Identify three key attributes of three different fabrics including at least one recycling or up-cycled fabric option	TK:Tp* TP:BD	Table of three potential fabrics with key attributes of each	• identify and describe materials that flugs are made from include polar-fleece, feaue fur, felt, etc • identify one performance property of each material • identify describe how the materials have been manipulated to make fluffy toys **Key stage 2 Brief Development
select materials for their intended design	select potential fabrics for their Flug -add specifications to brief	TP:BD**	Modified Brief	• explain the outcome to be produced • identify and describe attributes for an outcome OR • describe the attributes for an outcome that take account of the need or opportunity being addressed and the resources available.

COPY THIS PAGE AS REQUIRED

Unit by: Wendy Fox-Turnbull, UW (adapted from a unit by Mairehau Primary School 2011) Date: June 2020

Technology Learning Intentions *The students are learning to...*	Learning Experiences *The students will ......*	Strand & AO/ PO	Technological Learning Evidence	Technology Success Criteria for Assessment at 3 or4 Key Stages/ AS used for Assessment (L6-8 only) *What are we looking for in the evidence?*
draw a sketch of two or three design ideas, select one, justifying selection	draw a sketch of two or three design ideas for their flug, select one and tell why they selected that one	TP:ODE	Sketches with one ticket. Articulation of reasons	
reinvestigate existing technologies to identify finer features	go back to existing toys to identify accessories which give features such as eyes, mouths, teeth etc.	NT:CTO	Table of items used for features e.g.	
draw selected design ideas in detail, annotate with suitable materials and items to make features and accessories	draw selected design ideas of flugs in detail, annotate with fabric types, colours and items to make features and accessories	TP:ODE	Drawing of designed Flug	
talk to technologist or technician in the field to identify how to undertake key aspects of their technology practice	talk to a pattern maker, clothing designer to identify how to make a pattern for a stuffed toy, discuss the need for seams and sewing inside out	NT:CTO	Co-constructed flow chart of process	
construct pattern for intended outcome	make the pattern for the Flug	TP:ODE	Pattern	
make a mock-up of designed technology outcome using cheap materials	make a mock-up of designed Flug with newsprint paper stapled and stuffed	TP:ODE	Mock-up	
evaluate design and make modifications to final pattern if needed	evaluate mock-up to think about improvements to their designed Flug and make modifications to their pattern if needed	TP:ODE	Changes made on final design drawing	
use specialist equipment safely	use needles safely, taking care not to drop any nor prick themselves and understand who to behave around sewing machines	TP:ODE	The finished Flug	
with assistance construct final outcome	with grandparents cut out and sew Flugs inside out, turn in right way and sew on accessories before stuffing and closing the gap.	TP:ODE		
			Oral report of best features	
evaluate final outcomes identify the best features of their own and others'	identify what they like best about their own and other's Flugs and place in class library corner and cuddle when needed.	TP:ODE		

Unit by: Wendy Fox-Turnbull, UW (adapted from a unit by Mairehau Primary School 2011) Date: June 2020

Figure 4.21 (Continued)

158 *Implementing the technology curriculum*

Figure 4.21 (Continued)

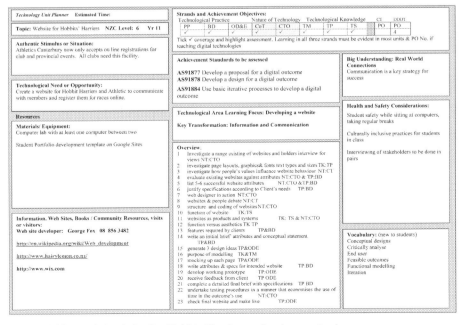

Figure 4.22 Level 6 website for Hobbit Harriers technology unit plan

Implementing the technology curriculum 159

Technology Learning Intentions *The students are learning to...*	Learning Experiences *The students will.......*	Strand & AO or Domain & LO or PO	Technological Learning Evidence	Technology Success Criteria for Assessment *(L6-8 only)* *What are we looking for in the evidence?*
1. investigate a range of technological outcomes to identify key features of system and how it is made up of a series of products	investigate a range existing of websites and identify features that are common to all websites and identify the individual products that make up the system	NT:CTO TK:TS	Table of products situated within a website system with features of each	**Designing and Developing Digital Outcomes (Progress outcome 4)** Students will need to investigate and consider possible solutions for the given context or issue. With support, they will use an iterative process to design, develop, and test digital outcomes, identifying and evaluating relevant social, ethical and end-user considerations. They use information from testing and apply appropriate tools, techniques, procedures and protocols to improve the quality of the outcomes and to ensure they are fit-for-purpose and meet end-user requirements.
2. investigate specific structure and make-up of technological outcomes	research website layouts, effective graphics and fonts and fonts, text types and sizes to identify six key attributes	NT:CTO& TP:BD	List of six attributes	
3. identify stakeholder values and subsequent influences on behaviour	interview a range of website holders including client for their views on what they think makes a successful website.	NT:CTO& TP:BD	Present a report linking values to behaviour	
4. evaluating other existing websites against established attributes	evaluate page layouts to determine effective fonts and text size from **http://www.wix.com** to establish specifications suitable for the client.	TP:BD	List of 5-6 early specifications e.g. specifications font and text	**An effective proposal for a digital outcome includes** • a proposed outcome statement including problem and/or issue, scope, purpose, context • the requirements (including specifications) • the end users
5. identify a need or opportunity from the given context and issue	following discussion with the president of Hobbit Harriers identify the technological needs for the website to be developed	TP:BD	List of client's needs, list of attributes and additional specifications	• the resources required (e.g., people, equipment, estimated timeframes for development) • using feedback and research to improve the proposal
6. write an initial brief/proposal by composing an initial conceptual statement and identify key attributes which justify the nature of the outcome	write an initial brief for Hobbits Harriers with the information in a conceptual statement and key attributes for a successful website. Justify inclusion of identified attributes	NT:CTO& TP:BD AS1.1 *	Initial brief with justified conceptual statement and attributes	• ensuring the proposal shows clear links between the requirements, end users and resources required. This includes justifying, with evidence, that the proposal meets the overall project requirements.

2 Unit by: Wendy Fox-Turnbull 2015 Modified 2020   Planner v 09 by Wendy Fox-Turnbull 2015 adapted from planner by Fiona Haynes, Paul Rodley, Dave Sam and Wendy Turnbull 1997

7. identify and understand relevant aspects of authentic technical practice and demonstrating understanding of and skill in basic concepts of a web site	interview a web designer in action while s/he constructs a basic web page. Practice basic techniques by constructing a mini site.	NT:CTO TP:TS	Define key procedures and mini site with three features	**When creating a digital media outcome students need to demonstrate that they can:** • use appropriate features of digital media software to edit and integrate digital media types to create a digital media outcome
8. discuss interactions between a technological outcomes and people	debate the function of website and role it plays in today's society	NT:CT	Class debate: Topic "Websites enhance business"	
9. recognise key functions of a specific digital technological outcome	identify and explore 4 favourite websites for each list and explain the key functions	NT:CTO	Explanation of key functions	• apply formatting techniques, design elements, and data integrity and testing procedures, to ensure the outcome meets the specifications
10. demonstrate understanding of coding of websites	undertake an exercise of developing coding for a basic website	TK:TS PO4	Coding for website	• follow legal, ethical, and moral responsibilities as appropriate to the outcome
11. demonstrate understanding that some digital technologies are a combinations of products and systems	re-explore 4 favourite websites for each identify two key products and underlying systems within	NT:CT	Tabulate products and systems within one website. Justify nature and purpose of each	• show accuracy and independence in the application of techniques and testing procedures
12. investigate people's opinions about the balance between the need for functional fitness for purpose and the aesthetic element of design	interview website users on how their views of aesthetics and function impact on their webpage use then explore a poorly functioning website and discuss the issues in relation to functionality and aesthetics	TK:TP	Class discussion about the issues of functionality versus aesthetics	• undertake techniques and testing procedures in a manner that economises the use of resources in the digital media outcome's production and use.
13. interview client to identify specific needs for intended outcome	interview president of HH to identify specific needs for their website	TP:BD	Interview questions and answers	
14. modify initial brief' conceptual statement and attributes according to new information gathered	modify initial brief conceptual statement with attributes and specifications for Hobbit's Harriers Website	TP:BD	Modified initial brief	
15. generate three design ideas that are informed on research to date and justify critically analyse each to determine final selection	Storyboard three potential designs for the Hobbit Harrier's web site. Write pros and cons for each one a identify preferred option	TP:ODE	Story board for each with pros , cons and preferred option identified	

3 Unit by: Wendy Fox-Turnbull 2015 Modified 2020   Planner v 09 by Wendy Fox-Turnbull 2015 adapted from planner by Fiona Haynes, Paul Rodley, Dave Sam and Wendy Turnbull 1997

Figure 4.22 (Continued)

160 *Implementing the technology curriculum*

16. investigate and identify three reasons functional modelling is undertaken	justify the advantages of modelling there options of the website before selecting the final one to be developed purpose of modelling	TK:TM	Poster to explain the advantages of functional modelling	Evidence to show that students can use basic iterative processes to develop a refined digital outcome includes
17. mock up main aspects of the final outcome to refine ideas	mock-up each page of the website and evaluate against attributes to refine ideas	TP:ODE	Mocked up web page	• planning a digital outcome to address a problem, need, opportunity, or interest
18. write remaining attributes and specifications for intended outcome taking into account previous research and investigation	refine existing and add other relevant attributes and specifications for Hobbit's Harriers taking into account their interview and website research	TP:BD	Updated brief with final specifications	• managing the development by decomposing the digital outcome into smaller components • trialling components of the outcome in an iterative manner • testing that the digital outcome functions as
19. develop working prototype	develop working prototype of website	TP:ODE	Working prototype	intended • describing relevant implications • using information from testing and trialling to
20. present to and receive feedback from client	present to Hobbit's Harriers committee and ask for specific feedback	TP:ODE	Action feedback in website	improve the outcome • trialling multiple components and/or techniques and selecting the most suitable
21. complete a detailed final brief with very detailed specifications	complete a detailed final brief with very detailed specifications for the Hobbit's Harriers Website	TP:BD	Final brief	• addressing relevant implications • sketches, wireframes or mock-ups of the outcome
22. undertake testing procedures in a manner that economises the use of time in the outcome's use	construct final website to meet the final brief and test it to ensure efficiency of use	TP:ODE	Completed Web page	
23. undertake a final check of technological outcome according to specifications	check final website and make live	TP:ODE	Completed Web page	

4 Unit by: Wendy Fox-Turnbull 2015 Modified 2020   Planner v 09 by Wendy Fox-Turnbull 2015 adapted from planner by Fiona Haynes, Paul Rodley, Dave Sim and Wendy Turnbull 1997

Links to Key Competencies: **Thinking:** Discovering an issue, developing a concept and proposal, determining a suitable solution **Relating to others:** Designing something that is fit-for-purpose, something that other people will be able to interpret and understand (solves the issue); interviewing stakeholders, dialogue with web designer, debate in class **Using language, symbols, and texts:** When creating a website, understanding how text, symbols and pictures combine for effective communication **Managing self:** Maintaining assessment documentation throughout the project, meeting checkpoints and submitting work on time **Participating and contributing:** Engaging in class activities	**Links to Curriculum Areas:** *Highlight and explain* **The Arts:** Key design principles **English:** Debating **Health and PE** **Learning Languages** **Mathematics and Statistics** **Science** **Social Sciences**	
Organisation Class and Students Class may need to be taken in a computer lab with an adjoining work space Students to work in pairs. Individual portfolios will reflect the aspects of technology practice of each student	**Links to Tātaiako** **Ako:** Practice in the classroom and beyond **Wananga:** Communication, problem solving, innovation **Whanaungatanga:** Relationships with both peers and stakeholders/users **Tangata Whenuatanga:** Place-based, socio-cultural awareness and knowledge **Manaakitanga:** Values - integrity, trust, sincerity, equity	**Values:** **excellence**, by aiming high and by persevering in the face of difficulties **innovation**, inquiry, and curiosity, by thinking critically, creatively, and reflectively **community and participation** for the common good **integrity**, which involves being honest, responsible, and accountable and acting ethically
Unit Evaluation *(to be written post–teaching) In this space annotate what changes need to be made next time you teach this unit of work.*		

5 Unit by: Wendy Fox-Turnbull 2015 Modified 2020   Planner v 09 by Wendy Fox-Turnbull 2015 adapted from planner by Fiona Haynes, Paul Rodley, Dave Sim and Wendy Turnbull 1997

Figure 4.22 (Continued)

Conceptual statement

The immediate context is established through a conceptual statement (later transferred to the given brief teachers write for their students). This has two parts, the first identifies the scenario that outlines the technological issue to be solved – the scenario or situation and the second briefly describes the need or what the students need to develop.

Materials and resources

The materials and resources that will be required during the implementation of the unit. The more detailed this section is, the easier the unit is to implement.

Learning needs and special considerations

The special considerations and support need to assist all students within the class referring to specific individuals if necessary as well as whole class needs.

Technological area

Identification of the technological area within which the unit is situated occurs next. Primary students must be exposed to all five technological areas multiple times over their time in Years 1–8. In secondary settings, teachers may well be specialised in one or two technological areas. Technology units frequently sit across more than one technological area, such as developing an electronic watering system for a garden will draw on knowledge and skills from designing and developing both digital and materials outcomes. A technological area learning focus means specific skills and knowledge unique to the identified technological area are taught explicitly. There may well be other incidental learning from other technological areas as units progress. On the planner, name and justify the key technological area in the appropriate section.

Big Understanding/enduring learning

Identify the "Big Understanding." This is the learning that teachers want the students to take away from this unit. We like to think of this as what we want the students to remember in 20 years' time. For example, they may not remember how to design and make a filter for water but they will remember that "people are able to improve natural resources for human consumption." The "big understanding" may also be linked to the need and context. For example, if the children are completing a playground unit the big understanding might be "the made-world is constructed to meet needs and wants."

Unit summary

A unit summary or overview is also written on the first page of the planner. This can come straight from the completed pathway and is best set out as bulleted episodes of learning.

162 *Implementing the technology curriculum*

Safety considerations

All safety considerations for the unit must be identified on the planner. If the unit has few hazards then this section will be sufficient; however, in a unit with numerous hazards, a more detailed plan will need to be completed and referred to in this health and safety section of the planner. Details on how to do this can be found in the Ministry of Education's Safety in Technology Education: A Guidance Manual for Schools. This is very important as teachers need "to be taking all reasonable precautions." By identifying hazards on the unit planner, teachers can prove that they were aware of the hazards. This must also be reflected within learning of the unit and often leads to specific teaching especially in the use of some equipment. For example, if you have identified the use of the hot glue gun as a hazard and you know the children have not used it before, you must include glue gun use and safety within your learning intentions and experiences.

Middle pages

Expansion of identified learning occurs on pages 2 and 3 of the planner. Each aspect of the pathway is expanded into a "lesson slice" (Table 4.6), the learning intention with a learning experience to explain how the students will learn what is intended, the strand and AO within which the learning is situated, evidence of learning that is produced as an integral part of the planned activity and success criteria describing successful learning.

Learning intentions

The identification and writing of clear learning intentions informs students of the TK and skills that are the focus of their learning within any one lesson. Teachers consider the knowledge (conceptual, procedural, societal) and skills (technical

Table 4.6 The lesson slice

Context-free learning intention (LI)	Learning experience (LE)	Links to NZC Strand: AO POs	Technological learning evidence (TLE)	Success criteria (SC)
What is the technology learning to enable students the required skills and knowledge to successfully complete their technology practice?	What will the students do to learn the intended learning? Experiences should be varied and allow for expert and community input	Identify the achievement object situated with a strand and a PO (if in the digital space) being meeting through the learning intention and experience	What will be developed to assess whether students have met the intended learning? This is tangible evidence	What will successful learning look like?

Implementing the technology curriculum 163

and information) students require. Learning intentions are written sequentially for teaching and are matched 1–1 with learning experiences and technological learning evidence. A learning intention (LI – sometimes called learning objective) is a statement of the intended learning of the lesson. One is written for each aspect of the pathway and also noted sequentially (order of teaching). There are several points for consideration here. Technology practice will be the focus of most units. Learning situated in the strands NT and TK enhance and expand students' understanding, knowledge and skills in areas that will inform their TP. Learning situated within the CT technological area should develop students' knowledge and skills to enable them to design and develop digital outcomes. Learning intentions should be context free in nature. Consideration must be given to the learning needs of the students. All classes have students working across a range of levels with multiple starting points. Keep in mind the immediate context, and the technological area identified. Later in this section we explore the concept of context-free learning intentions further.

In the writing of quality learning intentions, teachers need to be conversant with formative assessment practices and principles. Students should take a significant role in their learning. It is therefore vital when planning a technology unit that learning is focused on technological learning. It is easy to get distracted, especially if the context is particularly engaging or exciting. To assist this focus, learning intentions for generic knowledge are context free. This does not mean that the context is not important, it is absolutely vital and given as the whole unit is contextually situated. Therefore, an opportunity occurs to separate technological learning from the context.

Context-free learning intentions and questioning increase students' involvement as they become more aware of the purpose, intent and scope of their learning. By making learning intentions explicit, teachers tend to focus more on actual learning than the activity or experience being used to stimulate student thinking. When writing learning intentions for specific TK and skills, it is easy to muddle context and technological learning so that neither become clear – developing "mucky brown paint" scenario rather than a clear pool of "curriculum colour" – because technological learning gets buried in busy activity related to context. The separation of learning intention and context ensures that students and teachers focus on technological learning and can have a dramatic effect on teaching and learning. Context becomes the "vehicle" through which learning occurs. Examples of context-free learning intentions in technology are given in Table 4.7.

Making the learning intentions and the context explicit facilitates the transfer of skills and knowledge to other contexts within, and across, learning areas. Table 4.8 gives examples of learning intentions muddled with their context and then separated to illustrate the clarity of learning that occurs when technology learning is separated from the context. At the bottom of the table we have left space for you to have a go at separating some muddled learning intentions.

To assist in the writing of the context-free learning intentions above, we drew on the Indicators of Progression or Technology Indicators found in Technology

164 *Implementing the technology curriculum*

Table 4.7 Learning intentions with context separated

Learning intention *Students are learning to.....*	*Context*
describe examples to illustrate the strengths and weaknesses of TM for risk mitigation (NZCL7, TK:TM)	School senior ball gown/ prom dress
use planning tools to manage time, identify and record key stages, associated resources, and actions to be undertaken, with progress review points clearly indicated (NZC, L4, TP:PP)	Meals for the elderly living at home
understand how the physical and functional nature of an outcome impacts on performance (NZC, L2, TK:PP)	Wooden JigSaw puzzles for an early childhood centre
explore critical environment issues and impacts of a commonly used technology (NZC, L6, NT:CTO)	Cell phones
draw 3D detailed plans of a structure using a suitable software programme (NZC, L3, TP:ODE)	A hutch for a rabbit
develop a feasible technological outcome that is justified through functional modelling and evidence from multiple stakeholders and test for a specific client from a range of perspectives: safety, user friendliness, fitness-for-purpose (NZ C, L8, TP:ODE)	Webpage for a local institution/club

Table 4.8 Muddled and contest-free learning intentions

Muddled learning intention with context *The students are learning to*	*Separated LT* *The students are learning to*	*NZC level, strand:AO*	*Immediate context*
develop a functional model of an improved potato peeler	develop a functional model of an improved commonly used device to meet a specific need	TP:ODE L4	Potato peeler
develop critical paths to plan what they need to complete their school production props	identify key stages, and resources required at each stage to ensure completion of an outcome is completed	TP:PP L3	School production props
critique the role of solar powered cars in the development of sustainable environments	critique the role of technology in the development of sustainable environments	NT:CTO L8	Solar car
establish the specifications for "Bed and Breakfast" pamphlets to address the needs of Mr and Mrs Fox	establish the specifications for an outcome to address the needs of the client in consideration of resources available	TP:BPL6	Bed and breakfast pamphlets
identify what does into a compost heap and what good compost should look like	identify the input/s and output/s of particular technological systems in an organic/living environment	TK:TS L1	The compost heap

Implementing the technology curriculum 165

Online. This is a very valuable resource that should be at the teacher's side when they plan. The other very useful resource is the POs in digital technologies. For example, from PO2 in CT "use algorithms to create simple programs involving outputs and sequencing" makes a perfect Learning Intention for TK:TS at L3 NZC (Students will: understand that technological systems are represented by symbolic language tools and understand the role played by the "black box" in technological systems).

Learning experiences

The learning experience (LE) will enable the students to meet the necessary learning intention. The learning experience is the activity that students experience that will allow the necessary learning about TP, concepts, processes and principles to occur. Over the course of a unit, students should experience a range of experiences. These might include such things as a visit, or visitor, research, interviewing, practical tasks to develop skills, oral and written activities, reflections or investigation.

Links to NZC achievement: strands objectives progress outcomes

Identify links from the learning intentions and learning experiences to the strands and AOs and POs identified in NZC. One learning intention and related experience may have links to more than one strand and several AOs or an AO and PO. What is important is that the students experience the full nature of TP rather than forcing learning into AOs that may not be essential to the process undertaken. This is why in technology we consider the necessary learning related to holistic technology practice before we situate the learning within the AO and PO.

Technological learning evidence

Next step is to consider and identify the evidence of learning the students will produce as an integral part of their learning. Each learning intention and associated experience usually produces some form of tangible evidence of learning. This technological learning evidence (TLE) provides proof of learning for the teacher and students themselves. They may include such things as: posters, charts and tables, interviews, written summaries or reviews, recorded discussions or oral explanations, concept maps, rough sketches, annotated drawings, 2D and 3D planning, role plays, debates, mock-ups, prototypes and developed technological outcomes. These can be used formatively or summatively for assessment when clear specific criteria have been identified.

On the planner, just identify the actual evidence only. Don't rewrite the learning experience. One or two words is enough! Remember TLE should be

166 *Implementing the technology curriculum*

tangible (written, oral, visual, dramatic, graphical) evidence that the learning has occurred and is able to be used for assessment if required. No extra assessment tasks should be needed in technology except in senior secondary for aspects of NCEA.

Achievement success criteria

The next step is to identify two or three key stages throughout the unit that learning needs to be assessed. In technology, it is not necessary to assess all learning intentions. We tend to cluster them together for assessment. For assessment purposes specific success criteria will describe and facilitate what we are looking for in the evidence of learning. Teachers need to consider what their students need to be able to do or know so that they can move on to the next learning outcome or aspect of their technology practice. At each key stage, determine and write specific criteria to be used as a measure of students' achievement. Write these in the Success Criteria column. One set of criteria may be used to assess more than one learning intention. Use the evidence of learning to assess how well the student has met the learning intentions clustered at each key stage.

The identification of where the key stages within each unit will be determined by a number of factors. In some cases, a key stage will occur at the point that enables a decision to be made about whether the students are physically or cognitively able to continue with the next step. This is especially the case with technical and procedural knowledge and information management knowledge or skills. A key stage might assess students' conceptual and societal knowledge. Teachers may ask themselves whether the students understand enough about their immediate context, existing technologies or stakeholders' views to continue on the path to successful learning. In other cases, they will determine the quality or success of the learning or technological outcome.

The criteria should be placed in a position so that they allow teachers and students to assess a range of learning rather than relating to specific AOs. When good quality success criteria are written they allow teachers and students to assess by determining whether the criteria have been met or to what degree they have been met. When writing criteria, teachers should consider very carefully the purpose of the learning experience or experiences. To do this they need to consider the knowledge (conceptual, procedural, societal, technical) that is essential and desirable to their students' TP within the unit. Once identified by the teacher in the unit plan, teachers are in a better position to facilitate student engagement in their learning. They should be highlighted to students and displayed during teaching episodes, and even co-constructed with the students. Co-construction can be achieved by using examples of successful learning or contrasting examples of learning from previous years, giving students an opportunity to identify what success looks, feels, sounds, tastes like. The co-construction of success criteria with the students assists students' engagement and motivation.

Back page

The final page in the unit planner template identifies the consideration of potentially critical links related to the wider NZC. It also offers a space to evaluate teaching and students' learning and offers a space to suggest changes to teaching and learning or the unit structure should it be taught again.

Links to NZC key competencies and values

This is where the teacher identifies links to the key competencies. These will be related to the needs of the class and they are often linked into whole class programmes, syndicate programmes, and in some schools, whole school programmes. Teaching of the key competencies may take place within the unit.

Links to NZC learning areas

In this section the teacher identifies links to other curriculum areas. Technology is a perfect vehicle for curriculum integration and can be a true motivation for learning skills and knowledge from other areas as students are able to see and make real-world connections to a wide range of skills and knowledge.

Bicultural considerations

Using the earlier section Bicultural Perspectives and Considerations as a guide, consider ways Māori Tikanga, values, technologies, technologists and te reo can be seamlessly integrated into the students' technology practice and wider learning to enhance learning for all.

Unit evaluation

The final section on the unit planner is a post-teaching evaluation of teaching and learning. Evaluating teaching and learning should not be confused with assessment. Assessment, both formative and summative, is about the specific learning and progress of individuals.

Evaluation of teaching and learning is more holistic. It draws on a range of sources of information including assessment data, teacher observations, conversations with colleagues, students' attitudes and opinions, among others. There are two aspects to unit evaluations, teaching and students' learning. We use questions to assist our reflection and suggest improvements for future teaching. Below are some questions you might use to guide your unit evaluations. The list is by no means exhaustive.

Teaching

- How well did the unit support the principles of the Treaty of Waitangi?
- Where the activities targeted at the students' needs?
- Where the students engaged and motivated during the unit?
- Was the unit resourced in a timely and appropriate fashion?

168 *Implementing the technology curriculum*

- Were the learning intentions clear and articulated to students?
- What barriers were encountered during the unit?
- How might these barriers be mitigated or avoided?
- Were students of all levels catered for?
- Did the unit include wider community or expert input?
- Did teacher questioning facilitate wider level thinking and learning?
- What could have been done better?
- What went really well?

Students' learning

- Were the needs of Māori learners met?
- How well did the student achieve in the unit?
- Were my relationships with students a barrier or an enhancer to learning?
- Were the activities and learning intentions pitched at the correct level?
- Did the students achieve the intended learning?
- How were high achieving students extended?
- How were low achieving students assisted?
- How well were diverse learners and students from all cultural backgrounds included in the learning process?

Word to the wise

A school's organisational structure and teachers' perceptions and beliefs about the purpose of technology education can lead to contradictions in the ways technology is perceived, valued, timetabled and taught, and the way three strands: NT, TK, TP are interpreted and enacted. These contradictions can be represented as the following:

- as a disparity between teachers' espoused perceptions and practice;
- in differing ways of thinking and attitudes towards technology education;
- through teachers' capacity to make meaning of the curriculum;
- teachers' ability to take pedagogical risks, replicate, or retreat to previously established practice;
- by senior management who direct prejudged students to, or from, "manual subjects";
- by senior management who timetable technology to clash with "academic" subjects effectively forcing students to select technology or not over other critical subjects;
- the prioritisation of literacy and numeracy as more important but separate to technology;
- by teachers who make decisions about the learning context, in consultation with students;
- by teachers who emphasise the development of practical skills with the view to manufacture high quality products and systems, and to accommodate community expectations.

Implementing the technology curriculum 169

The ways that technology education is represented in a school are likely to reflect any of the above list and impact the nature of the programmes of work that students are exposed to. In junior secondary schools, programmes of work need to be carefully planned to support students' developing understandings and experiences in a range of technological areas. If schools have a more traditional approach to learning, students are likely to rotate between four technological areas in Year 9, spending approximately a term in each. The rationale for this is that students are then well positioned to choose a technological area in Year 10.

An alternative approach to programme design has been observed more recently in the Innovative Learning Environment schools. In these schools, there can be a shared focus (e.g. through Impact projects), and teachers work collaboratively, in pairs or larger groups, to address the curriculum. Such approaches have seen a trend where Principals in secondary schools are seeking Primary trained teachers who have traditionally had a wider understanding of the differing learning areas and think more holistically about the curriculum.

We advocate for a coordinated approach to technology programme design in primary and secondary schools alike. During their years through primary school students should experience technology through all five technological areas multiple times (3–4 over eight years) in a range of authentic immediate contexts. This approach requires planning and liaison between primary and intermediate schools or specialist technology centres. When students move from primary to intermediate it is very important that their new technology teachers move them forward from where they are at rather than assuming all students have had limited technology learning. Students should enter intermediate at Levels 3 or 4 of NZC. The same applies as students' transition into secondary school. Technology is a compulsory curriculum until the end of Year 10. Technology departments should plan and develop programmes of work based on the curriculum components to ensure coverage and progression occurs for all students regardless of the technological areas within which they work. For example, no matter whether a student is in food technology, resistance materials or digital technologies the planned programme should plan for all students to cover the same AOs each term. Typically, Year 9 students rotate through a range of technological areas and may select two options in Year 10.

Technology education in early childhood

How and why students' progress in their technological thinking in the early childhood sector is less defined and structured than in the primary and secondary sectors. Guy Claxton and Margaret Carr suggest three adverbial dimensions: robustness, breadth and richness, which can assist teachers when assessing students' understandings of technology and developing their TP. First, robustness can be thought of as a tendency to respond to learning in a positive way when conditions for learning are not as supportive as they once were. Robustness is a matter of tolerating and managing the emotions of learning. The second dimension, breadth, is concerned with the understanding that what is learned in one

170 *Implementing the technology curriculum*

domain can be transferred to other settings, sometimes known as knowledge transfer. For example, developing skills in working collaboratively in one area slowly develops into the skill of developing collaborative skills and taking leadership roles is a range of other domains. Richness is the third dimension and involves the development of flexibility and sophistication. In summary the main goals for technology in early childhood are to ensure students gain positive dispositions to exploring and using technology, that they develop resilience when engaging with and learning about new technologies in increasing complex ways and that they understand that skills and knowledge learned in one context may be transferred to other contexts.

Unfortunately, many early childhood teachers are unsure what to teach in technology and are frequently found to have limited understanding of technology education. This is mainly due to the fact that few have professional experience in technology education. ECE is based on a holistic approach to education, with care, socialising and learning at the heart of programmes. ECE also offers a holistic approach to technology. Technology education is not taught specifically as it is in the primary and secondary sectors; however, technology is both implicitly and explicitly mentioned in the three ECE curricula (Sweden, England and New Zealand) studied by Wendy Fox-Turnbull in her study into ECE childhood technology. The study identified four common aspects related to the teaching of technology within ECE settings. These aspects are student engagement in:

- exploration of the made-world;
- communication of ideas about the made-world;
- independent engagement in and with technology;
- contribution to the made-world through making and construction in a range of contexts with a range of materials.

Teachers in early childhood centres are encouraged to give their students opportunities to engage with and develop cultural heritage values, traditions, language and knowledge, to be reflective and to work collaboratively. The study also identified a number of desirable skills and dispositions within ECE curricula for example curiosity and initiative. These are all critical components in technology practice.

Summary

This chapter has provided a detailed explanation of how technology is organised in NZC and implemented. Detailed explanation of critical aspects and components provides insight into the intent of the curriculum. The detailed explanation and modelling of the unit planning process enables student teachers and teacher new to New Zealand to undertake the process themselves. Careful scaffolding of this process facilitates thorough planning to meet the needs of technology in NZC. The unit planning process is illustrated by the modelling of two units of work, one at NZC Level 1, the other at Level 6 through each stage in the unit planning process. The recommended process outlined in this chapter is especially important for less experienced teachers as it scaffolds teacher thinking to ensure units are planned to enable our students to design and develop quality technological outcomes situated within need-based authentic contexts.

Bibliography

Black, P., & Wiliam, D. (1998). *Inside the black box – raising standards through classroom assessment* (1st ed.). King's College.

Clarke, S. (2005). *Formative assessment in action: Weaving the elements together.* Hodder Murray.

Clarke, S. (2008). *Active learning through formative assessment.* Hodder Education.

Claxton, G., & Carr, M. (2010). A framework for teaching learning: The dynamics of disposition. *Early Years: An International Journal, 24*(1), 87–97.

Curriculum Advisory Group. (2017). *Curriculum advisory group report: Digital technologies/hangarau matihiko.* http://education.govt.nz/assets/Documents/dthm/Nov-17-update/Digital-Curriculum-Consultation-CAG-Report.pdf.

Darling-Hammond, L. (2008). *Powerful learning.* Jossey-Bass.

Department of Education. (2014). *Statutory framework for the early years foundation stage: setting the standards for learning, development and care for children from birth to five.* Department of Education. https://www.gov.uk/government/uploads/system/uploads/attachment_data/file/335504/EYFS_framework_from_1_September_2014__with_clarification_note.pdf [Record #704 is using a reference type undefined in this output style.].

Fox-Turnbull, W. (2012). Learning in technology. In P. J. Williams (Ed.), *Technology education for teachers.* Sense Publishers.

Fox-Turnbull, W. (2018). Implementing digital technology in the New Zealand curriculum. *Australasian Journal of Technology Education, 5,* 1–18.

Glatthorn, A., Boschee, F., & Whitehead, B. (2009). *Curriculum leadership: Strategies for development and implementation.* Sage Publications.

Grimsey, G., & Phillipps, M. (2008). *Evaluation of technology achievement standards for use in New Zealand secondary school computing education: A critical report.* https://itp.nz/Activities/Reforming-Education.

Jenkins, M. (2017). *Digital technologies/Hangarau Matihiko consultation final report.* http://education.govt.nz/assets/Documents/dthm/Nov-17-update/Martin-Jenkins-DT-HM-consultation-report.pdf.

McGee, C. (2011). Teachers and curriculum decisions. In *The professional practice of teaching* (pp. 76–96). Cengage Learning.

Ministry of Education. *Technology Online: Technology in the NZC.* Retrieved 13 July from https://technology.tki.org.nz/Technology-in-the-NZC.

Ministry of Education (1995). *Technology in the New Zealand curriculum.* Learning Media.

Ministry of Education (2007). *The New Zealand curriculum.* Learning Media.

Ministry of Education. (2017a). *Digital technologies – Hangarau Matihiki, draft for consultation.* MinistryofEducation.https://education.govt.nz/assets/Documents/Ministry/consultations/DT-consultation/DTCP1701-Digital-Technologies-Hangarau-Matihiko-ENG.pdf.

172   *Implementing the technology curriculum*

Ministry of Education. (2017b). *Strengthening digital technologies Hangarau Matihiko in the curriculum*. Retrieved 3 November from https://www.education.govt.nz/ministry-of-education/consultations-and-reviews/digital-technology-consultation/.

Ministry of Education. (2017c). *Te whāriki a te kōhanga reo*. Ministry of Education.

Ministry of Education. (2017d). *Technology in the New Zealand curriculum*. Ministry of Education. Retrieved 20 February from http://nzcurriculum.tki.org.nz/The-New-Zealand-Curriculum/Technology.

Moreland, J., Jones, A., & Chambers, M. (2001). *Enhancing student learning in technology through teacher technological literacy*. University of Waikato.

Skolverket. (2010). *Curriculum for the preschool Lpfö 98 revised 2010*. Fritzes Kundservice.

Snape, P., & Fox-Turnbull, W. (2013). Perspectives of authenticity: Implementation in technology education. *International Journal of Technology and Design Education, 23*(1), 51–68. https://doi.org/dx.doi.org/10.1007/s10798-011-9168-2.

Stables, K., & Kimbell, R. (2000). Unorthodox methodologies: Approaches to understanding design and technology. In Marc de Vries & I. Mottier (Eds.), *International handbook of technology education: Reviewing the past twenty years* (pp. 313–330). Sense Publishers.

Starkey, L. (2016). An equitable curriculum for a digital age. *Curriculum Matters, 12*, 29–45.

Te Tāhuhu O Te Mātauranga, (2008, 2017). *Te Marautanga o Aotearoa*, Te Tāhuhu O Te Mātauranga, Ministry of Education.

5 Classroom narrative

This chapter introduces you to students' experiences in technology. Alongside this, is a narrative from teachers, to illustrate professional thinking and the knowledge and skills required to inform teaching practice in culturally situated school contexts. Technological practice is a means to realise students' thinking and design ideas in order to solve technological problems. This chapter is organised as a narrative in which two fictitious children work their way through early childhood education (ECE), primary and secondary schools. Some of the units are loosely based on actual experiences of the authors. The children's experiences and activities in technology education are described. In parallel to this will be a teacher's dialogue about the planning and thinking that has gone into the technology learning undertaken by the students. Our narrative begins when our two imaginary children who are in their last year in ECE (Early Years). It then tracks them through their technology learning in Years 1–3 (Junior Primary School), Years 4–6 (Middle Primary School), Years 7–8 (Intermediate School), Years 9–10 (Lower Secondary School) and Years 11–13 (Senior Secondary School). Our children, Cooper and Aria, are four years old when our narrative begins. Cooper is a European male and Aria a Māori female.

Early years (4 years old)

Cooper and Aria played together in the sandpit building a house with a garage and two doors. After playing in the sandpit for 30 minutes, Aria moved on to build a roadway and garage from blocks with another friend Imran. Aria and Imran drove their ride-on cars all around their newly constructed roads. Later they gathered two more friends, Lotty and Yung, to help build several more roads and houses.

Cooper and Kaleb then joined the group to help make a bridge over their "river" so they were able to take their cars over it. Mary and Aroha, Centre staff, assisted the children, helping them to imagine a stream and to identify that a bridge might help cars navigate it.

After lunch, Aria and Cooper played a matching game called "Memories" on one of the computer laptops. Aria had trouble navigating the digital mouse. She started to get angry and began to cry. Mary talked to her about taking time to

174 *Classroom narrative*

Figure 5.1 Examples of pull-along toys

learn new skills and that having trouble was perfectly normal. She suggested that Aria's skills would improve if she practised and tried not to get angry. Cooper comforted Aria and assisted her to learn this new skill.

In the afternoons, over a period of a week, the staff introduced a challenge to the older children by announcing that the following week the Centre was going to have a series of "pull-along" toy races and that the children themselves could make their own toys for race day. This learning brought back happy memories for Aria, when she played with the Pōtaka tā with her Koro. On the first day, the staff had a range of pull-along toys for the children to play with, similar to those illustrated in Figure 5.1.

With Mary and Aroha the following day, the children explored the pull-along toys to see what features made them "pull-along" toys. The children told their teachers that the toys needed a string to hold on to and that they all had wheels. They told their teachers that the toys looked like animals, and cars, and trains. The teachers asked the children what they noticed about the wheels. Cooper had noticed that the wheels went "round and round." Aria told Aroha that she noticed that most of the toys were colourful and fun to play with.

On the third day, the teachers took the four-year olds, including Cooper and Aria, for a walk around the block from their Centre to look at other turning wheels. Aria noticed that when the car wheels turned the cars moved as well. Aroha asked the children if the cars went round and round like the wheels. Cooper noticed that they didn't go around but went along. Back at the Centre, the children were able to identify that the wheels on the pull-along toys helped them move along as the children pulled them. The next day, the children were given a range of small boxes, wheels, axles and other materials to explore and experiment with. Cooper noticed that only the wheels went around and that an axle joined two wheels. The children had fun putting together pairs of wheels which they then put aside to use on their pull-along toys later. Finally, on the fifth day, the children were given a range of materials including grocery boxes, kitchen rolls, cardboard, large buttons and sticky tape to build a pull-along toy for their race. Aria opted to draw her idea before she made it. Cooper didn't, he went straight to the boxes and started to join them together with a sticky tape. The teachers assisted the children with joining materials if needed. Zeeka, another teacher, had a low melt hot glue gun to join some things at the children' request. Later the same day, the children painted their toys and then they were attached a string to the front. Early the next week, both Cooper and Aria took place in a carefully planned and managed pull-along toy race. Afterwards the children were able to tell their teachers that their toys were made by them, that they all had wheels and string and that some toys were better than others.

Teacher commentary

Te Whariki Exploration | Children are critical thinkers, problem solvers and explorers Mana aotūroa | Children see themselves as explorers, able to connect with and care for their own and wider worlds (p. 46).

In this unit, the students were given opportunities to demonstrate a number of key ideas and capabilities from Strand 5 of Te Whāriki – Exploration. These include the capability to solve problems, looking for patterns, classifying and guessing. Initially students were introduced to an example of their made world – the pull-along toy. During their walk around the block, students were given opportunities to classify vehicles with wheels and note patterns in relationship to wheels and movement. They guessed how the wheels might turn and why the whole vehicle does not turn. Back in class, they observed the pull-along toys' movement mechanisms, comparing and explaining what happened when the toys were pulled. The students were given opportunities to plan their ideas and use trial and error to design and build their toys. During this process Mary, Aroha and Zeeka engaged the students in reflective discussion, asking about their designs and design decisions. Students were asked what made their designed creations pull-along toys, what they liked best about their design and why. The students were introduced to the word "technology" as being the "stuff" in their world that has been made by people for a specific reason. The students discussed why they made their toys and what good toys needed and what they help children to do. During this unit, the students were encouraged to pursue a project for a sustained period of time and offered degrees of challenge in construction activities. Curiosity and the ability to inquire into, research, explore, generate and modify working theories about the human-made world is a key to students meeting goals and learning outcomes identified in the exploration strand of TeWhariki.

Education (Early Childhood Services) Regulations 2008 require all licensed providers to take all reasonable steps to keep students safe. In order for teachers to take the students out of their ECE Centres, teachers need to check the policy of their Centre and undertake all critical steps, identified in that plan and by the Ministry of Education.

Years 1–3 (5–7 years old)

During their first three years at school, Aria and Cooper participated in one technology unit each year. This section describes two of these units, followed by the associated teacher commentary.

176 *Classroom narrative*

Flugs

Early in the school year, the city where Cooper and Aria lived was hit by a significant natural disaster. The children in the class were stressed and missed their parents during the school day and asked their teacher Miss Maxwell if they could make some cuddly toys for their classroom. Miss Maxwell thought it was a wonderful idea and suggested to the children that they also design their fluffy toys. Miss Maxwell explained that designing meant that the students could plan the colours, shapes and fabrics for their proposed toys and that all the toys would be unique. The class with Miss Maxwell decided that their toys would be fluffy, ugly monsters or "Flugs," and that they needed to be friendly – like some Taniwha. Miss Maxwell reminded the class that in Māori mythology, taniwha could live in dark caves, or even the sea, where there were dangerous currents or giant waves.

Aria wondered about the *life* of her flug and wondered what materials she would use to make it. She remembered her Koro saying that she needed to treat all things (alive or otherwise) with respect. All students were going to be able to design and make one each.

The first activity required students to bring their favourite soft toys from home to school. Cooper noticed that all the toys had faces with eyes and a nose. Some had mouths and some did not. Aria identified that the toys were soft and cuddly and most had legs, or arms and legs. After a play session with the toys, the children were also able to identify that the toys were small enough for children to carry around, but big enough to give a good cuddle to. They also noticed that most were made of fluffy material.

During the next technology lesson, the students were divided into groups to investigate the properties of different materials. Each group was given a swatch of fabrics to investigate. Cooper's group was asked to check out whether the fabric could be washed and still remain soft and cuddly. They took each sample and washed it in a basin of warm soapy water, rinsed each one, and placed outside to dry. When dry, they talked about how the washed samples had changed. They recorded their findings on a worksheet Miss Maxwell had given them.

Aria's group had two tasks to do with their fabric examples. The first was to rank them from most cuddly to least cuddly. They also recorded these findings on the worksheet Miss Maxwell had given them. After this activity, Aria's mother, Ngatai, assisted the children in Aria's group to undertake a burn test. Ngatai took each sample in a pair of tongs and attempted to burn it by lighting the fabric square with a long-nose lighter. The children watched carefully from a distance but were able to see that some fabrics burnt very quickly, some melted, and others did not burn very well at all. Each group reported their findings to the class and made their recommendations for the best fabrics to use for their toys. The children and Miss Maxwell then listed a few things they needed to think about and plan for when designing their flug.

Classroom narrative   177

The students decided that their toys needed to:

- be soft and cuddly;
- be safe;
- be big enough to cuddle;
- have eyes and a nose;
- have four legs or two arms and legs;
- be washable;
- last a long time.

Next time, during the technology-focused activity, Cooper and Aria drew what they wanted their flug to look like and then Miss Maxwell invited Mr Carnegie, a clothing designer, into the class to talk about making a pattern for their design. The children learned about seam allowances and about making a mock-up in paper – just to check their design would work. Mr Carnegie also showed the children how the material has a good side, on the inside, for cutting and sewing and then how the toys were turned inside out for stuffing. Mr Carnegie told the students that when the seams were on the inside and the fluffy side of the material is on the outside, the toys are neater and cuddlier.

The students then drew their shapes on folded newsprint paper, cut them out, stapled together around the sides and stuffed them with newspaper to mock-up their design ideas. Aria noticed that the arms in her mock-up were too skinny and too hard to stuff, so when she made her final design she made the arms wider. Cooper initially decided he wanted his flug to be made of brown fur fabric but after seeing some of the colours available in polar fleece he changed his mind and went for blue instead.

Once the students had finalised their pattern, the children pinned them onto the fabric and cut out their flugs. The children learned that making a mock-up helped them realise what shapes and designs would work and which would not and that their final flugs were better because of it. Miss. Maxwell and Cooper's dad (Tane) brought their sewing machines to school that day and as the students finished cutting out their flugs the adults sewed the seams leaving a 57-cm gap so the children could turn their flugs the correct way. Before the flugs could be sewn some children had to add ears and hair into the inside to be sewn into the seam.

Later in the week, the children were very excited because it was the school Grandparents' Day. Aria had three of her grandparents attend, Grammy, Koro and Nanny. Cooper's grandparents all lived in the North Island so he didn't have any at school that day but it didn't matter because Aria's Grammy helped him. When the grandparents arrived in the class, each child was assigned a helper. The grandparents took guidance from the children and used the drawings to guide the sewing on of external features such as buttons, patches, mouths and ears. Once completed, the children stuffed their flugs with a material called Dacron and the grandparents then helped to sew up the "stuffing hole."

178   *Classroom narrative*

Afterwards, all the flugs lived in the library and when Cooper, Aria and the other class members needed a cuddle because another earthquake occurred or because they were sad, they were able to get a hug, no questions asked.

Teacher commentary

This unit was situated within the technological area of designing and developing materials outcomes (DDMO). Students undertook purposeful investigation in relation to the properties of suitable materials for stuffed toys. The unit was actually taught in Christchurch although obviously Aria and Cooper, our fictional characters were not actually involved. The flugs unit was an excellent example of an authentic context for learning. Students were highly motivated, as they perceived that there is a real and purposeful need for the intended outcome. The Christchurch Earthquake severely affected the lives of the children in Christchurch. Many lost homes, some lost loved ones and all experienced ongoing aftershocks with associated stress.

There are several resources available to teachers, to assist them to work with children then they are coming to terms with traumatic or life-changing events (e.g. Hā Ora, a resource website designed for this purpose). Rather than avoiding such significant events, projects like these can help children to find ways of coping with significant and traumatic events in their lives.

More recently, we have experienced the COVID-19 pandemic. Situations such as these can deeply affect children. Engaging the students in an activity that met their needs was a very empowering experience. They were engaged in brief development (BD) and modelling as, after they sketched and mocked up their design, they were able to recognise changes that were needed to alter their brief.

The schools' "Grandparents' day" coincided with the unit. The grandparents were therefore able to assist the students with their sewing. If this was not the case, inviting grandparents or people from a local old people's home to the school for the sewing day would have been an excellent opportunity to involve school and community. When inviting parents, grandparents and other experts into school to assist students with their technology projects, it is important for teachers to brief the adults that all design decisions must be that of the students. The adults are there to follow students' design instructions and to make helpful suggestions. They are not there to do the project for the students. The final focus of this unit was for the students to understand that the flugs they made were a technological outcome and that they were designed for a specific purpose, which in this case was to help them feel comfortable at school after the earthquakes.

In this unit, students were involved in learning across all three strands of the technology curriculum. Learning situated in the nature of technology (NT) strand occurred in the achievement objective (AO) characteristics of technological outcomes (CTO). The students looked at and critiqued existing cuddly toys to identify key characteristics and features of each and in general. They also explored vehicles with wheels on their walk about. In the technological knowledge (TK) strand, the students worked in the AO technological modelling (TM) to understand that making a mock-up assisted the success of their final design and in technological products (Tp) to understand that the properties of materials impact on their design decisions and the success of their final outcome. The remainder of the activities were situated with the technological practice (TP) strand in the AO BD when they identified the technological need for something to comfort and the attributes of their flugs. Planning for practice (PP) when learning how a clothing designer does things, identifying the tasks they need to do and resources required to complete flugs on time. Outcome development and evaluation (ODE) when they drew their designs, made their mock-ups, evaluated their designs and made their flugs.

Treasure hunt with Bee-Bot

Easter was approaching and the Easter Bunny came to the class to give the children the Easter Egg farm map with hidden Easter treasure and worker robot bees (Bee-Bots) who could help them find the Easter eggs that he was going to hide on Easter morning. Aria and Cooper were very excited. Easter Bunny told the class that they needed to programme the Bee-Bots to help find the treasure (see Figure 5.2). During the second lesson, the children were shown a video about a robot for the home – Meet Jibo: The Social Robot of the Future.

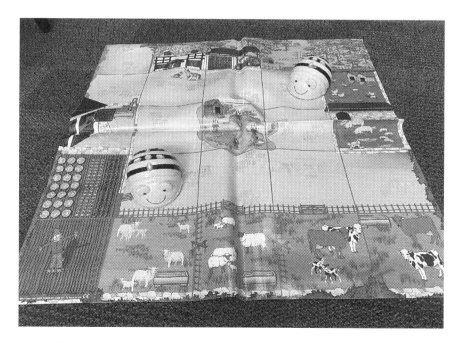

Figure 5.2 Bee-Bots on the farm

180 *Classroom narrative*

Cooper was very excited to see that you could talk to a robot and that it could answer back. Aria was interested to find out that robots could do things for people and thought it would be great to have "Jibo" to provide help in dangerous situations where it would be too risky for humans, such as if there was a natural disaster.

The next day, the students learned about programming computers and giving instructions that needed to be very accurate and in the correct order. In maths they learned about going forward and backwards a specific number of steps. They also learned about turning left and right a quarter turn or 90°. They discovered with four 90° turns and walking the same number of steps between each turn that they could walk in a square.

The Bee-Bots arrived in class later the same day and the students were taught how to make the Bee-Bots travel in a square just the way they did in maths that morning. They also investigated how to make the Bee-Bots do left and right turns. They then had to write three or four instructions in a row and then give these instructions to the Bee-Bots. They found out that these instructions for the robot became its programme and that all computers needed programmes to tell them what to do or how to do it. Early in the second week of the unit, the students were introduced to a large transparent grid of 30 cm × 30 cm plastic squares that was put on the classroom floor. Initially the students practised telling a partner to move across the grip according to the instructions they gave. This was exemplified by Cooper who told Aria to "move forward three squares, turn 90° (degree) left, move forward 6 steps, turn 90° right twice, then move forward another five squares and stop."

In the next lesson in groups, the students programmed their robots to travel around a smaller grid (15 cm × 15 cm) in a similar way. Finally, they were ready to have their Easter Bunny Easter Egg hunt. Whaea Ruth, their teacher, drew a map of the school and showed the students where on the map the eggs were hidden. Each group of children then programmed their Bee-Bot to travel from their "classroom" on the mat to the Easter Bunny's treasure. The Easter Bunny came to watch as each group programmed their Bee-Bot to find the treasure. When they were successful, he gave them each an Easter egg.

Teacher commentary

This unit is situated within DDDO and draws on progress outcomes (PO) from computational thinking (CT). The Bee-Bots are an excellent tool to develop early ideas related to computer programming. Many of the skills and knowledge needed also align with mathematics as the students need to understand sequencing instructions and rotation in 90° increments, direction such as forward and back, left and right. This is the beginning of CT and leads to an understanding of computer science. Research suggests that having an understanding of CT and computer science assists people to make critical choices when selecting and using technology. The Bee-Bots unit was an opportunity for the students to begin to understand technological systems (TSs), with inputs and related outputs. Given that the robot was already made, the students were able to develop an understanding that a programme for a computer is also technology and that not all technology is a physical product, or "thing," but are systems also.

The unit demonstrates how the POs in the new digital technological areas work together to enable students to design and develop technological outcomes situated within the three strands of technology. In this unit the students were involved in NT by developing an understanding of what technology is and how and why a robot is technology (CT) and CTO when learning about Jibo (see https://youtu.be/yyLdXY5nUFA). Although Jibo is no longer made, the YouTube segment allowed the students to see the role a robot might play in their lives. In the unit, students also learned about TSs in TK as well as undertaking their own TP in ODE.

Years 4–6 (8–10)

Over the three years Cooper and Aria were in the middle syndicate of their school, they undertook one technology unit in both Years 4 and 6 and two units in Year 5 – five units in total. Two of these units are described in this section.

Savoury yoghurt

Matua Mohammad, the CEO from the local "Oh Dairy Me Diary Company," visited the Year 4 learning space, Cooper and Aria's Year 4 class. She explained to the students that the company was going to experiment with a range of savoury yoghurts. She asked the class to assist her by developing a range of savoury flavoured yoghurts that could be taste tested by the food technologists at the factory. Their teachers Mr Rahed and Mrs Burgen outlined what the students were asked to do on the teacher-given brief outlined in Figure 5.3.

To begin the unit, the students discussed what yoghurt was and shared their experiences with yoghurt. Aria shared that her mum made their yoghurt in a yoghurt maker with water and then added fruity flavours after it was made. Cooper noticed that, at the supermarket, yoghurt was found near the milk and cheese where it was cold. Mrs Burgen shared the story about how the first yoghurt was made accidentally many years ago in Turkey from goat's milk. Next, the class with their teachers wrote a list of the tasks that they thought they might need to do to design and develop the savoury yoghurt. Mr Rahed told the students that they were going to be undertaking technology practice and that identifying the key stages of the process, and the resources needed, was an important part of this. At the beginning of each lesson the students discussed where they were up to and what changes they had made to the task list and why.

After discussion about how to walk on streets and cross roads safely, the next day, the students walked to the local supermarket to look at the existing yoghurts on the shelves. The children had a worksheet to complete while at the supermarket and also listened to the store's manager (Mrs Walker) who talked to them about their yoghurt range. She also showed them some products that

182   *Classroom narrative*

SAVOURY YOGHURT GIVEN BRIEF

Conceptual Statement

Situation/context/issue

There are many people throughout the world, from many cultures who enjoy yoghurt as part of their diet. However, most flavoured yoghurt in the New Zealand market is fruit-based and sweetened with sugar. Not all people enjoy fruit in their yoghurt and some people cannot have sugar. The "Oh!, Dairy Me" Company has approached us to develop a range of savoury flavoured yoghurts.

Technological Need

Develop a new savoury flavoured yoghurt for the "Oh!, Dairy Me" Company that is tasty and will appeal to a range of people who cannot eat fruit or do not like it.

Attributes and Specifications

The given attributes (features) are as follows. The new flavoured yoghurt must:

- ✓ be savoury flavoured;
- ✓ be tasty;
- ✓ be hygienically produced;
- ✓ reflect the company's environmentally friendly philosophy;
- ✓ dairy based.

Figure 5.3 Savoury yoghurt given brief

could be classified as savoury. Back at school, they discussed the things they had noticed about the existing yoghurts such as current flavours, size and shape of containers, and labelling. They then learned how to do taste testing, keeping everyone safe. They learned about how to use a range of senses such as sight, smell, feel and taste to assess the yoghurt. They also learned that they could not share spoons with anyone and that they could not put a licked spoon back into the yoghurt. Aria reminded everyone that they would need to say a karakia mō te kai before they ate. Karakia are prayers or incantations, which can be used to start a meeting (karakia timatanga), close a meeting (karakia whakamutunga) or Bless food (karakia mō te kai).

They then used these new skills to taste test the yoghurts bought from the supermarket, identifying four things that made a good yoghurt. After class discussion, it was agreed that these were that yoghurt needed to taste good, have a smooth texture, look inviting, and not be too sour. Mr Rahed called these attributes and the students added these to their brief. The following day, the students took home a questionnaire (Figure 5.4) to their families so they could get an idea of how yoghurt is used in people's everyday lives.

Classroom narrative   183

What Part Does Yoghurt Play in Your Life?

A survey for the families of pupils in Room X XYZ School

Name:_____(Rm.9 Pupil) Name:_____(Family Member)

Please help us with our yoghurt study by answering the following questions:

1.   **What do you think of Yoghurt? How often would you consume yoghurt? When?**

2.   **Do you use yoghurt in cooking, if so how?**

3.   **What type of yoghurt do you usually buy(e.g. low-fat, plain, flavoured, diary food etc.)? Why?**

4.   **What brand names and size of yoghurt do you usually buy? Why?**

5.   **What flavours of yoghurt do you like best (top two or three)?**

6.   **Are you concerned about ingredients of yoghurt?**

Figure 5.4 Questionnaire taken home

When the questionnaires were returned, the students were put into six groups. Each group was given all the answers to one question. In maths, they learned about bar graphs and practised by creating a bar graph from the results. Each group then shared their findings with the class, their graphs were displayed on the classroom wall. Their maths lesson concluded with the class jointly writing a concluding statement for each question.

In the next technology lesson, the students were introduced to the idea of sweet and savoury flavours. They were given a range of savoury foods (such as grated cheese, carrot, kūmara, onion, capsicum, pūhā, tomato, bacon, cucumber, mint, corn, salmon, olives, pikopiko and chives) to taste and describe. They were then introduced to a number of spices and sauces that enhanced savoury flavours such as turmeric, kawakawa, cardamom, caraway, mustard and tabasco, horopito, Worcestershire and soy sauces. Before the students started the unit, Mr Rahad had sent a note home to parents telling them about the unit and

184 *Classroom narrative*

checking if the students had any food allergies, intolerances, or cultural and religious preferences related to food and food preparation practices. Cooper's dad mentioned that their family did not eat pork products so Mr Rahad made sure that Cooper did not sample the bacon.

Mrs Burgen and Mr Rahad grouped the students, putting Aria and Cooper in the same group, with two other students. In the next lesson, the students continued to use safe taste testing practices to sample a variety of neutral yoghurts, to identify which could be used as the base for the savoury unit. Figure 5.5 shows the results sheet used as the students sampled three neutral yoghurts: home-made yoghurt, yoghurt from a yoghurt maker and a commercial neutral acidophilus yoghurt.

After they had selected their base, each group identified three savoury flavour combinations to try. At the beginning of the next lesson, the students were

---

Taste Test a Yoghurt Base

Name:_____

Date: _____

Technology is age old and forever.

Rate each on a scale of 1-5: 1 being lowest and 5 being highest

Attributes/ Base	A	B	C
Flavour			
Texture			
Colour			
Sourness			
Sweetness			
Aftertaste			

The yoghurt most suitable as a base for our savour yoghurt is _____ because_____

_____

Safety Notes

- **Wash hands thoroughly before working with food**
- **Use each tasting spoon only once**
- **Never put a used spoon back into a container of yoghurt**
- **Do not taste yoghurt if you have dairy allergies**

Figure 5.5 Taste test form used by the students

Classroom narrative   185

reminded about thorough washing of hands and how to prepare food safety, and how to use a knife and grater for chopping and grating. They then made a test batch of base yoghurt flavoured with their three savoury flavour combinations. The students were reminded about how to taste test safely, not sharing spoons or reusing dirty spoons. Mrs Wong revisited the class this day and brought with her one of the company's food technologists. They assisted the students during their testing by giving them feedback on their flavour combinations – thus helping the students' final selection. After this lesson, the food technologist spoke to the students about what food technology is, what a food technologist does, and how and why they do it.

The next day, the students finalised their savoury flavour and wrote their group's final brief giving it to Mr. Rahad so he could make sure he had enough ingredients for the whole class. Two days later, the students made 300 g of their yoghurt. They put the final product into sterilised glass jars and then attached the labels they had made during their literacy class. The final products were presented to Mrs Wong the following day. Her food technologists evaluated the products and sent students their feedback, the following week.

Teacher commentary

This unit was situated within DDMO and was essentially about the development of a new food product. Food technology is not about learning to cook and following a recipe. That is not to say that cooking skills and the ability to follow a recipe are not critical skills in food technology. They are two of the building blocks needed to achieve the final outcome, a new or modified food product.

When investigating yoghurt, its history, its varieties and savoury flavours the students were developing their understanding of the nature of yoghurt (NT:CTO). They were also learning how materials (ingredients) impacted on final products and therefore engaged in (TK:Tp). The food technologist's visit was a critical aspect of this unit aimed at developing their understanding of authentic food TP. This is a critical aspect of the component planning for practice (TP:PP) and was one assessment focus for the unit. The students were involved in the construction and ongoing maintenance of the task list and identified resources they might need. The Indicators of Progression tell us that at L3 students should be able to identify the key stages of their practice, the resources needed and understand how and why changes are made. This unit saw PP co-constructed with the teachers initially, and then independently, as each student's practice started to differ from others. In subsequent units in Years 4–6, students would move to doing this completely independently.

Another major consideration in the savoury yoghurt unit was student health and safety. Understanding safe practice is also part of TP:PP. Undertaking it occurs in TP:ODE. This was considered through two areas. The first was the consideration of dairy and other food allergies. Obviously, within the yoghurt unit, this was a major consideration. When planning a unit such as this, parents must be informed. Letters need to be sent home outlining the unit and

186   *Classroom narrative*

requesting information on all allergies. Teachers need to discuss with their students what food allergies are and why it is important to be respectful of others. In terms of the yoghurt, if there is a child with a dairy allergy in the class, a non-dairy alternative, such as soy or coconut yoghurt, should be provided as a base for that child's group. Other foods can be avoided by excluding ingredients from recipes. At Years 5–6, students can be encouraged to take responsibility for not sampling inappropriate foods. For students younger than this, we recommend the avoidance of any potentially dangerous foods. The second safety consideration was the taste testing. How to safely undertake taste testing for themselves was a priority and taught very explicitly. Disposable tasting cups and teaspoons is probably the best way to go. Teachers must emphasise that used utensils are not placed back in the food products or to be used by anyone else.

Props for our school production

During Year 6, Aria and Cooper's class was involved in designing and developing the props required for their class's section of the senior school production. The school theme for the term was the Olympic Games. Two of the students had written the script for their class's item titled *The Olympics – 1896–1936*. In the early stages of the unit, the students worked with the school's Year 1 children, who were doing the same unit but developing props for their own class item. The first lesson involved the identification and definition of props and the types used in professional productions. The students watched two clips of stage productions, identifying the types of props used. The lesson culminated with the writing of a definition of a prop. This learning was consolidated in the next lesson when a speaker from the local theatre company talked to both classes about his role as props manager and the types of props they used. Figure 5.6 shows a range of props shown to the students. They included clockwise from bottom left: actual real items, plastic fake items, items with exaggerated humanised features and those items adapted for a different purpose (coconut shells for making horse trotting sound).

Following these lessons, the students co-constructed a set of desirable attributes for the props. They were able to identify that props needed to be realistic, durable, visible and accurately located in a historical and cultural sense. The students then practised identifying and critiquing a range of objects in relation to their suitability as prop. For this they used the PCQ (Pros, Cons and Questions) strategy in which they identified the pros and cons of a range of objects as prop and at least one question about each potential prop. To assist with the "Q" section the students drew on their knowledge of de Bono's six thinking hats that they had used in Social Studies earlier in the year. Edward de Bono has developed a number of useful strategies to assist critical thinking. One popular strategy used in primary schools is Six Thinking Hats. This strategy scaffolds thinking from a range of perspectives, each identified by a different coloured hat. The blue hat facilitates thinking about processes, the white hat about the facts. Red Hat thinking comes from a feelings perspective and a green

Classroom narrative 187

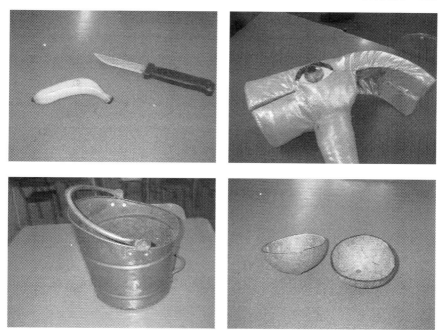

Figure 5.6 A range of props shown to the students

hat – creativity. When thinking with a yellow hat the benefits are considered and the back hat the cautions and difficulties.

The second area of research undertaken in this unit was to research artefacts from the 1896 to 1936 era. The students' Given Brief was for their prop items to be for the Olympic games during this era. Students identified a number of materials and design styles, beginning with Victorian and concluding with Art Deco styles – typically used during this time. The students learned that metals, fabric, card, wood and glass were the main materials of the time, with no plastic available. At this time, it was interesting to see both Cooper and Aria draw on their information learned from watching movies, reading books from the era studied, and more recently, from their shared experiences at the local Iron Māori event that the school hosted.

Having read the script written by their peers, the students also listed potential items that might have been needed for props in the class item. This list included a radio microphone, a radio, Olympic medals, Olympic torch and a podium. Each group selected one prop to design and produce before the dress rehearsal. Miss David, the class teacher, assisted the students to plan their practice so that it would be completed on time, by identifying tasks and necessary steps. Aria's group chose to develop a 1930s style radio microphone and Cooper's group a set of three Olympic medals. Now the students were ready to write their group's initial brief including their intended outcome, the earlier attributes, plus others

188 *Classroom narrative*

identified as a result of their earlier research. They also had a specific completion date, the dress rehearsal.

Following the writing of the initial brief, the students returned to research by investigating how their specific artefact was historically located. Cooper was very excited when their group discovered that medals from the Olympic Games of this era did not have ribbons. They therefore decided to include a cushion upon which the medals could sit. As new facts emerged and ideas formulated, the students continued to add information to their brief as a record of their final outcome. Sketching some design ideas and sharing these with other group members was the next step to the students' project. Because this was a collaborative project, in which each group was developing only one prop, the students had to compromise to ensure the group ended up with the best possible design. One of the members in Aria's group had quite a different idea about how their microphone should look (Figure 5.7), thinking it would be handheld. After sharing their designs, she understood that the microphone needed to be self-standing.

Once initial sketching was completed, the students selected and produced a detailed drawing of their selected design and made a mock-up to test their design ideas. The mock-ups were taken to a range of stakeholders for feedback. Cooper's group took their mock-up to other staff in the school and Aria's group each took it home to show it to their parents as they were potential audience

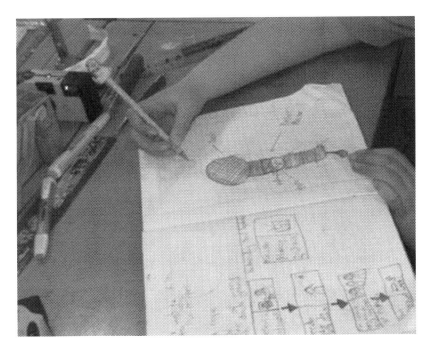

Figure 5.7 One child's sketch of a microphone

Classroom narrative 189

members and therefore stakeholders. Both groups also took their props to the show's producer, Mrs Caddy. The students asked her, as the key stakeholder, a range of questions to ensure they got valuable feedback to inform their TP. They then made modifications to their designs and wrote their final briefs according to the feedback given. The props were constructed. Both Aria and Cooper's groups selected to use papier machè as a construction material. Miss David took a class lesson on papier machè before they started to ensure that students knew how to do it correctly.

The final production near the end of the school year was a very exciting time for the students. Cooper, Aria and their friends agreed that their class had the best props of any class. All the props lasted the three productions and were easily recognised by the audience. In the final lesson of the unit, Mrs Cooper asked the students to think about the steps they had undertaken to design and make such outstanding props and how the steps contributed to such successful props for their class production.

Teacher commentary

Situated in DDMO the Props unit was the second technology unit the class had undertaken during the year. For this unit the primary learning focus was the role of stakeholder feedback, in the design and evaluation of technological outcomes. This unit progressed this idea by using the mocked-up designs to gain specific feedback from stakeholders. The mocked-up props were evaluated against the attributes that the students used to guide the questioning of their stakeholders (TP:BD). The second focus was the role of modelling, especially in terms of how creating a mock-up contributes to TP. The Year 6 students learned in their prior unit that developing a mock-up improves the quality of the outcome (TK:TM). Understanding the role and purpose of props and knowing the types of objects that made up a range of props was a critical aspect of this unit (NT:CTO). Further evidence that the NT strand is a critical aspect of technology education. The construction and ongoing evaluation of the props was situated in TP:ODE. The concluding discussion was situated in TP:ODE (final evaluation of function and performance of the props) and TK:TM as conversation led to the understanding that the drawing and mocking-up of design contributed to the quality of the final props.

Working collaboratively was another important feature of the learning in this unit. Because the students worked in groups of three to develop one outcome, they had to reach a compromise when opinions differed. This was assisted through a range of strategies, some of which were to teach the students to articulate and justify their design thoughts, being open to feedback and comments, listening to feedback and ideas from group members and finding a compromise when needed. Clear links can be drawn here to the New Zealand curriculum (NZC) key competencies: thinking –listening to others views and finding value in aspects or all of what they say and using language, symbols, and texts to articulate their design ideas. Managing self occurred through development of

190 *Classroom narrative*

understanding that their ideas may not be the best; relating to others in their group when sharing their design ideas and understanding others' ideas. This of course meant that the students were participating and contributing to their group design ideas and process.

Both units mentioned in this section offered numerous authentic opportunities for interdisciplinary integration. For example, the Yoghurt unit integrated health (benefits of dairy protein), mathematics (measurement of ingredients and graphing preferred flavours) and science (living world – growing organisms; the nature of science; undertaking testing – only changing one variable at a time). The Props unit integrated English (oral articulation of design ideas and decisions; reading for prop research), mathematics (measurement, symmetry, scale), social studies – understanding era and influences on design and fashion and art (drawing, papier machè and painting techniques).

Years 7 and 8

When at intermediate, our students went to specialist teachers for technology. Both students, although in different classes, experienced a rotation of food technology, textiles, resistant materials, electronics and digital technologies over the two years.

Immigrant biscuits

In Year 7 Food technology, Aria's classroom teacher and technology teacher worked together so the students could utilise facilities from both classrooms for the project. The students were introduced to the topic through a guest speaker, Maya Salaamed – a recent immigrant to the city. She explained to the students how hard it was to come to a land with unfamiliar sights, sounds, customs, and food, and being so far removed from family. She also talked about how much familiar sounds, tastes and smells meant to a person who is surrounded by the unfamiliar.

The class was divided into two mock companies, each of which was charged with developing a packaged biscuit product that would welcome new immigrants from that country to New Zealand, and also give them a "flavour of home." Each "company" was given an immigrant culture for which they had to develop a welcoming gift. Each group appointed a chief executive officer (CEO) and was divided into three teams – biscuit production, packaging and labelling. In their usual classroom, the students had created a Curriculum Vitae (CV) and written letters to "apply" for their preferred team. Final teams were selected by the teachers with all students getting their first or second choice. Once sorted into their teams the students identified the key stages of the process that needed to be coordinated across the teams. The teacher used this list to complete the top half of the herringbone timeline (Figure 4.8) for all students and gave a copy to each team leader who collaborated with team members to identify and sequence team only tasks.

Next, the students started on a range of research tasks. The first asked students to research the immigrant cultural group they had been given. This included insights into the culture's customs, sights, sounds, flavours, traditions, symbols, colours and icons. The second research task was to undertake specific research related to their team. This included investigating existing biscuits, how they are produced and production methods for the biscuit production team, food packaging regulations and existing designs for the packaging team. The labelling team investigated regulations and the Australia New Zealand Food Authority (ANZFA) website. Each team reported key findings and other relevant details to other teams in their company. This discussion was facilitated by their CEO. Their next learning was related to quality assurance and fitness for purpose.

Matua Wiremu, the quality assurance manager from a local biscuit company, spoke to the students via a Zoom meeting to discuss regulations and processes used by the company to ensure consistent quality of product. He described product tests conducted in a laboratory or test bakery to ensure consistency in biscuit dimensions, colour, weight, texture and flavour. He explained how some of these tests could be replicated in the classroom by students.

Colour measurement

When biscuits bake, there are three phases of cooking:

1 The structure and texture of the biscuit develops.
2 Moisture reduces.
3 The surface of the biscuits brown as a result of caramelisation, dextrinisation, and the Maillard reaction. These processes only occur with high temperatures and if the biscuits have lost their moisture.

The quality of a biscuit can be determined by its colour. In Industry, hyperspectral cameras are used to measure colour, and the parameters for browning depend on the type of biscuit (e.g. Anzac or Shortbread). In the classroom, paint colour charts can be used to determine fitness for purpose and assist students to make visual decisions about the quality of the biscuit. Students can ask the stakeholders what their preferences are to also determine one of the biscuit's attributes. When students cook the biscuits, they can match the biscuit colour to the chart of shades of brown from very light to dark (Figure 5.8), to assure fitness for purpose.

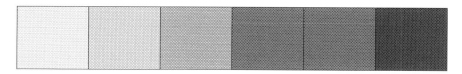

Figure 5.8 Biscuit colour chart

192 *Classroom narrative*

Maintaining biscuit colour across a batch is easier to achieve when individual items are of the same size and thickness. During production in a classroom, this can be achieved by having frames or rollers to maintain consistency, which can be custom designed by students.

Next each person in the class brought the package of their favourite food to class. They performed a number of experiments to determine protection and freshness. For example, the freshness of biscuits can be determined by break resistance and fracture properties.

Fracture testing

The amount of fat (e.g. butter) used in a biscuit recipe impacts the product's fracture properties. Usually, a biscuit's fracture properties can be determined by hand with a three-point bending test. Biscuits with elastic behaviour fracture at a small strain. If a biscuit fractures from the bottom side upwards it indicates a higher fracture stress. Students can adapt their recipes to change the strain/ fracture properties and achieve different biscuit compositions to address stakeholder organoleptic preferences.

Cooper was in the biscuit production team and very surprised to find out that biscuit meant "twice baked," and that biscuits were invented in early navy times as hard tack for sailors. His group also found out that in North America the term "biscuit" means something quite different to New Zealand, being rather more like our scone. He realised that you cannot make assumptions that everyone has the same ideas about things. Cooper's group developed their early ideas in the specialty food technology room by sketching how their biscuit might look. They then proposed a range of shapes, flavours and finishing (in this case, icing), identified from their immigrant culture research. They then selected three to test, wrote recipes for each and compiled lists of ingredients. Test batches were made the following session and baked with a base biscuit recipe (see Figure 5.9). The students added their identified flavour combinations. Once their mixtures were made they also tested shapes, thickness and cooking times for colour and texture.

Aria was appointed kaiārahi (team leader) of the labelling team and as such she needed to work closely not only with her own team but also that of the biscuit and packaging teams. She developed the team's critical path after they had collaboratively identified all the tasks that were needed to develop the outcome for the "presentation day." Within her team, Aria allocated different aspects to team members, depending on their strengths and interests. For example, Jenny took responsibility for fonts and colour, Tāne for layout, Frank for nutritional and company information, and finally Aria took responsibility for images.

All team members produced initial design ideas which they shared with each other, each person with a responsibility made the final decisions in that area if a consensus could not be met. Their teachers had provided the students with a technology resource portfolio to record all their ideas and decisions. Aria met

Classroom narrative   193

ONE HUNDRED AND ONE BISCUITS

Ingredients

500g butter

½ C white sugar

5 C Flour

5 tsp baking powder

1 can condensed milk

1 pinch salt

Instructions

Preheat oven at 180 °C and prepare baking trays

Cream sugar, butter and add condensed milk

Sift together flour, salt and baking powder,

Add slowly mix to combine

Add other desired ingredients (to flavour) *

Roll rounded teaspoon of mixture into balls, flatten slightly (can be rolled and cut also)

Bake for 10-12 minutes or until golden

*Biscuits can be flavoured to suit, using a range of spices (sifted with dry ingredients), nuts, dried fruits, confectionary, such as 100&1000's chocolate chips, white chocolate etc.

Figure 5.9 A base recipe that might be used in this unit

with the CEO and other team leaders regularly to ensure everything was on track. When considering a range of ideas, the students were encouraged to use the strategy PCQ (Pros, Cons and Questions) to assist their thinking. Aria's team was expected to develop a legal label for the packaged biscuits and therefore needed to engage with Food Standards Australia New Zealand (FSANZ) and the Ministry of Primary Industries Food Labelling Guide.

Aria's team familiarise themselves with these requirements, but also felt that it was important to recognise the bicultural nature of New Zealand on their packaging. They wanted to ensure that both te reo Māori and English were used. Once the label was designed, layout, fonts, colours, images considered and after the biscuit team had finalised the recipe, but before the label team were able to print their final label Aria used an online Nutritional Panel Calculator to facilitate the production of an authentic, legal nutritional panel as seen in Figure 5.10 which was included into the biscuit's labelling.

Within each "company," all three teams had to work very closely together. For example, the labelling team needed to know the exact list and quantity of ingredients before they could calculate their nutritional panel. The biscuit team could not bake the final biscuits until the packaging was completed – so

194 *Classroom narrative*

One Hundred and One Biscuits

Total ingredient (raw) weight:	1187.00 g
Total (cooked) weight:	1210.74 g
Weight change:	2.00 %

Nutrition Information

Servings per package:	12.00		
Serving size:	10.00 g		
		Average Quantity per Serving	Average Quantity per 100 g
Energy		211 kJ	2110 kJ
Protein		0.5 g	4.6 g
Fat, total		3.4 g	34.3 g
- saturated		2.2 g	22.4 g
Carbohydrate		4.4 g	44.1 g
- sugars		1.7 g	17.0 g
Sodium		52 mg	518 mg

Ingredient name: Sugar, white, granulated or lump
12A10050
Amount: 192.00 g

Energy:	1700 kJ	Fat, total:	0.0 g	Carbohydrate:	100.0 g	Sodium:	0 mg		
Protein:	0.0 g	Fat saturated:	0.0 g	Sugars:	100.0 g				

Ingredient name: Butter, salted
04A10060
Amount: 500.00 g

Energy:	3036 kJ	Fat, total:	81.5 g	Carbohydrate:	0.0 g	Sodium:	776 mg
Protein:	1.1 g	Fat saturated:	53.8 g	Sugars:	0.0 g		

Ingredient name: Baking powder
14B10098
Amount: 20.00 g

Energy:	34 kJ	Fat, total:	0.4 g	Carbohydrate:	0.0 g	Sodium:	11800 mg
Protein:	0.1 g	Fat saturated:	0.0 g	Sugars:	0.0 g		

Ingredient name: Flour, wheat, white, plain
02A20061
Amount: 450.00 g

Energy:	1498 kJ	Fat, total:	1.2 g	Carbohydrate:	73.0 g	Sodium:	2 mg
Protein:	10.8 g	Fat saturated:	0.2 g	Sugars:	0.0 g		

Ingredient name: Milk, canned, sweetened, condensed, regular
09A20018
Amount: 25.00 g

Energy:	1415 kJ	Fat, total:	9.2 g	Carbohydrate:	54.9 g	Sodium:	105 mg
Protein:	8.3 g	Fat saturated:	6.1 g	Sugars:	54.9 g		

NOTE: All nutrient values shown above for these ingredients are per 100g EP
Working values may differ from final NIP due to rounding.
Printed: 04:49 Wednesday, 2 September 2020

Figure 5.10 Nutritional panel for base biscuit recipe

the biscuits were fresh. The packaging and production team had to agree on biscuit size and shape. The labels needed to fit the packaging and all teams needed to collaborate on colouring and imaging to be portrayed. The "grand finale" of the unit involved an invitation to members of the immigrant cultures to attend a special presentation of the gifts at a school assembly. Again the students were involved in the organisation of the assembly and the afternoon tea which followed.

Teacher commentary

At Years 7 and 8, students in New Zealand are entitled and funded for specialist teaching in technology education. This means that technology education is often provided by another school or technology centre, or that students have specialist facilities within their own school. Client schools and teachers at this level should always liaise with their technology providers for three main reasons:

1 to ensure that the students are receiving technology education as outlined in NZC;
2 to ensure that the programmes offered are holistic in nature, offering all strands of the curriculum;
3 to work with the centre to ensure ongoing learning and facilitate opportunities for curriculum integration.

When undertaking food technology, students are engaged in DDPO. This unit was aimed at L4, but with some learning occurring at Level 3 NZC. The company approach used for the Immigrant biscuits unit is a good way to motivate students and to do things a little differently. Although the students are working in different areas within the company the underlying technology theory or "generic" skills and knowledge remained the same across the teams and class. For example, all students were involved in the collaboration of the whole class and team aspects of their herringbone timelines and involved in the ongoing monitoring of team tasks and resources (TP:PP). They all learned about the societal influence on products through research of products from cultures other than their own, to determine how cultural influences can affect design (NT:CT).

Team research into aspects of their specific products included ways of finishing biscuits, food packaging and food labelling (NT:CTO). This research enabled the identification of attributes required for their product. Each team was then able to write an initial brief for their team that differed from the teacher's given brief and the other team briefs within their company thus all students undertaking aspects of brief development (TP:BD). Understanding of the impact and influences on design functionality of intended materials was also applicable across teams and undertaken by each (TK:Tp). The concept of "materials" however differs for each team. In foods technology ingredients are the "materials" of foods. Packaging materials is reasonably clear but labelling the concept of materials related to software and programmes used to produce the label. All students were involved in the design and development of their technological outcomes (TP:ODE). So we can see that despite working in differing contexts students are still able to progress within the relevant technology AOs.

Scooter racks for schools

In Year 8, in the resistant materials class, Aria, Cooper and peers were asked to identify some problems or issues within the school community. The group identified that many students were riding scooters to school and on arrival the students dumped them in a large pile. This looked messy, was hated by the teachers, and was very frustrating for students at the end of the day. They decided to develop a scooter parking system to solve this authentic school-based problem.

196 *Classroom narrative*

To assist them their teacher, Mr Brentell, approached the "Futureintech Neighbourhood Engineering" programme coordinator who facilitated the students working with qualified engineers throughout their project. Whaea Waimārie, a young engineer, assisted the students in their understanding of the suitable materials, design aspects and range of possible production systems. Shee came to the class four times during the project to give the students feedback on their ideas and provide information and guidance when needed. The students drew designs by hand and on the computer using Google Sketch-up. They tested and critiqued a variety of existing designs and talked to a number of potential users and other stakeholders, such as staff and the school caretaker. They also drew on personal experience to identify a number of potential attributes for their scooter racks. These racks needed to be strong, durable, made of sustainable materials, weather proof, affordable, light weight and lockable.

The group went through a long "trial and error" design and modelling process to develop a range of design ideas for parking the scooters. They visited a local factory to see how sheet metal can be cut and manipulated. They eventually selected 4-mm galvanised steel for their final material as it met many aspects of the brief – it was strong, durable and weather proof. Mock-ups of several design ideas were made first in cardboard then plywood to allow product testing, before the final design was determined. Three final versions developed. The final designs were sent to a local manufacturer for production.

The students became intimate with the whole design and manufacture process. They were very proud of their final outcome, which was very successful and was manufactured for a number of schools around New Zealand, thus generating funds which went on to assist funding in the school's technology department. During the project the students also learned about patents and the concept of intellectual property (IP).

Teacher commentary

IP is pertinent where technological designs are perceived to be new, original, creations of the mind. Intellectual property rights (IPRs) belong to the innovator for a limited time and ensure that they can determine how their creations are used, and to return some investment on their design. From a Māori worldview, IP includes the body of knowledge from their ancestors, as well as Māori creativity, cultural practices, and language. Here, IP can be seen as a way to prevent exploitation and cultural appropriation, and ensure Mātauranga Māori (Māori knowledge) is protected.

This project was a structural project within the technological areas of design and visual communication (DVC) and DDMO. It was taught at Level 4 of NZC. It exemplifies how in the primary sector DVC can be combined with another technological area so that designs and drawing occur within an authentic project. It also exemplified the integrated nature of all the components of technology. Technology also offers an excellent opportunity for collaboration with industry. In the scooter example a Young Engineer was used to facilitate this process. Young Engineers is a group within Engineers of New Zealand (ENZ).

Technological modelling (TK:TM) was a critical component of this unit. It exemplifies the close relationship modelling has with DVC. DVC at this level teaches skills and knowledge needed for effective drawing and modelling of designs – both of which are types of modelling, understanding design styles and influences, and strategies for creativity. These aspects shape designerly thinking.

The unit also exemplifies the close and intertwined relationship between the AO. Product evaluation (TP:ODE) was another important component of the scooter unit. When an authentic context like this, the identification of possible attributes (TP:BD) was a critical component of product evaluation. The purpose of modelling was twofold: (i) it develops understanding on the role modelling plays in technological development, as suggested above (TK:TM) and (ii) it assists in product and process evaluation (TP:ODE – students own practice and NT:CTO others' products and practice). The latter of these informs students planning of their practice and identification of resources needed (TP:PP). Robust attributes (TP:BD) were established using a range of activities such as investigating existing products (NT:CTO), their materials and joins (TP:Tp), historical research (NT:CTO), dialogue with clients and other major stakeholders (TP:BD), peer and self-critique of their design ideas (TP:ODE) were vital strategies for guiding and evaluating design decisions and products.

Years 9 and 10

On their arrival at secondary school Cooper and Aria discovered that technology occurred through a rotation of options in Year 9, and the subsequent selection of two choices in Year 10. In Year 9 they spent one term in digital technology, food technology, resistant materials and textiles. In Year 10 they selected two of these, one for each semester.

Te reo readers

In digital technology, the students' first project was focused on the sustained school relationship with an authentic client and developing a quality outcome using basic computer programmes for text, layout and illustrations (DDDO). The Principal from the local primary school, Whaea Tūmai, had previously approached the high school and asked if the Year 9 students could develop early readers (books) in te Reo (see http://cybersoul.co.nz/). This project was an integrated unit with languages (te reo) and technology, and required students to choose a pūrākau (Māori legend: see https://kauwhatareo.govt.nz/) and retell it. Pūrākau refers to the base (Pū) or roots of a tree (rākau), an image used by Māori to represent the interconnectedness between the social and natural environment. Pūrākau is also a methodology used to communicate Māori knowledge, values, protocols and worldviews.

198 *Classroom narrative*

Figure 5.11 Example of te reo readers

In their next lesson, the students listened to Matua Rawiri, a teacher of Year 1 students, talk about junior readers as seen in Figure 5.11, the role, length and layout of the books and how they were used to reinforce basic vocabulary, using repetition and prediction, with assistance from the illustrations. Matua Rawiri agreed to be the students' mentor throughout the unit.

This lesson was reinforced with a follow-up lesson on technology and how books are Tp. The students looked at some junior readers to examine peoples' changing perspectives over time. In their te reo language class the students worked on identifying the top 20 basic sight words and other vocabulary around their topic. They also recapped the notion of sentence structure and began writing the text for their readers.

In the next technology session, the students explored a range of different junior readers to identify layout, length, fonts, numbers, size of words and illustrations. As a class they identified a list of attributes that junior readers needed to meet. These were emailed to the client for review. The students identified attributes are listed below with the additions from Whaea Tūmai in italics.

Te Reo readers must:

- use basic sight and high frequency words;
- be colourful and engaging;
- be suitable for five-year olds;
- introduce no more than five new words;

Classroom narrative   199

- be 10–15 pages long;
- have clear links between text and illustrations;
- be strongly constructed and durable;
- use suitable bicultural images where appropriate.

In the next session, the students were taught about the computer programmes and systems that would be used in this project. They developed an understanding of how systems within the computer and Internet worked and how they were interrelated. They were introduced to two programmes (Storyboard Creator and Snapfish), identified the features of the programmes, and how aspects within each programme were linked. They then identified the relevance of the programmes in relation to their project. In the computer lab the students recapped their skills by inserting text and graphics into "Word" documents. They also investigated suitable fonts and font sizes for their books. When ready to plan their design ideas they initially listed the pages they wanted and what they wanted on each on page.

In the next lesson they were taught to use an application to develop a storyboard (Storyboard.com) of their proposed junior reader. Self and peer assessment was used to evaluate their storyboard design against the identified attributes. They also sent their ideas to their mentor for feedback and made alterations according to the feedback received. When ready to produce their readers they created their books on *Snapfish* and ordered one preview copy to present to their target age school children. The class then visited the primary school, each student reading their book to a small group of students before gifting them to Mrs Averill at the school. After the reading session and presentation, the students evaluated their books and identified any potential changes before several copies of each were created. Each student made suggested changes before sending the file to the client school for them to use as they wished.

Teacher commentary

As the students transition into secondary school, a considered approach to technology education becomes even more vital for students to be supported to advance in all the AOs, to prepare them for their senior secondary learning and arguably more important for their lives in a technological world. A programme of work should be developed within each technology department across the technological areas and year levels to ensure all students receive a good understanding of the AOs in technology regardless of the options selected and the specialist skills and knowledge needed for advancement into Years 11–13 and NCEA assessment qualification.

Due to the rotational NT in Years 7–10, and the optional nature of subjects in Years 11–13, students in the same school will experience technology learning in different contexts and technological areas. For example, all students in Year 9 might learn about Brief Development and the Characteristics of Technology in Term 1. In Term 2, the focus might be on PP, CTO and TM, regardless of whether students are in digital technologies, food, materials or textiles

200   *Classroom narrative*

technology. Careful programming across all year levels will be most successful when faculty cooperation is an expectation. All staff need to have a strong understanding of technology education, and how it is best implemented and assessed.

Years 9 and 10 are an excellent opportunity for students to work collaboratively and cooperatively on single projects. Among other benefits when working collaboratively, students must talk about, explain and justify their ideas and thinking. When working on one project students are forced to consider the views of others, in order to progress. We frequently hear criticism about students working collaboratively, because of the need to assess students individually. There are two ways around this, both of which depend on the nature of the assessment. In technology, both product and process are assessed. To assess "product" in a collaborative project, students can be given different areas of responsibility. Assessment judgements can be made on the success of individual components of parts, rather than the whole. Students' understanding, skills and knowledge can be recorded independently and individually and assessed in a holistic manner. Students' ability to write a design brief, respond to stakeholder feedback and make necessary judgement is quite independent from the context of the technology content. However, assessment rubrics can be designed to make judgements about both curriculum and technological area content.

This Pūrākau unit was purposefully planned to engage the students at the beginning of the year with an authentic context, to design and develop a digital outcome. It was based at Levels 4–5 of NZC. A range of generic understandings of technology education were developed, within the context of digital technology. The students were also introduced to the notion of technology subsystems with systems and their connections functionality and fitness for purpose. Technological systems (TK:TS) was a critical teaching and learning focus. The students were guided to understand that the properties of a subsystem relate to its performance. They were given the opportunity to analyse a range of examples of TS that contain at least one subsystem and identify subsystems within TS explaining their properties. The students used examples to gain insight into how the selection and interfacing of subsystems relies on understanding the transformation and connective properties of subsystems to ensure the best "fit" with the required system specifications. To assist the teacher in the identification of learning that is curriculum based and also meets the needs of the revised technology curriculum-digital technologies progress outcome 3 (PO 3) was used.

https://technology.tki.org.nz/Technology-in-the-NZC/DDDO-Progress-outcomes-exemplars-and-snapshots/(tab)/PO3

> … They [students] identify the key features of selected software and choose the most appropriate software and file types to develop and combine digital content.
>
> Students understand the role of operating systems in managing digital devices, security, and application software and are able to apply file management conventions using a range of storage devices. They understand that with storing data comes responsibility for ensuring security and privacy.

The students were also assessed on the quality of their final outcome for fitness for purpose using the developed specifications in the final brief (TP:ODE and TP:BD).

Kai ora

In Year 10 Aria selected food technology, then textiles as her technology options. In food technology, there was a class discussion facilitated by the classroom teacher, the students agreed that their parents and caregivers were very busy people and at times they felt pressured to provide quick and nutritional meals for their families. In groups of four the students then set out to develop a product that was a nutritionally balanced, "all in one" meal, for a family of four. This product was to be appropriate for storage either in a refrigerator or freezer. It also needed a sauce of some kind.

A food technologist, James, was invited to talk about food production. Initially James spoke to the class about how they could test their products for quality, with a specific focus on food safety. James taught the students about hazard analysis critical control point (HACCP), a management system in which food safety is managed during food product development. This is a necessary process throughout product development, to analyse and control the hazards from raw material production, procurement, handling, manufacturing, distribution and consumption of the finished food product.

James asked the students to identify and sequence the tasks that were needed to complete their fast food dish on time, and to identify the potential hazards from the input → process → output stages of production. As a group they completed a critical control point (CCP) pathway as part of their PP (Table 5.1). James and their teacher, Mrs Kingsbury, assisted the students in their identification of potential hazards, to negotiate the most effective ways to prevent harm. The plan was for students to have a shared dinner at parents evening. Parents were to be asked for feedback. Obviously the dish needed to be completed in time for this. Aria found it helpful to have the tasks listed out so she knew what was required of her group.

Over the next two weeks, the students had food technology twice a week. They co-wrote their initial brief, which outlined the task for their group. They then investigated online and existing fast foods at the local supermarket. During the practical classes, the students tested their products, according to the nature of the attributes and specifications identified in their brief. This enabled them to make judgements about fitness for purpose, and the effect of storage on their final outcome. In groups, students tested the differing components of fast food dishes. For example, they trialled a range of sauces, conducting viscosity testing, to determine the appropriate consistency for the sauce in their dish. They also stored them in both the refrigerator and freezer, to see how the product's consistency, viscosity and quality changed during these processes.

Using all of their findings, students developed the type of dish they wanted to trial. Aria's group settled on a chicken and pasta based dish for which they then

Table 5.1 An example of a CCP pathway: fast foods

Step date	Process	Potential hazard	Justification	Hazard to be addressed – CCP	Control measure	Critical limits
1	Co-write an initial brief in collaboration with a range of potential clients (parents and caregivers)	N/A	N/A	No	N/A	N/A
2	Investigate fast foods	N/A	N/A	No	N/A	N/A
3	Sample a range of fast foods for investigation	Bacterial and viral bugs from others, e.g. legionella, Norvovirus, colds, strep throat, mumps and meningitis	Sharing utensils and dishes can facilitate this process	Yes	Cleaning no utensils to be reused	Utensils and dishes to be washed in water at least 55°C at tap (60°C at cylinder), with detergent and thoroughly dried before, between and after tastings
5	Identify attributes and initial specifications for the dish	N/A	N/A	No	N/A	N/A
6	Determining the recipe for trialling and adding to the brief	N/A	N/A	No	N/A	N/A
7	Trialling the food product	Enteric pathogens: e.g. *Salmonella*, verotoxigenic – *E. coli*	Enteric pathogens have been associated with outbreaks of foodborne illness from undercooked chicken	Yes	Cooking	Oven temperature:___ °C Time; rate of heating and cooling Heating ___ min Cooling ___ min

(*Continued*)

Table 5.1 (*Continued*)

Step date	Process	Potential hazard	Justification	Hazard to be addressed – CCP	Control measure	Critical limits
8	Taste testing test	Passing on and receiving bacterial and viral bugs from others as above	Sharing utensils and dishes can facilitate this process	Yes	Cleaning no utensils to be reused	Utensils and dishes to be washed in water at least 55°C with detergent and dried before, between and after tastings
9	Modifying recipe according to feedback given and complete final brief with all specifications	N/A	N/A	No	N/A	N/A
10	Prepare final convenience food	Enteric pathogens: e.g. *Salmonella*, verotoxigenic – *E. coli*	Enteric pathogens have been associated with outbreaks of foodborne illness from undercooked meat	Yes	Cooking	Oven temperature:___ °C Time; rate of heating and cooling Heating ___ min Cooling ___ min
11 Sept 2	Present convenience foods at parents evening. Receive feedback	Bacterial and viral bugs from others as above	Sharing utensils and dishes can facilitate this process	Yes	Cleaning no utensils to be reused	Utensils and dishes to be washed in water at least 55°C, with detergent and dried before, between and after tastings
12	Reflect on feedback where improvements could be made to products and process	N/A	N/A	No	N/A	N/A

204 Classroom narrative

wrote a manufacturing plan, and trialled their dish several times. Their product was tested by a staff member who had been trained as sensory evaluators. Sensory analysis provides a scientific approach to testing the products. A popular way of recording results is through the use of a radar chart (also known as a star diagram – Figure 5.12). Rather than choosing generic terms like "flavour," the

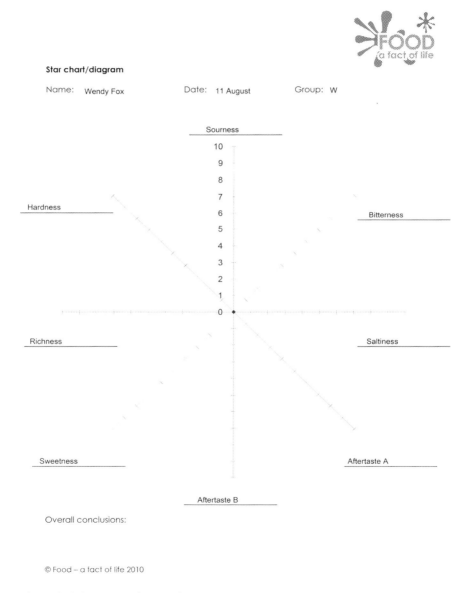

Figure 5.12 Sensory evaluation diagram

particular attributes of the product should be identified. For example, if a sauce should be "cheesy" sensory evaluators will need to make a judgement about this characteristic.

From the feedback received, Aria's group modified their recipe, added all specifications to the final brief and prepared their final plan. Their final practical class was the same day as parents evening, so all dishes were fresh and only needed to be reheated before dinner was served. After dinner, parents filled in anonymous evaluation forms, which they left beside each dish. In the final class the student read their feedback and undertook a final evaluation of their dish and the process they undertook.

Teacher commentary

When considering the Tp, the main focus is on the form and function of materials. It is important to remember that the materials in food technology are the ingredients. This means that students need to consider a range of possible ingredients when developing food products and identify the properties and function each brings to the potential product. This should enable the students to discuss and justify ingredient selection in terms of performance properties and impacts of the final outcome.

When undertaking PP at Level 5 students should have previously been exposed to a range of planning tools so that at this level they can analyse a range of tools and select and or modify the one most suitable to the needs of the project. The tool exemplified above is a modified version of a "Task List," incorporating food safety, using HACCP. All forms of planning need to be annotated with justified changes as the students move through their TP.

Year 11: design and visual communication

In Year 11, Cooper chose to take DVC as his technology option. As a result of his recent engagement in the national Climate Strikes, Cooper had a passion for New Zealand's native birds and believed that they are a vital part of both our eco-system and local communities. During his major project, he was keen to explore and develop ideas to address the fact that there had been an observed decrease in natural nesting spots in New Zealand backyards for teh native birds. This was because of an increasing urban population, less space, and various associated challenges (e.g. cats) resulting from urbanisation.

As part of his research, Cooper investigated the challenges that native birds faced in New Zealand and reviewed existing birdfeeders. He identified and consulted with a stakeholder (his mum), and then designed a nesting box specifically for tūī. Cooper was also keen to ensure that his design resembled organic forms, to blend into the kōwhai trees that the tūī love to feed on. His stakeholder had a preference for sustainable, easily resourced materials.

206 *Classroom narrative*

Teacher commentary

It is a common practice in senior secondary schools for students to engage in a major project over three terms. It is important that students have an overview of the key stages for this project to develop. These key stages are often broken into smaller and negotiated aspects, to ensure that the learning outcomes are met. During this project, Connor demonstrated his achievement of BD at Level 6 of the NZC because he was able to:

- identify a need or opportunity from a (given) context or issue;
- establish a conceptual statement to justify the nature of the outcome and why it should be developed;
- establish the specifications for an outcome and show consideration of the environment in which the outcome was intended to be situated, using available resources;
- justify and communicate specifications to account for key and wider stakeholder considerations and allow an outcome to be evaluated as fit for purpose;
- generate design ideas which were informed by research and the critical analysis of existing outcomes, then evaluate his design ideas to develop a conceptual design for a feasible outcome;
- evaluate the conceptual design against the specifications and suitability of materials/components, to determine fitness for purpose.

Connor also showed his achievement in the DVC area because he:

- showed in-depth information about the intent of his design features, in this instance, by developing a body of related sketches that included exploded, sectional and sequential views to explain design features;
- developed freehand sketches to explore and communicate his design ideas, which were created unassisted by the use of instruments or any digital technologies;
- demonstrated isometric, perspective, oblique and planometric freehand sketching techniques;
- produced examples of sketching techniques, including quick rendering, crafting and the use of line hierarchy.

Senior secondary programmes of work provide an opportunity to develop personalised learning contexts in negotiation with students. In this instance, Connor was passionate about sustainability and was keen to develop a design, which addressed a personally meaningful need in his community.

Year 13: designing and developing material outcomes

In Year 13, Aria chose to continue to pursue her senior pathway with materials (textiles) technology. She was unsure what she wanted to do when she left school but thought that by studying technology, she could continue to refine her self-management and design skills.

Classroom narrative 207

Aria was told that she needed to develop her own context for learning and was keen to develop an outcome that would focus on the Māori tradition of weaving. She already knew that the leaves from harakeke (New Zealand flax: see http://www.alibrown.co.nz/gathering-flax.html) needed to be cut carefully to preserve the centre shoot, and strip the fibre (muka). She has observed that before the fibre was cut, a karakia (prayer) was said, to protect the plan and harvester, and acknowledge the harakeke as a taonga (a spiritual and sacred treasure). The fibre could then be washed, beaten and rolled by hand into threads, which could then be dyed. Aria was aware of female family members who had learned about the ceremonial and spiritual aspects of weaving, and hoped to work with them as key stakeholders, when she was developing her textile outcome. She also understood that she would need to give her first outcome as a gift and thought that her teacher would appreciate it.

Before committing to the nature of her final outcome, Aria tried out an approach to finger weaving, called whatu. She knew that this was a type of weaving, which could be used to make Māori cloaks (Kākahu) for people of rank by stretching a cord between two pegs, hanging warp threads from the cord, and then incorporating finer weft threads. She also understood that such cloaks could take several years to make, and that she might have to find an alternative outcome, which used the same technique.

Next, Aria explored decorative weaving (Tākino), which was traditionally used for the borders of garments, or tukutuku, a type of weaving used to adorn the inside walls of meeting houses. She had consulted with her Kaumatua about the required tikanga (Māori custom) when developing this type of outcome. He recommended that she talk to her whānau further, to ensure that she explored a wide range of culturally appropriate opportunities. She considered developing a woven container as a gift for her tuakana (elder sister), who was pregnant. She knew that her sister was keen to recognise the Māori custom, where parents choose to take the placenta home, and plant it beneath a tree in a purpose made vessel (ipi whenua), as a means to reinforce the baby's connection to the place of its birth.

Coincidentally, Aria's Horticulture teacher gave her the contact for a stakeholder who was keen for her to explore how indigenous plants (like harakeke) could be used to develop future-focused solutions, using traditional methods. Aria developed designs, models and prototypes of biodegradable plant containers (Figure 5.13), which supported a plant's growth until such a time that it needed to be planted. Her designed outcome ensured that once the plant reached this stage, the container could be buried, with the plant in it, to allow it to thrive. She decided upon the weaving style of raranga as her technique.

Teacher commentary

It is generally accepted that in Year 13, students can work with more independence and explore ideas that might be suited to production, in response to authentic technologist's needs. Figure 5.13

208 *Classroom narrative*

For example, in this context, Aria worked independently through the trialling and production of the plant pot. She completed the processes accurately and efficiently to maximise her time and effort and meet the predetermined deadlines set by her external technologist. She also sought knowledge from her aunts to ensure that tikanga (Māori protocol) was followed, when cutting and working with the harakeke.

Aria's portfolio work reflected comprehensive discussion about her TM, and she provided photographic evidence to show how she resolved issues, and to defend and validate the decisions she made during the product development phases. She explained in detail how composition of the harakeke changed from its natural (raw) state into how it looked in the final product, and explained the processes used to ensure performance. Her research led to her understanding that harakeke could be used for a variety of other applications, such as a medicinal gel, or even a new type of Pōtaka tā that her Koro introduced her when she was little (a traditional Māori game)!

Summary

This chapter provides some insight into Cooper and Aria's TP and illustrates their schooling journey in technology education. The narrative provided description of their participation in a range of learning and in authentic contexts, each at a different NZC achievement level, in a range of technological areas. The teacher narrative also presents some of the teaching and learning decisions, and assessment opportunities, which link to the student's activity. The narrative chapter outlines the philosophy underpinning technology education, as translated into classroom practice, and student's learning technology education.

The Epilogue chapter reflects the key ideas represented in the book and our reasons for highlighting them for both student teachers and existing practitioners of technology education in New Zealand.

Bibliography

de Bono, E. (1992). *Six thinking hats for schools* (Vol. Book 2 Middle-Upper Primary). Hawker Brownlow Education.

Ministry of Education. (2017a). *Te whāriki a te kōhanga reo*. Ministry of Education.

Ministry of Education. (2017b). *Technology in the New Zealand curriculum*. Ministry of Education. Retrieved 20 February from http://nzcurriculum.tki.org.nz/The-New-Zealand-Curriculum/Technology.

6 Epilogue

Our aim for this book is to assist understanding, planning for, and the implementation of technology education in the New Zealand classroom. To do this it explores differing understandings of technology, and subsequent approaches to implementing the subject in the classroom. Teachers new to New Zealand and from around the world have different views and beliefs of technology. This book is written by teacher educators, who acknowledge that students come into Initial Teacher Education (ITE) programmes with vastly differing understanding and experiences of technology.

Technology education in New Zealand has had a short but checkered journey. Before it was first implemented, a PPTA (Post-primary Teachers' Association) moratorium delayed professional development for many. At that time, some principals believed the curriculum would never reach implementation and did little to support it. In the primary sector, implementation occurred as a part of the new curriculum framework roll-out, meaning teachers were left to manage the significant changes in six existing learning areas – before even considering the addition of technology as a new aspect of the curriculum. This change occurred over a period of six to seven years. Teacher professional learning and development (PLD) was limited. Over this time schools applied for a place in each learning area PLD programme, many giving priority to other learning areas. When technology was finally gazetted as a compulsory subject, many primary teachers had not engaged with or held misconceptions about the nature of technology education. The issues were further compounded by the fact that few teachers experienced PLD in technology, and very few (if any) had been taught it themselves.

During this time intermediate and secondary programmes were largely skill-based, and philosophically very different from the technological practice-based programmes that are so critical to the enactment of technology education. In intermediate schools "manual teachers" were suddenly called technology teachers. In secondary schools, teachers of cooking, sewing, home economics, woodwork, metalwork, resistant materials, typing, computing, and technical drawing were suddenly expected to become teachers of technology. This diversity equated to teachers with different ideas about technology and how it should be taught. The learning area was combined to include teachers from different backgrounds

210   *Epilogue*

and practices – such as those from trades, industry-business sectors, individuals with design-based degrees and no work experience, which brought vastly different ideas about the nature of technology.

A more recent governmental agenda of improved literacy and numeracy levels further exacerbated the issue in primary schools. Schools responded by increasing the amount of time spent on reading, writing and maths. Changes in entry criteria to teacher education qualifications also excluded many people with practical trade backgrounds, which perpetuated the severe shortage of technology teachers in New Zealand. A number of teachers of technology from other countries were subsequently employed. These teachers, including Liz Reinsfield, brought their own understandings of the nature of technology education, and often received little (or no) PLD to counter the professional "cultural shock" they experienced during their transition to a new country. In the secondary school context, it remains the responsibility of an individual to analyse his or her own practice and ensures it aligns with curriculum expectations and/or supports student success. Most recently, the emphasis on digital technologies in the curriculum places technology at risk of being marginalised to become solely digital or skill-based programmes.

For the reasons mentioned above, there are diverse understandings of the nature and purpose of technology education in New Zealand. Programme design and delivery vary greatly, and are heavily influenced by historical factors, and the priorities of the differing technological areas. Conversely, research findings assert that delivery of quality technology education requires common understanding of the philosophy and nature underpinning this learning area, as well as a strong rationale for teaching it. It is for this reason that this book began by outlining the key factors to ensure a foundational understanding of technology, and by then discussing the philosophy of technology in Chapter 2.

The relationship between technology and society underpins the notions presented in Chapter 2, which begins by developing the readers' understanding of technology as an innate human activity. This idea strengthens the argument that technology should be a foundational subject in a school. Understanding that technology is both process, and designed and developed systems/products counters the superficial view that technology is solely limited to digital devices.

A generic view of technological knowledge and process is presented in Chapter 2. When undertaking technology practice, students are exposed to and taught knowledge and skills common across the technological areas (generic knowledge), as well as knowledge and skills specific to each technological area (specific knowledge). Understanding which is which is important. Generic knowledge develops and is transferable across technological areas. Specific knowledge develops and is transferable across projects, within a technological area. Chapter 2 concludes with a discussion about the relationship between science and technology. Common misconceptions are illustrated when media promote a view that scientists have developed a new product (such as a vaccine). In reality, they are technologists drawing on scientific knowledge and processes, to design and develop a technological outcome.

Epilogue 211

In Chapter 3 we focused on developing understanding of why technology should be taught in schools. The six rationales were presented to illustrate that arguments for introducing technology to the New Zealand curriculum (NZC) framework (in the early 1990s) are just as valid today. However, this chapter explains that because of its original conception as a practical subject (such as cooking and woodwork), many have difficulty in seeing the benefits of practical subjects in today's classroom. As machines and computers can now perform many of the tasks and skills that were traditionally taught in practical subjects of the latter half of the 20th century, the need to change is evident. The greatest difference between technology education and its predecessor subjects is the academic needs-based focus.

To assist understanding of the transition from a practical skill-based subject we provided a brief history of the evolution of technology in New Zealand schooling. This focus provides a means for teachers to reflect upon their own understanding of technology and aims to motivate a change in thinking to recognise the subjects' dual focus (academic and practical). Chapter 3 also highlighted the notions of technological literacy (or technacy). Technological literacy is also a term with multiple definitions and understandings. Some limit its definition to being able to use technology, but it should be much more encompassing – hence the use of the term technacy.

Critical to the understanding of this duality is the role authenticity plays in technology. In Chapter 3, we emphasised the importance of notions of authenticity and presented a range of models of technology practice. Some of these models were from a holistic-macro perspective, acknowledging the roles of society and culture in technology practice; others are conceptualised from a micro approach, focusing on the design and make aspect of technology.

Technology education is ideally suited to innovative teaching practices and environments. The descriptions of different teaching approaches recommended for technology were provided in Chapter 3, to assist teachers to develop a range of pedagogies for the enactment of technology, suited to both traditional and innovative learning environments. These approaches situate technology for future-focused approaches to teaching and learning, and offer authentic contexts for inquiry and problem-based learning – thus preparing students for their lives in an ever-changing technological world.

Chapter 3 concludes with sections about the importance of *talk*, and students drawing on their cultural and social funds of knowledge. Valuing students' cultural and social knowledge not only informs technology practice from different perspectives but also gives credence to the variety of knowledge and practices that otherwise might be overlooked. Knowledge is often shared through talk when students are working collaboratively. We recognise this is a valuable tool for cognitive development and note that on a pragmatic level facilitates immediacy in response, and requires less time than other more traditional ways of idea sharing.

Our aim for Chapter 4 was to explain technology in *The New Zealand Curriculum* (MoE, 2017b). We provided clarification of the nature of technology in the curriculum and made connections to how this translates into

212 *Epilogue*

classroom practice, which is critical if the aims and goals for technology are to be attained. In the chapter, we provided an overview of the three curriculums, from which teachers in New Zealand can teach technology. Although technology in the NZC was the focus of this chapter, the structure and components of the three curricula are discussed to assert the importance for all students to engage with and critique technologies as suggested in the nature of technology strand of NZC, Te Whaitake o te Ako i te Hangarau (Concepts of Hangarau) strand of Marautanga o Aotearoa (Te Tāhuhu O Te Mātauranga, 2017) and in the Exploration strand of Te Whāriki (MoE, 2017a), students should also collaboratively and individually design and develop quality technological outcomes as identified in the technological practice and technological knowledge strands of NZC, Te Hanga o Tēnei Wāhanga Ako (technology practice) strand of Marautanga o Aotearoa as well as the Exploration strand of Te Whāriki

We began this chapter with a brief overview of the structure and organisation of technology in NZC and then described the technological areas in detail, providing some further history relating to the development of the technological areas. This intended to provide readers with further insight into the intentions of the differing technological areas. For example, at first glance it might be difficult for students to understand processed technologies, until there is awareness that this area consists of both food and biotechnologies, but can also include broader contexts, including the development of new materials – such as textiles and construction materials. It is acknowledged here that the latter two, whilst perceived this way in industry, are less likely to be conceptualised in this manner in the school context.

In the section pertaining to technological areas, we provided a brief history of the development and implementation of digital technologies to give insight into the thorough (and somewhat controversial) process of including digital technologies within technology. This was a deliberate decision to ensure readers understand the place that digital technologies have in the technology curriculum. We also wanted to promote the view that the teaching of digital technologies must occur within authentic contexts to minimise the risk that it could defer to a skill-based "tick-box" approach to the curriculum. It is also hoped that this chapter may be of particular interest to researchers.

Transformation is a critical notion for technology. The NZC promotes the idea that technology practice transforms materials, information and/or energy. Although mentioned in NZC, these three transformations are not explored or written about elsewhere, and are excluded from the 2017 revised Technology in NZC iteration. In Chapter 4 we unpack the three transformations, with a view to assist students' understanding of the scope and breadth of technology practice.

The idea of immediate contexts was also introduced in Chapter 4. The term *context* can be confusing, because like the term *technological literacy* people have different understandings of its meaning. In technology education, some people refer to each of the technological areas as contexts; for others the context refers to materials used – such as wood; for food and others it describes how specific projects are conceptualised. The latter definition is associated with the immediate context in Chapter 4. We suggest possible immediate contexts at each of NCZ's eight levels. This list is not exhaustive, and teachers are encouraged to identify their own immediate contexts to meet the needs of their students, in their local communities.

The technology components and achievement objectives are the backbone of technology in NZC. Considerable effort has been made to give detailed descriptions of the components in Chapter 4. Some examples of how they might be unpacked for deeper understanding are provided. Subsequently, we explored the nature of students' technological practice – in contrast to Chapters 2 and 3, which emphasised the practice of technologists. In Chapter 4, we identified differences between technologists' practice and that of student technologists, to show the importance of a teacher's role to intervene, as appropriate, to support students' success.

Chapter 4 concluded with detailed explanation and modelling of the unit planning process. A number of strategies can enable both student teachers and existing teachers to plan and implement technology education – as it is intended. We began with the pre-planning preparation stage because of its importance in providing the foundation for quality units of work. The planning process might seem time consuming, and even laborious, but in our experience, it is worth it. As student teachers and teachers become more experienced, the time it takes to plan is likely to decrease. However, such processes are still recommended as they scaffold a teacher's pedagogical thinking, to ensure that students are best positioned for designing and developing quality technological outcomes, as they are situated within needs-based authentic contexts.

We are particularly proud of Chapter 5 in this book. The narrative approach was used to bring the technology curriculum to life. The stories of Aria and Cooper personalise the journey of technology learning. The teacher commentary situates the learning and highlights the pertinent aspects of the curriculum. Following our two fictitious characters through their technology schooling journey provides insight for the reader – to imagine what teaching technology might *look like* at different year levels. The progression between achievement levels is indicated in very subtle and different ways.

This book provides a means to support technology teachers at various stages of their professional journey. When engaging with the narrative provided in Chapter 5, we recommend that readers do so in conjunction with the achievement objectives and Indicators of Progression very close to hand.

Bibliography

Ministry of Education (MoE), 2017a. *Te whāriki a te kōhanga reo*. Ministry of Education.
Ministry of Education (MoE), 2017b. *Technology in the New Zealand curriculum*. Ministry of Education. Retrieved 20 February from http://nzcurriculum.tki.org.nz/The-New-Zealand-Curriculum/Technology.
Te Tāhuhu O Te Mātauranga, 2017. *Te Marautanga o Aotearoa*, Te Tāhuhu O Te Mātauranga. Ministry of Education.

Index

Note: Page numbers in *italics* and **bold** refer to figures and tables respectively.

achievement objectives (AOs) 99, 100, 213
achievement standards (AS) 104
achievement success criteria 166
alterity 74–75
anchored instruction 45
apprenticeship models of learning 44–45
areas of technology, NZC 101–116; 1995, 2007 and 2017 **102**; computational thinking 109-110; control technology, 112; design and visual communication 114; designing and developing digital outcomes 111–112; designing and developing materials outcomes 111–112; designing and developing processed outcomes 112–114; digital technologies 103–109; Fox's model 114–116; immediate contexts for learning 117–119, **118**; positioning senior secondary specialist areas 114–116
artefactual determinism 36
attributes 123, **125**
Australia New Zealand Food Authority (ANZFA) 191
authentic activity: cultural 54; within immigrant biscuit context 72–73
authenticity 7; and technology 41–42; in technology 46
authentic pedagogy 55–59; Slavkin's six suggestions for 56
authentic teachers 55–59
authentic technological practice 47–54; anchored instruction 45; apprenticeship models of learning 44–45; case study 68–74; complex design process 52–54; constructivism 42; and culture 42–46; cyclic design model 52; enculturation 43; expert knowledge 43; feminist theory 45–46; situated cognition 43–44; technological practice, models of 47–51

Bell, Tim 106
Benson, Steve 33
big understanding 161
biotechnology 112–113
biscuit colour chart *191*
brainstorm/brainstorming 145; Hobbit Harriers, website for *147*; school, flugs for cuddles at *146*
brief development (BD) 123–125, *124*, 178
Bronowski, Jacob 13

CAG *see* curriculum advisory group
Carr, Malcolm 24
Carr, Margaret 169
Centre for Science, Mathematics and Technology Education Research (CSMTER) 33
CGC *see* Convergent Growth Conversation
characteristics of technological outcomes (CTO) 120
characteristics of technology (CT) 120
Chief Executive Officer (CEO) 71, 132
classroom narrative, of technology education 173–208; early years (4 years old) 173–175; years 1–3 (5–7 years old) 175–181; years 4–6 (8–10 years old) 181–190; years 11 (DVC) 205–206; years 13 (DDMO) 206–208; years 7 and 8 190–197; years 9 and 10 197–205
Claxton, Guy 29, 78, 80, 169
cognitive apprenticeship 43; learning theory 44–45
Compton, Vicki 34
computational thinking (CT) 97, 99, 109–110
conative classrooms, characteristics of 58–59

Index 215

conceptual statement 123, 161
constructivism 42
control technology, 112
Convergent Growth Conversation (CGC) 77
Cosgrove, Mark 13, 14
Cowie, Bronwen 36
Creech, Hon Wyatt 34
critical control point (CCP) pathway 201, **202–203**
critical path 128–129, **130–131**
cultural locatedness 28
culture, authentic practice and 42–46
curriculum: hidden 40–41; New Zealand curriculum (*see* New Zealand curriculum)
curriculum advisory group (CAG) 106; recommendations of 107
Curriculum Advisory Group Report 106
cutting room floor 19–20

Dakers, John 14
DDMO *see* designing and developing materials outcomes
DDPO *see* designing and developing processed outcomes
design and visual communication (DVC) 114; year 11 205–206
Design Brief 16
designing and developing digital outcomes (DDDO) 97, 99, 107, 110–111
designing and developing materials outcomes (DDMO) 99, 102, 111–112, 116; technological area of 178; year 13 206–208
designing and developing processed outcomes (DDPO) 112–114, 116; biotechnology 112–113; food technology 113–114
DGC *see* Divergent Growth Conversation
digital technologies 103–109; education in 107–108, 109; history of 103–109
Divergent Growth Conversation (DGC) 77
DVC *see* design and visual communication
Dyson, James 20

early childhood curriculum (ECE) 7, 98, 170
Edison, Thomas 20, 78
Education Council of New Zealand 107
enculturation 43; participatory 86–89
enduring learning 161
expert knowledge 43

face-to-face communication 76–77
feedback loop 134
feminist theory 45–46
Ferguson, Don 33
fit-for-purpose digital solutions 110
Fleer, Marylin 74
flow chart 132–140; DDDO and 134; decision-making and 134; outcome development and evaluation 135–136; simple *133*; students' technological practice and 136–140
FOK *see* Funds of Knowledge (FOK)
food technology 113–114
Fox-Turnbull, W. 47, 106, 170; model of student TP *137*
fracture testing 192–194
Funds of Knowledge (FOK) 28, 79; participatory enculturation 86–89; passive observation 89–90; sources of 86–90

Gawith, J. 47, 136, 138; model of technology practice 49–50, *50*
generating-testing-and-selecting (GTS) cycle *17*, 21; developmental nature of 20; values guiding 19
grounding 76
GTS cycle *see* generating-testing-and-selecting cycle
Guy, Terry 33

Hangarau curriculum 97, 106; first draft proposed models for *108–109*; released draft *109*
Hawe, Eleanor 33
Hawe, Jones 33
herringbone timeline 129, 132, *132*
hidden curriculum 40–41
homo faber 16
homo sapiens 16
human civilisation, evolution of 13
human development, technology and 10–12
human technology, definition of 13

idea generation: brainstorming and discussion for 18; technology and 17–18
Immigrant Biscuit *70*, 71
Information and Communication technologies (ICT) 104
Initial Teacher Education (ITE): adult students 69; educators 4; programmes 209
innovation 37

216   *Index*

innovative learning environments (ILEs) 59–60; schools 169
intercognitive conversations 77–78
International Journal of Technology and Design Education 4, 82

JiTT *see* Just-in-time teaching
Jones, Alister 24, 34
Just-in-time teaching (JiTT) 40–41, 45

Kimbell's Reflective Active Capability model *51*, 100–101, 136

learner-centred pedagogies 40
learning: apprenticeship models of 44–45; authentic 44; cognitive apprenticeship 44–45; enduring 161; evaluation of 167–168; guided inquiry 65–68; immediate contexts for 117–119, **118**; inquiry 65; needs and special considerations 161
learning experience (LE) 169
learning intentions 162–165; with context separated **164**; muddled and contest-free **164**

Manaakitanga 142
manipulating materials 116
"manual teachers" 209
Maori learners 28, 142
Maori pedagogies 143
Maori Tikanga 167
Maori values 63, 71, 97, 142
materials: manipulating 116; and resources 161; transforming 116–117
Matthews, Paul 106
McMahon, Julie 106
McNae, Rachel 36
middle pages, technology unit planning 162–166; achievement success criteria 166; learning experience 165; learning intentions 162–165, **164**; NZC achievement, links to 165; technological learning evidence 165–166

National Certificate in Educational Achievement (NCEA) 104, 138, 166; ASs 141; Assessment framework 115
National Curriculum Framework 33
nature of technology (NT) 9–10, 25, 34, 82, 99, 119; socially embedded 31; transformative 37; value-laden and values-driven 22

NCEA *see* National Certificate in Educational Achievement
Newcomen, Thomas 12
New Zealand Computer Society 105
The New Zealand Curriculum 96–97, 211; revised 105; technology as learning area in 99–101
New Zealand curriculum (NZC) 2, 24; areas of technology 101–116; framework 211; key competencies and values, links to 167; learning areas, links to 167; level *156–160*; "Nature of Technology" 46; organising structure of technology in *100*; purpose of 40; rationale for teaching technology 25; strands and components 119–132; technological literacy under 34; technology in 96–97, **97**, 211–213; TOCF nature of technology level 4 **83–85**; transformations 116–117, 212
The New Zealand Curriculum Framework 33
New Zealand Qualifications Authority (NZQA) framework 4

organising structure, of technology in NZC 100
outcome development and evaluation (ODE) 135–136

Pacey, Arnold 35, 47
participatory enculturation 86–89
pathway of teaching 149–151; Hobbit Harriers, website for *151*; school, flugs for cuddles at *150*
PCK *see* pedagogical content knowledge
PCQ (Pros, Cons and Questions) strategy 186–187
pedagogical content knowledge (PCK) 3, 90
pedagogy 26–27; authentic 55–59; contemporary 29–31
planning for practice (PP) 126
planning units of work, in technology 140–169; bicultural perspectives and considerations 141–143; brainstorming 145, *146–147*; final or back page 167; key elements 140–141; middle pages 162–166; pathway of teaching 149–151, *150*, *151*; preparatory research 143–144; pre-unit planning steps 144–145; scoping 145, 148, *148*, *149*; unit planning steps 151–162; unit

Index 217

preparation and preplanning 141; word to the wise 168–169

PLD *see* professional learning and development

Post Primary Teachers' Association (PPTA) 3, 209

PPTA *see* Post Primary Teachers' Association

Pre-service Technology Teacher Education Resource (PTTER) framework 4

pre-unit planning: immediate context 144–145; learning needs 144; technological area 145

professional identity 39–40

professional learning and development (PLD) 209; contracts 3; counter professional "cultural shock" 210; plan 107

progress outcomes (POs) 99–100, 110–111

prototype 18

PTTER framework *see* Pre-service Technology Teacher Education Resource framework

rationale, for technology education 3–5, 24–29; culture 27–28; economic justification 25–26; environmental rationale 28; motivation 27; pedagogy 26–27; personal justification 29; vocational (trades) *vs.* general education 26

refrigeration 11–12

Reinsfield, E. 25

ritual knowledge 39

scoping 145, 148; Hobbit Harriers, website for *149*; school, flugs for cuddles at *148*

self-concept 39–40

sensory evaluation diagram *204*

situated cognition 43–44

Slavkin, M. L. 56, 57

social interaction, in technology 74–86; alterity 74–75; dialogue 75–76; face-to-face communication 76–77; grounding 76; intercognitive conversations 77–78; interpsychological level of functioning 74; intrapsychological level of functioning 74; language and 74; Symbolic Interactionism 76; technology observations conversation framework 78–86

society, technology and 13–14, 35

Sociocultural Conflict Theory 76

sophistication and flexibility of thinking across achievement objectives **81–82**

specifications 123

Spendlove, David 79–80

S.S. Dunedin (ship) 11, *11*, 12

strands and components, of curriculum 119–132; brief development 123–125, *124*; characteristics of technological outcomes 120; characteristics of technology 120; critical path 128–129, **130–131**; herringbone timeline 129, 132, *132*; key task lists 126–128, *127*, *128*; nature of technology 119; planning for practice 126; technological knowledge 120; technological modelling 120–121; technological practice 122–123; technological systems 121–122; technology products 121

student engagement 61, 170

Symbolic Interactionism 76

Tangata Whenuatanga 142

Tataiako competencies 142, 156

teaching approaches, in technology education 59–75; authentic technology practice 68–74; guided inquiry learning 65–68; implications for classroom 68; innovative learning environments 59–60, 62–64; inquiry learning 65; integration 61–62; interdisciplinary integration 64; learner-centred classrooms 60–61

technological areas *see* areas of technology

technological content knowledge (TCK) 3

technological determinism 35–36; perspectives of *36*

technological development 12–13; dversity and 14; human and 14; knowledge and capability 16; values and 15

technological frames 36

technological knowledge (TK) 1, 13, 99, 120, 210

technological learning evidence (TLE) 165–166

technological literacy 34–38, 211, 212; definition 1; innovation 37; key competencies 37–38; technical determinism 35–36

technological modelling (TM) 120–121

technological practice (TP) 16, 99, 122–123; authenticity and technology 41–42; authentic practice and culture 42–46; authentic teachers and

218 *Index*

pedagogy 55–59; culturally authentic activity 54; Fox-Turnbull model of student *137*; Gawith's model of *50*; hidden curriculum 40–41; Kimbell's reflective activity capability model of *51*; Pacey's model of 48–49, *49*; professional identity 39–40; self-concept 39–40; students' 136–140; thinking and knowledge for 38–59

technological systems (TS) 112, 121–122

technology: as academic subject 29–31; classroom narrative 173–208; common views of 9–10; cutting room floor 19–20; development process 17; generation of ideas 17–18; and human development 10–12; nature and perspectives of 9–10; planning units of work in 140–169; potential behaviours underpinning success in **82**; practices 16; science and 20–22; and society 13–14, 35; technological development 12–13; testing-and-selecting 18–19; and values 14–16

technology education 31–34, 211; in early childhood 169–170; *vs.* educational technology 2, *2*; evolution of 31–34; first draft proposed models for *108–109*; New Zealand is *vs.* other countries 34; rationale 24–29 (*see also* rationale, for technology education) ; released draft *109*; subject's formative years 32–34

technology education programmes: authentic teaching and learning, sources for 71; using authentic learning 44

Technology in the New Zealand Curriculum 4, 31, 33, 34, 140; meaning of "authentic" in 46

technology observations conversation framework (TOCF) 78–86; nature of technology level 4 NZC **83–85**; socialisation and 80, **81–82**

Technology Online 34

technology products (TP) 121

technology unit planner template *152–154*

testing-and-selecting 18–19

Te Whariki curriculum 98, 107

Tikanga Maori 63

TLE *see* technological learning evidence

TOCF *see* technology observations conversation framework

transformation, in technology 116–117, 212

transforming energy 117

transforming information 117

transforming materials 116–117

Turnbull, Wendy 40

unit planning 151–162; big understanding or enduring learning 161; conceptual statement 161; learning needs and special considerations 161; materials and resources 161; NZC level *156–160*; safety considerations 162; technological area 161; unit planner template, technology *152–154*; unit planner template guidelines, technology *154–155*; unit summary 161

unit summary 161

values: guiding GTS cycle 19; problem solving and 14; technology and 14–16

Vygotsky, L. S. 42, 44, 74

Wananga 142

Whanaungatanga 142

Williams, P. J. 25

Wiremu, Matua 191

Zuga, Karen 42, 45

Printed in the United States
by Baker & Taylor Publisher Services